BROADCAST NEWS PRODUCING

Although you may recognize the names of news anchors and reporters, news producers remain mostly anonymous. The on-air people get most of the glory, but you couldn't have a newscast without the behind-the-scenes work of the producers. To the thousands of producers across America who grind out broadcast news on a daily basis, this book is dedicated.

Special mention goes to Mike McHugh and Matt Ellis, who had what it took to become the very best producers in the business.

Ora et Labora: 1 Corinthians 1:31

BRAD SCHULTZ

University of Mississippi

BROADCAST NEWS PRODUCING

SAGE Publications
Thousand Oaks ▪ London ▪ New Delhi

For information:

Sage Publications, Inc.
2455 Teller Road
Thousand Oaks, California 91320
E-mail: order@sagepub.com

Sage Publications Ltd.
1 Oliver's Yard
55 City Road
London EC1Y 1SP
United Kingdom

Sage Publications India Pvt. Ltd.
B-42, Panchsheel Enclave
Post Box 4109
New Delhi 110 017 India

Printed in the United States of America on acid-free paper.

Library of Congress Cataloging-in-Publication Data

Schultz, Brad, 1961-
Broadcast news producing / Brad Schultz.
    p. cm.
Includes bibliographical references and index.
ISBN 1-4129-0671-7 (cloth)
  1. Television broadcasting of news. 2. Television—Production and direction.
3. Radio journalism. 4. Radio—Production and direction. I. Title.
PN4784.T4S35 2005
070.4′3—dc22

                                    2004005705

04 05 06 07 08 09 10 9 8 7 6 5 4 3 2 1

Acquiring Editor:	Margaret H. Seawell
Editorial Assistant:	Jill Meyers
Project Editor:	Claudia A. Hoffman
Copy Editor:	Catherine Chilton
Typesetter:	C&M Digitals (P) Ltd.
Indexer:	Will Ragsdale
Cover Designer:	Janet Foulger

Contents

Preface   ix

Introduction   xi

1. What Is a Producer?   1

Newsroom Structure   3

    The Station Manager   3

    The News Director   4

    The Assignment Editor   5

    Reporters and Photographers   7

    The Production Department   8

    The Engineering Department   9

    Sports and Weather   10

    The Traffic Department   12

    The Sales Department   13

    Studio Personnel   14

    Other Station Departments   14

What Else Does a Producer Do?   15

The Producer's Role in the Newsroom   16

Thinking More About It   21

2. Producing Today's News   23

The Evolution of News Production   23

Network News   25

    Emphasis on the Bottom Line   25

    Emphasis on Anchors   27

	Emphasis on Entertainment	28
	Emphasis on Technology	29
	Implications for Local Producers	31
	Thinking More About It	34
3.	**The Producing Process**	**37**
	Story Ideas and News Value	37
	Rundowns	39
	Skeleton Rundowns	45
	Blocks and Stacking	47
	Finishing Strong	60
	Scripting	62
	In the Control Room	66
	Thinking More About It	69
4.	**Writing**	**71**
	Overview	71
	Communicating an Idea	71
	Using Available Elements	73
	Audience Understanding	73
	Ten Suggestions for Better Broadcast Newswriting	74
	Writing for Packages, V/Os, and VO/SOTs	83
	Voiceover	83
	Voiceover–Sound on Tape	84
	Packages	85
	Summary	85
	Thinking More About It	86
5.	**Producing for Television**	**89**
	Alternative News Formats	90
	Live	91
	Roundtable	93
	Town Hall Meeting	94
	Debate	94

Election Night	95
The Call-in Show	96
Alternative News Strategies	98
Breaking News	99
Summary	101
Thinking More About It	101
6. Weather and Sports	**103**
Weather	103
The Producer's Role	104
Severe Weather	106
Credibility	108
Good Relationships	111
Sports	111
Special Sports Programming	112
Sports Producers	114
Working With the Sports Department	119
Thinking More About It	121
7. Producing for Radio and the Internet	**123**
Radio	123
How People Use Radio News	124
News on Talk Radio and All-News Stations	125
News on Music Stations	130
Public Broadcasting	132
The Internet	134
Internet Producing Strategies	134
The Future of Internet News	142
Thinking More About It	143
8. Surviving the Newsroom	**145**
Theories X, Y, and Z	145
Theory X	146
Theory Y	146
Theory Z	147

Newsroom Relationships   148

    Working With News Directors   148

    Working With Anchors   152

    Working With Reporters   154

    Personal Relationships   154

Thinking More About It   158

9. Issues in Producing   **161**

Quality Versus Ratings   161

Live Reporting   164

News Cutbacks   168

Market Size   172

Ethics   175

    Honesty   175

    Visual Bias   176

    Personal Biases   177

    Creating the News   178

Consultants   180

Thinking More About It   183

10. The Job Market   **185**

The Numbers   185

Finding a Producing Job   187

    What Stations Want   188

    Where to Look for Jobs   190

The Job Search Process   192

    The Cover Letter   192

    The Resume   194

    The Resume Tape   196

    The Interview   197

Summary   198

Thinking More About It   199

References   **201**

Index   **207**

About the Author   **217**

Preface

During a recent university advising session, a freshman student told me that she was in broadcast journalism because she wanted to "travel, make good money, and be on TV." Obviously, this is not what broadcast journalism is about, and the student ultimately decided to transfer to the business school. But this attitude is pervasive among college and high school students, who constantly read about the million-dollar salaries and celebrity status of today's TV news anchors. Today's journalism and broadcasting schools are crammed with people who see broadcasting as a path to personal fame and fortune.

Students need to know that there's another side to the business, without which these famous anchors and reporters wouldn't even make it on the air. Every newscast has to have a producer, someone responsible for putting the show together and making sure it runs smoothly. This is the unglamorous behind-the-scenes work of putting together a broadcast news program. News producers aren't well known, and they certainly don't enjoy the perks or salaries of on-air performers. They labor anonymously at big and small stations all across the country, often working 12+ hours a day, cranking out newscasts. Many times the stress level is off the charts, leading to cases of premature burnout.

Why would anyone want such a job? Well, there are several benefits to working as a news producer. Because so many people want to be on the air, there are fewer people who want to be producers, so producers have traditionally been in high demand. That makes it easier for producers to get into the business and then move up to higher paying jobs. The work is also considered much more stable compared to on-air positions, which have a lot of turnover. Producing is also considered a pathway into higher management, such as news director or even station manager.

Once you get behind the glamour of a news anchoring position, the job itself is not very interesting. Most anchors, especially those in larger markets, do nothing more all day than write a few stories and read them on the air (in fact, anchors are known in England by the more appropriate name of news *readers*). Producing is a constant challenge that involves a variety of skills: news judgment, writing, resource management, deadline pressure, delegation of authority, and so on. The good producer must bring all of these skills to bear in every newscast, and sometimes just getting the show on the air is a supreme accomplishment.

To some people, this challenge is irresistible. They view producing as a thrill ride, a roller coaster without seatbelts. Every day they climb to the top of the coaster and careen down the hill at breakneck speed. What many would view as insurmountable obstacles, they see as simply bumps in the road that must be overcome. Every twist and turn of the track is different, and they often finish the ride exhilarated and out of breath.

There are others who get into the business for much more practical reasons. As the realities of the broadcasting business become clearer, many frustrated on-air performers eventually drift into producing. Some people simply don't have the ability to perform on the air but still want to work in radio or television. Others see producing as the first step on a management track that they hope leads to news director or, someday, station manager.

Whatever your interest in broadcast producing, I hope you will find what you're looking for in this book.

Introduction

Why write a book on broadcast news producing? Actually, there are several reasons. Primarily, the demand for talented, trained producers in the broadcast industry continues to grow. New technology has led to an explosion in the number of channel offerings and an increased demand for programming. Many cable and satellite channels have filled the void with news, some of it on a 24-hour-a-day basis. Think of all the news you can access now from such sources as CNN, Fox News, CNBC, MSNBC, and other sources, not to mention local news providers. All those programs need producers to get the news on the air, and the result is that news producers are in demand like never before.

Traditionally, news producers learned their craft the old-fashioned way: by going to work at a station and getting some hands-on experience. Unfortunately, many producers got thrown right into the fire with a minimum of training. News is a demanding business, and producers generally don't have the luxury of waiting until they feel comfortable to start producing. News directors expect a producer to immediately jump in and put together a solid newscast. Expectations are high, and the learning curve is short.

This book is meant to help those producers by giving them the basics they need to know. Certainly, newscasts vary in style from station to station, but they really aren't all that different. Most of them have the same look and feel, which suggests that there are some basic producing strategies common to the various news media. This text will introduce you to some of those basic strategies and provide the groundwork for putting together a good newscast in radio, television, or even on the Internet.

There is more to news than just the newscast and more to producing than putting out the same old show every day. This book will introduce you to producing special shows, such as debates, town meetings, and election night coverage. It will also give you an idea of how components within your show work, such as sports and weather, which will be helpful when you have to produce a special extended show on these topics.

This book also aims to go beyond the mere "nuts and bolts" of producing and get you to think more about putting together a good newscast in the theoretical sense. What is news? What makes a good newscast? What should my relationship be with the news director? What are some of the issues that news producers must deal with on a daily basis? My hope is that this book will help you find the answers to these and other questions. It also focuses on the most practical question students have: How do I find a job? Compared to on-air people, producers often have an easier time getting into the industry and then moving up to better markets. Matt Ellis started as an on-air reporter for a small station in West Virginia. Frustrated with what he perceived as his lack of ability to get better jobs, he switched to producing. Ellis became head writer of ABC's *Good Morning America* in New York and is now news director at WBZ-TV in Boston.

Matt Ellis is one of several industry professionals who have contributed practical advice and information to this book. Unlike Ellis, Mike McHugh went into producing right out of college and worked his way up to assistant news director at WBBM-TV in Chicago, where he was responsible for the 10:00 p.m. newscast. He and other broadcast producers share their thoughts about the practical and theoretical side of putting together a good newscast.

Very few books on the market address these subjects. Most of the books you see today on broadcast "production" focus on the technical end of the business—audio and video setups, camera placement, and so on. That is important information, but it's hardly useful to the person who has decided to make a career of producing broadcast news. Whether you are already committed to becoming a broadcast producer or perhaps thinking of making a career change, I believe this text will give you the information you need to get your producing career going.

What Is a Producer? 1

A sking what a producer is or does is a little like asking "how deep is a hole?" Ask a hundred different people and you'll probably get a hundred different answers.

The short answer is that a producer does anything and everything to get a newscast on the air. They are with the newscast from beginning to end, not just the half hour or so that the newscast is on the air. Producers are involved in the editorial meetings that lay out what the newscast will eventually look like, and then they are there in the control room when the show actually goes on the air. Depending on the size of the station, this process can be extremely short and simple. But usually, it is a lengthy and exhaustive process that challenges every skill the producer has: planning, writing, editing, resource management, delegation of authority, and decision making under deadline pressure, just to name a few.

First and foremost, producers must produce a newscast of a predetermined length. For most television producers, this means a half-hour or hour-long show; radio producers deal with much shorter programs. That is the reality that faces every producer when he or she begins each work day. A certain amount of news time must be filled for the show to go on the air. The time constraints cannot be ignored, delayed, or forgotten. Many producers liken them to a hungry beast that must be fed every so often. Feeding the beast requires a variety of skills, including news judgment and value, putting stories in the correct order, and making sure the show gets on the air properly. Ultimately, producers are judged by the quality of the on-air newscast.

But producing is far more than simply putting a show on the air, as computer software can now easily arrange a newscast with a minimum of effort. Obviously, much of the difficulty lies in the process. Producers must oversee the various components of the production process, and

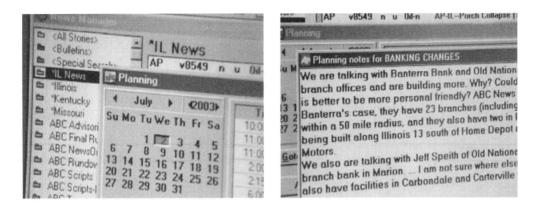

Figure 1.1   Producers Must Process Hundreds of Pieces of Information Each Day,
                   Usually Under Deadline Pressure

SOURCE: Photographs by Mary Lou Sheffer. Printed by permission.

these components have a tendency to break down or operate dysfunctionally. News vans will break down or live shots will fail. Photographers will get lost on the way to a story, or reporters will change story assignments. Breaking news will often force producers to rearrange a newscast at the last minute. There could be problems with the production, engineering, or traffic departments, all of which affect the newscast.

Technology has also made the role of the producer more complex. Improving technology, from digital communication to satellite transmission, means that producers must now deal with more information, and in less time, than ever before. Oftentimes, critical decisions must be made in seconds. In case of failure or the need to make a sudden change, producers must know exactly where to go and what to do next. In this sense, critical decision making under deadline pressure is one of the most important attributes of the news producer.

Producers must also be amateur psychologists. The producer is responsible for pulling together the people that contribute to the newscast and getting them to work together as a team, which is not always easy. Newsrooms are filled with jealousy, personal animosity, and strained relationships. Reporters may balk at working with certain photographers or vice versa. As silly as it sounds, producers will sometimes have to referee serious arguments in the newsroom, if they're not a part of the argument themselves. Even when everyone tries to work together, people can misunderstand their assignments, leading to confusion and delay. All of this takes place under the watchful eye of the news director, to whom the producer must report.

The producer is also expected to contribute to the content of the newscast. Reporters will cover most of the bigger stories, but producers usually write many of the other stories in the newscast. Thus producers must be good communicators, writers, and editors.

Finally, despite the need for producing on a daily basis, there is also a long-range aspect of producing. As a member of the news management team, the producer provides input to the news director about the direction of the newscast. Does the look of the newscast need changing? What components of the newscast need to be reevaluated for the future? More frequently, producers must engage in long-range planning for special event programs. Often, months of planning will go into the production of news programs for election night, political debates, local roundtable discussions, and so on. The producer plays a pivotal role in this planning, as he or she will be the one in control of the program on the day that it airs.

By now, you should be thinking of the producer as someone who must possess a variety of important skills. Much of this relates to the producer's position in the newsroom and his or her place within the station's news structure.

Newsroom Structure

Every news organization has some sort of hierarchical structure or organization, most of which are very similar. The producer deals with almost every one of these departments in the process of putting together a newscast.

THE STATION MANAGER

At the top of the structure is the station owner, general manager (GM), or station manager (SM). Many times, especially at smaller stations, these roles will all be handled by one person. But because of increasing consolidation and corporate ownership in the industry, a station manager or general manager will usually run the station on behalf of the station owners.

Very seldom does a producer deal with a station manager. The manager is more concerned with the day-to-day operation of the station, of which news is only a small part. Some managers prefer a more hands-on approach to news and want to get heavily involved in the news production process. More often, however, they will delegate responsibility for the department to a news director and stay out of daily news decisions. Managers do have ultimate hiring and firing responsibility at the station, and that may be the only time producers actually talk to them.

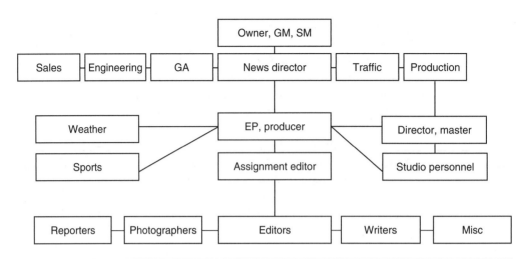

Figure 1.2   Typical Television and Radio Newsroom Structure

Note: EP indicates executive producer; GA, general administration; GM, general manager; Misc, all others under the assignment editor; SM, station manager.

THE NEWS DIRECTOR

The news director has direct authority over the newscast producers and is responsible for the overall news product of the station. Unlike that of a producer, this responsibility is not just the nuts and bolts process of getting shows on the air. News directors are more concerned with large-scale issues, such as overall news quality, audience feedback, and long-range planning. This is not to say that news directors have no interest in the day-to-day workings of the newscast, but having delegated most of that responsibility to producers, they are free to focus on the news department as a whole.

Producers work very closely with the news director in planning the newscast. Most days, the news director, producer, and several reporters will take part in an editorial meeting to discuss what stories merit coverage in the newscast and how to cover them. The editorial meeting usually gives the producer a good idea of what the newscast will eventually look like. By the end of the meeting, producers know what stories will be covered, the importance of each story, and which reporters will be working on them. The news director usually takes a strong hand in the editorial meeting, outlining what he or she would like to see covered. Once these decisions have been made, the news director usually turns over the show to the producer.

The news director will talk with the producer several times a day to check on the progress of the newscast. A producer might go to the news director with any major problems or concerns but usually does not need approval to make minor changes to the show. As with station managers, different news directors have different management styles. Some are very hands-on and want to get involved in the actual news production process. Others prefer to delegate that responsibility to the producer. Unless there are major problems or breaking news requires drastic changes, the news director typically lets the producer put the show together.

Ideally, the news director should be available to give feedback to the producer after the show. This can be done in person, when the news director and producer sit down to discuss the newscast, or it can be done in the form of a written critique distributed to the entire newsroom. Either way, it is important for the producer to know the strong and weak points of the newscast. Unfortunately, not many news directors take time to do this because of time restrictions or other deadlines. Many times, the only time the producer knows how the news director feels about the show is when it goes badly. In those cases, feedback is often immediate and forceful.

The relationship the producer has with the news director will have a direct bearing on the quality of the newscast in general and the producer's future in particular. It is virtually impossible to produce a good newscast if the news director and producer are not working together and do not share the same news philosophy. It is also unlikely that both parties would remain in such a situation, and usually the producer would want to find another job. This is why it is essential for the producer to cultivate and maintain a good working relationship with the news director. This does not mean that the two have to be friends, but rather suggests such things as good communication, trust, and respect.

For more on the relationship between the news director and producer, see chapter 8.

THE ASSIGNMENT EDITOR

Aside from the news director, producers work most closely with assignment editors. Assignment editors are responsible for the coordination of news coverage, which primarily means assigning reporters and photographers to cover certain stories. They have to juggle the schedules of all the people going out to cover news, making sure that reporters have enough time to do their stories. Many times, assignment editors will have reporters cover two or three shorter stories a day or will pull reporters off one story and send them to another.

In addition, assignment editors are responsible for coming up with story ideas. They take part in the daily editorial meetings, monitor other local news media, and listen to police and fire scanners for breaking

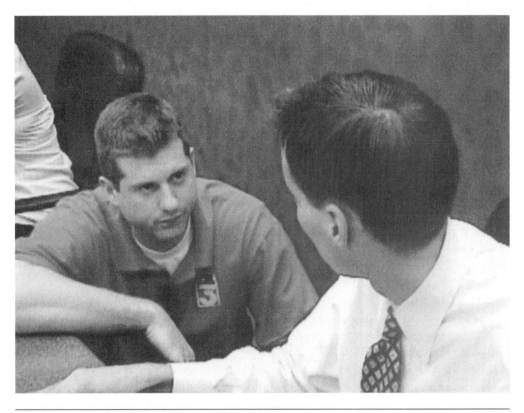

Figure 1.3   Assignment Editors Must Stay in Constant Contact With News Personnel
SOURCE: Photograph by Mary Lou Sheffer. Printed by permission.

news. They also sort through the mounds of information that come into a station every day, including news releases, meeting announcements, and story ideas phoned in by the audience as news tips. It is a job of constant communication and activity, especially during times of breaking news.

The producer needs to stay in constant contact with the assignment editor to see what, if any, changes need to be made to the newscast. The assignment editor will be one of the first to know if coverage of a story falls through or the story needs to be changed in format. For example, if a reporter gets delayed coming back from a story, that story might need to be moved to later in the newscast. Assignment editors can warn the producer of potential problems in these areas.

Technically, because the producer is in charge of the newscast, he or she has authority over the assignment editor. But it is a much better situation if the two work together, instead of one trying to control the other. Producers who become too authoritative with assignment editors (or other newsroom personnel) find that those people are much less willing to contribute to a quality newscast. The assignment editor position is one of the most thankless jobs in the newsroom, but it is absolutely vital in terms of helping the producer with the newscast.

REPORTERS AND PHOTOGRAPHERS

Even though the assignment editor coordinates the activities of reporters and photographers, it is really the producer who depends on them the most. Producers must know how reporters are covering their stories. Constant communication is essential, for if reporters deviate from their assigned coverage, it is likely to mean that the producer will have to make changes to the newscast.

After the editorial meeting, reporters and photographers get their story assignments. This includes not only the type of story but the format. There are different ways to cover stories, depending on their importance, the resources available, and the deadline involved (see chapter 3). Generally, more important stories are covered as live or packaged reports, and other stories are limited to voiceovers or short interviews.

Producers expect that reporters and photographers will cover their stories in this predetermined fashion, unless circumstances dictate otherwise. There are many circumstances that could change the way a story is covered, including equipment breakdown, the need to switch reporters to another story, or lack of time to meet deadline. It is imperative that reporters and photographers keep in constant communication with the producer so any changes can be made promptly. No producer wants to make a major change to the newscast minutes before show time.

At the same time, producers must have backup plans available in the event that such changes must be made. If a reporter is assigned to cover a story as a live shot and engineering loses the live signal right before the story goes on the air, the producer must have alternatives. These are things that a good producer considers ahead of time, well before the show ever starts.

Most producers do not try to dictate the content of reporters' stories. They understand that reporters and photographers have specialized training in this area and are also much closer to story sources and information. However, producers should feel free to suggest things that would help improve the reporter's presentation, such as different people to talk to, possible locations for live reporting, and other places to get information. Aside from this, producers want to know two main things from reporters: the format and the length of their stories.

Most of the problems between producers and reporters come from poor communication. Producers need to clearly define what they expect from reporters on their stories, and reporters need to maintain constant contact with producers to make them aware of anything that would require changes to the newscast. Chapter 8 goes into more detail about the relationship between reporters and producers.

THE PRODUCTION DEPARTMENT

The production department is technically not part of the news department and spends much of its time putting together commercials. But this department has a prominent role during the newscast, as it is responsible for the technical part of getting the show on the air. The key person in this regard is the technical director, who sits in the master control room during the newscast and supervises the audio and video presentation of the show. Audio personnel adjust audio and microphone levels, graphic artists work with chyrons (any printed material that appears on the screen), and tape operators roll taped stories at their appropriate time. Much of this process is becoming streamlined as more stations switch to digital technology. For example, many stories are now simply stored as computer files and not even put on video or audiotape.

Before the newscast, the producer and technical director may discuss the basics of the newscast—what stories go where, the specific technical needs, and any out of the ordinary requests such as special graphics. An hour or so before the show, the director will go over the list of stories and mark them to his or her specifications. Copies will be distributed to other members of the production team working in master control so that everyone is aware of what is going on.

During the newscast, the producer watches from master control but leaves the technical part of the show to the director. The producer focuses more on timing and organizing the show (see chapter 3). Stories are constantly being dropped, added, changed, and moved within the newscast, and all these decisions must be made by the producer. The producer must also make sure that the show times out correctly. This means it must begin and end at a certain time, and these times are usually very rigid. To account for changes in time, producers will add or drop stories or ask the news anchors to speed up or slow down in their presentation. Oftentimes, certain segments of the show will be adjusted to compensate for time problems. If the show is running long, for example, a producer might have to cut the sports segment from 3 minutes to 2½.

The producer is not expected to know how the production department works or how to "punch" the show from master control. Technical directing is a highly specialized skill, beyond the scope of producing. However, the producer should realize that no matter how well the show is put together, it does not mean anything if the show cannot get on the air. Producers should make every effort to create an effective working relationship with the technical director that is built on solid communication.

THE ENGINEERING DEPARTMENT

The engineering department is in charge of protecting, maintaining, and improving the technical equipment associated with running a media outlet. In a news sense, this particularly applies to electronic news gathering (ENG) equipment, such as cameras, microphones, news vans, and satellite trucks. Engineers spend some of their time on preventive maintenance and trying to keep equipment from breaking and much more of their time fixing equipment that has already broken. This last job is especially important, considering that the high cost of new technology makes it difficult to replace equipment.

Like the production department, the engineering department is not a part of the news department but still plays an important part in the newscast. Producers assume that reporters and photographers will have working equipment to cover stories. If some of the equipment is not working, it will influence how a producer puts a show together. For example, if the station live truck is inoperable, it would eliminate certain options for covering a story. Producers need to know if certain ENG equipment is not working or is unavailable.

Beyond that basic knowledge, producers rely more on engineers for satellite transmission and live story coverage. Certain stories require the downloading of satellite feeds, which is particularly true in the case of network newsfeeds. Most organizations have relationships with larger media outlets that involve these outlets providing national and regional news material on a daily basis. Because this information is sent by satellite, it is imperative that the satellite reception process works properly. Producers count on many of these stories to use in their newscasts and rely on engineers to keep the process running smoothly.

Engineers are more directly involved in the news process when the story involves a live report, which has become quite frequent in modern news reporting. Many stations want to go on location, either by satellite truck or microwave unit. The microwave unit is the more common method: the kind of news truck with a high mast that sends a microwave signal back to the station. Engineers have to make sure that the signal has a clear "line of sight," which means there are no trees or tall buildings in the way that could interrupt the signal between the truck and the station. Even a good signal has an effective range of only around 60 miles, and it can also be disrupted by high winds or rain.

A more sophisticated process is the use of a satellite truck. The truck bounces the signal off an orbiting satellite, which sends it back down to the station. There is no limit to its range, but engineers must have the exact satellite coordinates to download the signal. Because of the expense of buying satellite time, stations usually only have a limited window in which to do their transmissions. As with microwave transmission, unforeseen problems can interrupt or erode a satellite signal.

Figure 1.4   Producers Depend on the Engineering Department to Keep Equipment
Working Properly, Especially Satellite Feeds

SOURCE: Photograph by Brad Schultz.

No matter what type of transmission is involved, producers must
work with the engineering department to coordinate live coverage.
Producers must be especially aware of time restrictions and requirements, satellite coordinates, and geographic realities that may affect live
coverage capability. Technology has made live reporting easier and more
common, but there are still engineering considerations that must be
taken into account.

SPORTS AND WEATHER

Sports and weather have their own departments, but the producer still
has control over these segments within the newscast. This relationship can
cause a lot of problems for everyone involved. Sports and weather people
naturally want to control their own segments, but the producer has the
power to change or influence them in relation to the overall newscast.

For the most part, weather and sports people produce their own material. The newscast producer gives them freedom in this regard, particularly

Figure 1.5   The Sports Department Produces Its Own Material but Must Coordinate Closely With News Producers

SOURCE: Photograph by Brad Schultz.

when it comes to content. However, there are certain limits, the most obvious of which is time. The producer tightly controls the time allotted for both segments. Weather usually gets more time (3 minutes or more) because it generates a great deal of audience interest, especially during bad or threatening weather. Fewer people have an interest in sports, which comes at the end of the newscast and gets less time (around 2 minutes, but this is shrinking in many markets). In rare circumstances, such as breaking news or election night, the sports segment can be dropped entirely. On the other side, either segment can get more time in cases when audience interest would be higher, such as for coverage of a local championship game.

Dropping sports entirely is an extreme example of how the producer can influence these segments of the newscast. There are much more subtle influences, such as having weather or sports go live from a particular venue. In situations where weather or sports become the dominant story of the day, the news department can co-opt the story. For example, if a prominent sports figure in the community were arrested, that would probably lead the news segment. The producer and sports department would need to discuss and coordinate plans for covering the story.

Many sports and weather departments complain that in such situations, the producer is not leaving them any material for their own segments. The best course of action is fully coordinated coverage involving the producer, news director, and sports or weather departments. This can help lay out exactly what each one will contribute to the newscast. In situations where the conflict is harder to resolve, the producer and news director have ultimate authority to determine the shape of the newscast.

For more details about sports and weather segments within the newscast, see chapter 6.

THE TRAFFIC DEPARTMENT

The traffic department at the station has the responsibility of keeping track of everything that runs on the air. Stations keep a log of every program and every commercial, and the traffic department has to make sure that they all run at their assigned times. In a sense, it is the "traffic cop" of the station's programming.

Producers must look at the station log to determine such things as commercial breaks and the length of the news hole. In a half-hour television newscast, stations will typically devote 8 minutes to commercials (often in the form of four 2-minute breaks). The time that is left over, minus time for the standard opening and closing shots and credits, is the news hole. That is the amount of news content a producer has to organize. Once sports and weather are factored in, the news hole runs about 12 to 15 minutes in a half-hour show.

Producers must pay special attention to commercial breaks, because commercials are what make money for the station. In a very practical sense, the show exists only to give advertisers a way to reach the audience. Advertisers are paying not only for their commercial but for a specific time within the newscast. A company selling snow blowers, for example, expects its commercial to run as close to the weather segment as possible. Part of the job of producing is making sure that all the ads in the show run, and at their assigned times.

Except in very rare cases, producers cannot drop, shorten, or switch commercials. Failure to get a commercial on the air means that the station will have to offer the advertiser a make-good, which is essentially free air time for the ad. If the producer needs to adjust time in the show, it can be done by adjusting the time of the news hole—lengthening or shortening certain segments (such as sports or weather) or dropping individual stories. If the show comes up short in time, public service announcements (PSAs) can be added. PSAs are unpaid promotions for government or charitable causes, such as antidrug messages.

Of course, there are certain extraordinary situations in which a producer might drop commercials from a newscast, such as in the case of extremely urgent breaking news. During the September 11 terrorist attacks, for example, most of the major networks ran their coverage commercial-free (at a cost of millions of dollars in ad revenue). But even in this situation, the decision to drop advertising usually comes from the news director or station manager. In short, a producer should seldom drop ads from a newscast and should only do so upon consultation with station management.

THE SALES DEPARTMENT

By now, it should be apparent how important advertising is to the newscast and to the station as a whole. The sales department has the responsibility of selling station air time to local and national advertisers—still the main source of revenue for most broadcast stations. Because the local newscast is often the station's most visible and successful program, advertising within it is highly desirable and fairly expensive. Exact advertising rates are determined by a variety of factors, most particularly the audience ratings for the show.

In theory, the sales department should have little say in news department affairs or in the content of a newscast. However, advertising within the newscast is a major revenue source, and sales executives want to make news advertisers happy. In some cases, the sales department will suggest certain types of news content to match advertiser needs. For example, during the summer, many television stations arrange to do a cookout from a viewer's backyard as part of the weather segment. Naturally, a hardware store or barbeque grill company would find this an attractive way to advertise.

The increasing cost of producing news has made this type of arrangement very common. But even in the case of a fairly harmless backyard cookout, it raises questions of conflict of interest. This can become a serious issue when the sales department tries to protect advertisers from unflattering news coverage. A local hospital that spends lots of advertising money in the newscast certainly does not want to see the station run an investigative story about the hospital's safety record. It is not unheard of for sales executives to try and protect their clients in such situations by suggesting less damaging news coverage.

Sometimes this can turn into a power struggle between the sales and news departments, and in such cases, producers should do everything possible to protect the integrity of the newscast. This becomes even more difficult as the line between news content and advertising continues to blur. In situations where a major conflict arises, producers should not try to carry the fight alone. When the sales and news departments collide, the news director and station manager will ultimately have the last say.

STUDIO PERSONNEL

Weather and sports will produce their own contributions to the newscast, and reporters take up a certain amount of time with their stories. But it is up to the producer to fill the rest of the newscast with other material, which is typically a combination of national, regional, and general interest items. The producer is responsible for writing, editing, and getting these stories ready for the air.

Fortunately, the producer can usually count on studio help to get this done, as most stations have a staff dedicated to this purpose. It can be composed of full-time staff or strictly volunteer personnel, but its main job is to help the producer fill the news hole. This includes such things as editing stories, logging and describing news feeds, communicating with other news staff, and studio camera work. The studio crew will do a variety of jobs to help put the show together, but the actual writing of news stories is left to producers or other professional news staff.

Some stations have editors and writers whose sole responsibility is to perform these functions. Tape editors do nothing all day but edit stories on tape for presentation in the newscast. Generally, only the larger markets and stations can afford these positions on a consistent basis. It is also worth noting that many of these support positions are filled by members of unions. In these situations, producers and other nonunion members are forbidden from doing the jobs themselves.

In some very small markets, the producer may not get much help in getting these jobs done. As a practical matter, that is why it is important for producers to get experience in these areas. Most news directors would prefer to have studio crew members available, however, so the producer can be free to concentrate on the newscast.

OTHER STATION DEPARTMENTS

Some stations have a promotion department, which tries to advertise or promote the newscast and increase its audience. Such promotion could take the form of billboards, mailings, personal appearances, and the like.

The promotions department might ask the news department to cover certain stories in an effort to maximize publicity. For example, many stations will go on the road and do their newscasts on location in different areas. The location could be a business, a planned activity, or a small town within the station's broadcast range. The sales department might also get involved, as this usually attracts advertisers in the area. The producer might work together with members of the promotion department to coordinate news coverage.

There are other departments at the station that have little or no effect on the producer. For example, the general administration department

(GA) is the bookkeeping part of the station, responsible for financial matters such as accounts payable, accounts receivable, inventory, and group health and insurance plans. Depending on the size of the station, it may include a human resources or personnel department in charge of hiring and firing.

Again, these departments are mentioned only within the context of the overall station, and they have very little impact on how a producer goes about his or her job. However, producers certainly have an interest in the general administration department when it comes to health insurance, getting enough newsroom supplies, and especially on payday.

What Else Does a Producer Do?

You should be able to see the relationship between the producer and other departments at the station. In the course of putting together a newscast, the producer constantly interacts with a variety of station personnel. Much of the success of a newscast depends on the relationship between the producer and these other people and how well the producer maintains that relationship. In addition to these important relationships, there are many things the producer does with little or no outside influence.

Primarily, the producer is a *content organizer*. This is the main job of a producer—getting the newscast organized, put together, and on the air. Other personnel and departments will contribute their input to the show, but the ultimate responsibility rests with the producer.

As we have already seen, the producer is a *staff overseer*. The position of producer is part managerial, in that producers do have authority over other newsroom personnel, including anchors, reporters, and photographers. Producers must be able to exercise that authority to get a newscast on the air. Obviously, no one likes being told what to do, and the best producers view their authority as more of a shared communication process. However, when the hard decisions must be made, producers must exercise control over their newscasts and their personnel.

Perhaps it is better to think of the producer as a *department coordinator*. You have seen the variety of departments that have some sort of stake in the newscast. A good producer works with these departments and coordinates their input into the newscast. Many times, a newscast will fail simply because the producer did not take these various inputs into account.

The producer also has a direct responsibility to the news director, and thus serves as a *management liaison*. As such, he or she is a communication link between the news director and the rest of the newsroom. Generally, when problems associated with the newscast occur, reporters and other personnel go the producer first. Only if the producer cannot resolve the problem does the news director get involved. The process also works the other way, in that the news director can work through the producer to filter information to other news personnel. Either way, the producer is considered a link in the chain of command that must be respected.

Although most of the producer's day is filled up with getting a newscast on the air, he or she must also be a *long-range planner*. We have already noted how producers work with the news director and other station management on long-range projects. This also emphasizes the unique role of the producer—part management and part labor. The producer is much like other newsroom personnel when it comes to writing, editing, and putting a show together. But the producer also serves a management function that comes with much more authority.

The career of Mike McHugh shows how many different things a producer has to do. McHugh worked his way up from a small television station in Bluefield, West Virginia (market size 149), to assistant news director at WBBM-TV in Chicago (market three), where he also served as executive producer on the 10:00 p.m. news (Table 1.1). Note that as McHugh's career progressed, his responsibilities shifted away from the actual production of news and more into management activities such as budgeting and planning.

The Producer's Role in the Newsroom

The roles and responsibilities we have discussed apply to almost all producers, regardless of where or for whom they work. But there are other factors that vary from station to station and market to market, and these factors can make the producer's role in the newsroom much different.

The *size of the news operation* often dictates a producer's exact responsibilities. Smaller newsrooms do not have as much support personnel, and producers will have a bigger share of getting the newscast on the air. This includes such things as writing, editing, and maybe even some reporting or anchoring. In many smaller television markets, one person will produce and anchor the newscast. This is becoming more common even in larger markets, as stations look for ways to reduce the growing cost of news.

More often, however, larger markets will have more support personnel, and the producer will have a more specialized role. Some stations have an extra layer in their management structure for an executive producer (EP), who oversees the producer. The EP is more like an assistant news director and works together with the producer to put the show together.

Table 1.1   News Producing: Mike McHugh

1984-1985	Producer and Anchor, WVVA-TV, Bluefield, WV Produced and anchored 6:00 p.m. and 11:00 p.m. nightly newscasts.
1985-1987	Executive Producer and Producer, WTHI-TV, Terre Haute, IN Produced 6:00 p.m. and 11:00 p.m. nightly newscasts.
1987-1994	Executive Producer, WISN-TV, Milwaukee, WI Responsible for planning, editorial oversight, special projects, series, and sports department for number 1-rated news station. Duties included evaluating personnel, hiring, and budgeting. Promoted from 6:00 p.m. news producer.
1994-1996	Assistant News Director, WTAE-TV, Pittsburgh, PA Senior newsroom manager, responsible for editorial oversight, development and implementation of news "brand" at top-rated news station. Responsibilities included the management of all newsroom personnel. Duties included hiring, research analysis, ratings strategy, all news content, and series planning and production.
1996-2000	Executive Producer, WBBM-TV, Chicago, IL Senior News Manager, responsible for editorial control and production of daily news program. Executed station management's vision of redefined broadcast (worked with four news directors in 4 years). Supervised producer, writers, reporters, and anchors to deliver product consistent with station's goal. Responsible for daily content and story development.
2000-2002	Assistant News Director, WBBM-TV, Chicago, IL Senior-level news manager, responsible for all news gathering, operations, and management of 130 news personnel. Wrote staff policies for editorial and administrative concerns. Coordinated all operational systems relating to news-gathering technology. Worked closely with corporate legal and human resources personnel. Managed nonunion and union employees through contract implementation, personnel reviews, and accountability procedures. Fiscal responsibilities included creating all news project budgets and developing systems for newsroom overtime and outside vendor expense tracking. Recruited news personnel. Served as station representative in CBS national negotiations with IBEW. Selected for the national developmental team to digitize *CBS Newspath*.

SOURCE: Mike McHugh (personal communication, March 2003).

Comparing a large-market station and a small-market station shows how station size can influence the role of the producer (see Table 1.2). WBBM-TV in Chicago is part of the third-largest market in the United States and has a very large news staff. Not only does the station list at least 19 producers, many of these producers have specialized positions. There is a senior producer, for example, in charge of special projects. This is a position not involved with producing on a daily basis but more concerned with occasional programming.

By contrast, WTVA-TV is in Tupelo, Mississippi, the country's 131st market. WTVA has only four producers, and most of them must also work in some other capacity, such as anchor or photographer. There is also not the same level of support staff, which would suggest that producers at the station have to do much more in terms of actually getting the newscast on the air.

The producer's responsibilities also depend on the *style of the news director*. Some news directors, especially those at smaller stations, take a very hands-on approach to the newscast. They want to get very involved in the production process, sometimes to the point of micromanagement. In these cases, the producer can have very little to do other than standing around and helping out where needed. However, it is much more common for news directors to take more of a hands-off approach and delegate authority to the producer. The news director might pitch in when the situation warrants, especially in the case of breaking news, but more often he or she will let the producer do the heavy lifting. It goes without saying that news directors can be hands-on, hands-off, or anywhere in between. This is something that producers generally learn on the job, when they sit down and actually start putting a show together.

It should also be obvious that what a producer does, and the kind of show that can be put together, depend a lot on the station's *available resources*. Every station has a different level of resources committed to the news product. Often, this is directly related to station size—the larger the station, the more resources available. But this is not always the case. Many smaller stations have a tremendous investment in news production, including such things as state-of-the-art ENG equipment, satellite trucks, and live vans. Resources are not limited to equipment, and many smaller stations have invested in human resources, such as more reporters, photographers, and so on.

The resources a station commits to news have a direct bearing on a producer's job. It is unreasonable to expect a producer to put together a newscast with lots of sophisticated graphics if the station does not have the necessary equipment. It could be something as simple as computer producing software or something complex, such as a new satellite truck. The escalating cost of news has led many stations to reduce the resources dedicated to news production—a major source of frustration for most producers. But whatever the level of resources at a station, the producer can only work within those limits.

Table 1.2   How Producer Responsibility Varies by Station Size

Typical Large-Market News Staff, WBBM-TV, Chicago, Illinois, 2003	
Carol Fowler	News Director
Todd Woolman	Assistant News Director
Scott Keenan	Managing Editor
Ed Marshall	Executive Producer of Special Projects
Karin Movesian	Executive Producer, *CBS 2 News This Morning*
Jill Manuel	Executive Producer, *CBS 2 News Weekend*
Julie Eich	Executive Producer, *CBS 2 News,* 10 p.m.
Christopher Selfridge	Executive Producer, *CBS 2 News,* 11 a.m., 4:30 p.m., 5:00 p.m.
Deidra White	Manager of Recruitment and Staff Development
Marda LeBeau	Senior Producer of Special Projects
Elizabeth Johnson	Producer, *CBS 2 News This Morning*
Cynthia Knox	Producer, *CBS 2 News This Morning*
Tracy O'Brien	Producer, *CBS 2 News,* 11:00 a.m.
Regina Griffin	Producer, *CBS 2 News,* 4:30 p.m.
Beth Fruehling	Producer, *CBS 2 News,* 5:00 p.m.
Traci Fitzmorris	Producer, *CBS 2 News,* 10:00 p.m.
Sue Brown	Producer, Saturday, Sunday *Evening News* Producer, Sunday 10:00 p.m. *News*
Laura Meehan	Producer, *On Call with Dr. Breen*
Greg Kelly	Dayside Assignment Editor
Kevin Kraus	Evening Assignment Editor
Chastity Parker	Weekend Assignment Editor
Rob Holliday	Weekend Assignment Editor
Chris Boden	Sports Producer
Norm Potash	Sports Producer

(Continued)

Table 1.2 (Continued)

Steve Goldberg	Sports Producer
Lissa Druss	Senior Sports Producer
Pam Zekman	Investigative unit
Simone Thiessen	Investigative unit
Ann Marie Pagan	Satellite Coordinator
Mike Adamle	Sports Anchor, Reporter
Michael Ayala	News Anchor, Reporter
Chris Boden	Sports Reporter, Producer
Michael Breen, MD	Chief Medical Reporter
Markina Brown	Weather Anchor, Reporter
Mary Ann Childers	News Anchor, Reporter
John Davis	News Anchor, Reporter
Stacia Dubin	Reporter
Mike Flannery	Political Editor
Vince Gerasole	News Anchor, Reporter
Kris Habermehl	"Chopper 2" (helicopter reporter)
Chris Hernandez	Reporter
Kyung Lah	Reporter
Steve Lattimore	Reporter
Suzanne Le Mignot	Reporter
Jay Levine	CBS 2 Chief Correspondent
Linda MacLennan	News Anchor
Antonio Mora	News Anchor
Carolyn D. Murray	CBS 2 Consumer Reporter
Mike Parker	Reporter
Cynthia Santana	News Anchor, Reporter
Howard Sudberry	Sports Anchor, Reporter

Tracy Townsend	News Anchor, Reporter
Dorothy Tucker	Reporter
Monty Webb	Meteorologist
Pam Zekman	Investigative Reporter
Small-Market News Staff, WTVA-TV, Tupelo, Mississippi, 2004	
Terry Smith	News Director
Producers	Three full-time
Assignment Editor	One full-time
Reporters and videographers	Seven full-time
News staff	Same person may at one time or another be producer, on-air talent, reporter, editor, sports (or may do several of these jobs simultaneously)

SOURCE: CBS 2 Chicago (2004); Terry Smith (personal communication, March 5, 2004).

Thinking More About It

1. Contact or visit a local broadcast station and talk with one of the news producers. If possible, try to find out the following:
   a. What do you do during the day?
   b. How much of your day is spent writing? Planning? Overseeing newsroom personnel?
   c. What is the organizational structure at the station? Who is the news director? The station manager? Does your station have an executive producer?
   d. Do you like what you do? What is the most difficult part? The most satisfying?

2. Research broadcast stations on the Internet by typing the station call letters into a search engine. Find out what you can about the station news department, including the names and duties of the station manager, news director, and producers. Do most stations have the same type of organizational structure, or does it vary from station to station? Does the news section of the website give any indication of what the producer does or what part he or she plays in the newscast? Is there a way to contact the producer directly, via e-mail or phone?

3. Watch a television newscast or listen to a radio newscast in your area.
   a. Is there a clear delineation between news and commercials? Is it possible to tell how much influence the sales department has in news presentation? Are there areas or stories that seem more like commercials than news? What specific stories can you find that suggest the influence of the sales department?
   b. What specific stories indicate a level of cooperation between the news department and other station departments, such as engineering or weather? How frequent is this coordination in the newscast?
   c. Did it seem like a good newscast that was worth watching, or did you get bored and want to tune into another station? Do you think the news producer did a good job? Why?

Producing Today's News 2

There are certainly basic skills involved in producing, and those will be discussed in later chapters. Such skills can usually be learned quickly and with a little practice. But good producers have more than just the basic skills of putting together a show. They also understand the "big picture" of producing: how to create an effective newscast given the realities of today's broadcast news environment. Understanding the current broadcast environment is important because it has evolved drastically over the years and continues to undergo major changes.

The Evolution of News Production

If you have ever looked at a tape of a news show from the 1950s, you know that television news has changed dramatically over the past several decades. Even going back to radio newscasts of the 1920s, it is obvious that news is produced much differently today.

As it does today, technology dictated much of what could be done in those years. The difference is that the technology was so new and primitive then, news producers were primarily concerned with getting the product on the air. With radio in the 1920s and television in the 1940s, the technology would often break down or fail completely. Pioneer radio sportscaster Harold Arlin remembers, "Sometimes the transmitter worked and sometimes it didn't. Sometimes the crowd noise would drown us out and sometimes it wouldn't. And quite frankly, we didn't know what the reaction would be—if we'd be talking in a total vacuum or whether somebody would hear us" (Smith, 1987).

Faced with these challenges, first radio and then television news emphasized the importance of content over style. When the *Camel News Caravan* on NBC became the first national network television news program in 1948, it was starkly simplistic. Anchor John Cameron Swayze read stories from behind a desk, looking at only a single camera. Most of the stories were "readers" (stories that had only words and no accompanying pictures or sound) because of the difficulty of processing and transmitting film. In fact, the newscast dramatized the fact that it had "Today's News Today!" because in those days it was extremely difficult to get same-day film of an important event.

As television finally moved past the stage of technological curiosity, the industry began to look more closely at the type and quality of the programming. Up until this time, programs had been fairly staid and traditional—more in keeping with the old radio formats. But now television could start to experiment with creative new formats uniquely suited to the medium. Many of these groundbreaking efforts came in news and documentaries, and most of them seemed to come from CBS. Edward R. Murrow helped pioneer the television documentary, and his *See It Now* programs had a great influence on American life and culture. CBS documentaries, such as Murrow's *Harvest of Shame,* became broadcast journalism landmarks.

CBS became dominant in radio and television news, thanks to the leadership of founder William S. Paley. Paley's news philosophy was simple: Hire the best people available and spend whatever it takes to create a high-quality news operation. Paley invested heavily in human resources, putting foreign correspondents in almost every corner of the globe. Men like Murrow, Eric Sevareid, Howard K. Smith, and, later, Walter Cronkite and Charles Kuralt gave CBS the reputation of "The Tiffany Network" when it came to news. Their newscasts provided a rundown of important national and international news stories, usually on very serious issues delivered in a no-nonsense style. The high ratings of these shows seemed to support the network news philosophy.

But the numbers were more a reflection of a lack of viewing options and qualitative audience research. In the 1960s, consultants and professional media firms (see chapter 9) introduced this research to show the disparity between what the networks were showing and what people really wanted to see. The research indicated that most people did not watch the networks because they liked the news but because it was the easiest way to get the news. Research also showed the popularity of anchors, who in many cases were even more important than the news content.

Networks were very reluctant to embrace these findings, and many news executives criticized consultants for sensationalizing local news. In 1976, CBS news anchor Walter Cronkite, annually voted "the most trusted man in America," publicly bashed professional media consulting as a "fly by night fad" (Allen, 2001). But the success of consulting on the local level, combined with new cable news options, changing audience demographics, and sagging ratings, eventually convinced network news executives to embrace a new definition of news.

Network News

In many ways, there is little difference between the way news is produced at CBS News in New York and the CBS affiliate in Portland, Maine. Producers and news executives determine which stories to cover, how to cover them, what resources to use, and how to best communicate the stories in the broadcast (see chapter 3). The main advantage network news producers have over smaller operations is an abundance of resources, both human and technical. There are more reporters to cover stories, more people back in the newsroom, and certainly more sophisticated news-gathering equipment (see chapter 9).

However, because of a changing news environment, the content, style, and presentation of network news has evolved over the years. Today it looks much different than it did during the days of John Cameron Swayze.

EMPHASIS ON THE BOTTOM LINE

Paley represented an era of the independent owner in broadcasting, someone who created a powerful network from the ground up and then maintained almost exclusive control over its operation. Today, broadcasting is simply too expensive for one person to own, in part because of the growing cost of new technology. Costs associated with the development of satellite transmission, microwave relay, and, now, digital technology have made it almost impossible for the "mom and pop" owners to survive.

The increasing cost of doing business has given rise to giant media corporations, which now control most of the industry, including the major networks. Even though the Federal Communications Commission tries to maintain control over how many broadcast stations a company can own, media author Ben Bagdikian (2000) says only six companies now control the country's most widespread news, commentary, and daily entertainment programming. As of late 2003, the Disney empire owned ABC, General Electric owned NBC, and Viacom owned CBS. These conglomerates often place much more emphasis on financial accountability than on public interest, and they demand that news shows demonstrate profitability. Unfortunately, the cost of news continues to rise, and fewer stations can make money from it (see Table 2.1).

Table 2.1   TV News Profitability, 1996 to 2000 (in percentages)

Station Response	2000	1999	1998	1997	1996
Showing profit	56	58	57	63	62
Breaking even	13	11	9	11	6
Showing loss	10	11	11	10	8

SOURCE: Papper and Gerhard (2001).

The best measure of financial success for the news is the ratings, and for network news, the ratings have dropped significantly in recent years. In July 2003, *The CBS Evening News with Dan Rather* recorded its smallest average audience in at least a decade, and maybe ever (Bauder, 2003). This continues a trend that has seen all three nightly network newscasts lose 4% of their audiences since 2000. As the networks have declined, cable news programs have made tremendous gains. During the 2003 invasion of Iraq, cable news viewership went up 300%, but network news programs went down 10%. Media researcher Andrew Tyndall said ratings for the network newscasts usually increase during war, and called the decline "unprecedented" (Carter, 2003).

Faced with declining ratings, network news is doing everything possible to make advertisers happy. Former network producer Lowell Bergman calls it "self-censorship," because networks discourage any reporting that would threaten the company's financial interests. Bergman said CBS network executives killed a story in 1995 on tobacco giant Brown & Williamson because then-CBS News president Eric Ober did not want to risk company assets on a story that would make a major advertiser look bad. "The problem today is that any obligation to report stories about unaccountable power, about individuals or institutions that are as powerful as you are, has been lost," said Bergman (2000).

There are certainly other manifestations of this emphasis on the bottom line. Almost all the networks have suffered through periods of budget cuts and personnel layoffs. The result is streamlined network news that does more with less, including smaller budgets and fewer personnel. The big question is whether such cutbacks have seriously affected the quality of the newscast. After layoffs at CBS in the late 1980s, Rather publicly called it a "tragic transformation from Murrow to mediocrity" at the network and added that it was becoming impossible for CBS to maintain the Murrow tradition of outstanding broadcast journalism (Allen, 2001).

EMPHASIS ON ANCHORS

Of course, Rather's indignation during this time did not prevent him from accepting a raise in his salary, to $3 million a year. That salary pales in comparison to the deal Katie Couric signed with NBC in 2001 ("'Today' co-host," 2001). The *Today Show* host agreed to a 4-year deal worth an estimated $60 million. Those figures reflect the importance network news has always placed on anchors, going back to the days of David Brinkley and Chet Huntley at NBC and Walter Cronkite at CBS.

It is obvious that network news anchors are powerful figures with extremely high salaries. Many of them also have some sort of executive producer function with the newscast, and as such have a strong influence over the type, format, and presentation of stories. Many of the older anchors, such as Cronkite and Rather, were traditionalists who viewed the news as a sacred trust. Their newscasts reflected not only the news philosophies of their networks but their own personal and professional beliefs. For example, in explaining to viewers why ABC did not cover a shooting in Seattle, Peter Jennings of *World News Tonight* noted, "These can be important stories, but they do not become important simply because a live helicopter picture is available to sustain cable news for hours at a stretch" (Wendland, 2000).

The reference to cable news is an indirect reference to how competitive network news has become, in large part because of the rise of new, young, cable news anchors. In the 1980s, CNN established itself as a force in national news primarily by copying the network news model. This included traditional solid reporting on national issues delivered by a mature anchor, Bernard Shaw. But in the 1990s, Fox trashed tradition and promoted itself as the news network for the young and hip. With a stable of young, brash anchors, including Bill O'Reilly and Shepard Smith, Fox eventually caught and passed CNN in the cable news race.

Many of these new anchors have come under fire for their style, but they remain unapologetic. Referring to criticism he received for coming on as too patriotic after the September 11 attacks, Smith said, "If you've got a problem with me putting on an American flag the day after that happens," he said, "you can change the channel" (Bartlett, 2003). Media writer Jim Rutenberg says this is exactly the kind of attitude cable viewers want, "[a] strong point of view and a good dose of showmanship; qualities that are anathema to old-line news organizations" (Rutenberg, 2002).

It is unlikely that Dan Rather or Tom Brokaw of *NBC Nightly News* will suddenly start becoming more edgy and opinionated, and that remains a clear dividing line between cable and network news. "The story mix [on the networks] night to night is fairly similar for the first 10 minutes and then you have variations," said CBS News President Andrew Heyward. "I don't see any one of them sharply diverging from the evening news tradition" (de Moraes, 2003). That's another reason the anchor has become even more important in today's crowded news marketplace—to help networks distinguish their product from the competition.

EMPHASIS ON ENTERTAINMENT

Although the networks' reliance on advertisers and ratings has not changed, the network news audience certainly has. Primarily, fewer people are now watching news in the early evening, traditionally the bread-and-butter viewing period for network and local news. There is also a growing "generation gap" in terms of the broadcast news audience. Broadcast news still dominates the over-50 age group, but many people under 30 simply do not bother, suggesting that this younger group may never pick up the habit. The percentage of people who watch the network evening news has declined among all age groups since 1980 (see Table 2.2).

Much of this was confirmed in a 2002 study by the Project for Excellence in Journalism (2002). The project's study revealed that by November 2002, 76% of stations had reported declines in news viewership. The trend was especially significant in the larger media markets, where 78% of stations reported that they were losing news viewers. Only 55% of people reported watching television news "yesterday," down from a high of 74% in 1994.

Other news consumers say they are simply too busy for broadcast news. In a 1996 study from the Pew Research Center for the People and the Press, many Americans said they don't watch network news because they don't have the time. This includes not only the younger news audiences but the older group, which traditionally has higher usage of television news. The growth of the Internet and other news outlets has made it much easier for news users to skip local and network news and get their information from other sources.

All of this has led the networks to shift their focus away from the traditional older, middle class audiences in favor of younger audiences critical for ratings success. This trend has been well established in other areas of broadcasting and media. The supermarket tabloids are testimony to the fact that Americans love to talk about celebrities and entertainers. Television shows devoted to popular culture, such as *Entertainment Tonight,* have become extremely successful, as have entertainment-oriented magazine shows and talk shows. Even as far back as 1977, Pulitzer Prize–winning television critic Ron Powers wrote, "TV journalism in this country—local TV journalism, in particular—is drifting into the sphere of entertainment" (Postman, 1985).

Tonya Harding, O. J. Simpson, and Princess Diana all reflected a growing culture of the celebrity, not only in society but in journalism, as well. Celebrities perfectly fit into the new definition of media: They are plentiful, can be recycled continuously, and may be forgotten instantly. Where

Table 2.2   Percentage of the General Public Watching Evening Network News

Age Group	1980 Audience (%)	1995 Audience (%)
Over 65	53	38
Over 50	45	30
35-49	23	12
18-24	16	6

SOURCE: Nielsen National Television Index (cited in "Changing channels," 1996).

once network documentaries investigated the problems of poverty and migrant workers, the airwaves have now become filled with favorite recipes, off-screen romances, and tawdry gossip. "We can no longer gather an audience simply by having news from around the world," says CBS News President Andrew Heyward. "Sometimes there's much more heat than light" (Gavel, 2002). Lowell Bergman (2000) is even more direct. "News no longer means what it once did," he said. "The very forms used by the broadcast news organizations emphasizing the 'star' correspondent over the substance of the story have undermined their credibility."

For example, CBS News took a lot of heat in 2003 for its pursuit of Jessica Lynch, the highly publicized Army private briefly held as a prisoner of war during the invasion of Iraq. In a request for an interview, CBS offered Lynch pitches for a TV movie, concert, and book deal. CBS chief executive officer Les Moonves later admitted that the network might have erred in making the offers to Lynch (de Moraes, 2003).

Even the way the networks covered the conflict was often more focused on entertainment than on hard news. Frontline reporting from the battlefields ignored most traditional techniques and focused more on personalizing the war through embedded reporting (see chapter 9).

Bergman (2000) noted, "There was once a fire wall between the commercial-entertainment side of broadcasting and the public service 'news' side. That fire wall has been breached."

EMPHASIS ON TECHNOLOGY

In almost no industry does the technology change as fast as in the mass media, and especially in broadcast news. What began with film cameras and magnetic weather symbols has now developed into satellite transmission, live reporting, digital photography and editing, and computerized animation. Historically, demand and technological innovation have created a situation in which broadcast equipment has a short shelf life. The cameras and other equipment introduced today could be obsolete in a matter of a few years. Digital television, for example, will require all-new technology that is radically different from today's standard analog systems.

New technology plays an important role in network news for several reasons. For one thing, it makes the newscast visually appealing, especially to coveted younger audiences. People who grew up with computers naturally want a newscast to incorporate the latest and most sophisticated technology, and the networks have obliged with dazzling graphics, effects, and animation. Commenting on the networks' coverage of the 2001 invasion of Afghanistan, Jill Geisler (2001) of the Poynter Institute noted that there were "uplinks. Videophones. Experts on the set. Maps that animate, maps to be drawn on, pointed to, stood before. Graphics of military assets: pictures and words to illustrate the capabilities of planes, missiles and ships."

Viewers also expect reporters, producers, and especially anchors to have a certain level of technical sophistication. As just a small example, anchor Peter Jennings began incorporating the Internet and e-mail into his *World News Tonight* newscasts in the late 1990s. "It provides an immediate way to connect with the audience, to be personal in a way that was simply impossible before," says Jennings (Wendland, 2000). Interactivity is one of the new buzzwords in the industry, and technology makes it possible for the audience to take more of an active role in the newscast. Many stations believe that getting the audience involved will increase its loyalty to the news program. Thus, online viewer polls, e-mail feedback, and interactive websites have become quite common. There is evidence to suggest that these devices are helping to maintain and grow news audiences. A Radio and Television News Directors Association (RTNDA) study (RTNDA, 1996) showed "strong evidence that news consumers want to interact with news providers and news makers."

On a more practical level, technology has helped the networks deal with their budget problems. Although most new technology is expensive, it is also smaller, easier to use, and sophisticated enough to stretch other station resources. For example, in his "Road to Anywhere" segment, ABC reporter Mike Lee (2002) spent a recent summer covering the globe with nothing but a small digital video camera, a mobile phone, and a laptop with video editing software. All of his pieces were produced as "one-man bands," without the aid of any photographers or producers. One-man bands have been extremely common in smaller markets for years, but the new realities of broadcast news have increased their use at larger stations and networks.

According to Mike Peacock (2001), president of the consulting firm MEDIAdvise,

> The trend of multi purpose television employees [the one-man band] has been established now at the network level and is gaining momentum across

all markets. The bottom line is that employees are required to do more and technological advancements have removed the obstacles. Cameras are lighter and more manageable, non-linear editing is easier and faster and lower third graphics insertion can be made in the software. Even traditional operations employing a staff of photographers, producers and reporters benefit economically and functionally from a more diverse workforce. Today's production environment, running at Internet speed, mandates a cross-culturalization. News reporters or producers trained in the visual language can take a camera by themselves and acquire quality footage.

Unfortunately, cheaper news is also often lower quality news. At the same time ABC and other networks reduced the number of their foreign correspondents and consolidated their news programs, they focused more on cheap, easy to produce content, such as Mike Lee's travels. No one would deny that such reports are interesting, but are they really news? "What is being lost," says longtime NBC newsman Garrick Utley (1997), "has long been forecast: the role of a few television network news organizations as a unifying central nervous system of information for the nation, and the communal benefits associated with that."

The growing dependence on technology raises an interesting question for producers—the importance of technology in a newscast. As with live reporting, just because we now have all these exciting technical gadgets, does that mean we should use them? Live coverage of the Iraqi battlefield is visually interesting, but what about the pain and anxiety it causes for the families of soldiers back home? "The worry for me always is that the technology will lead us, and we won't lead technology," says Brokaw. "We have to be in charge" (Grossman, 2002).

Implications for Local Producers

There are very few secrets in broadcasting, and what works for one station or network usually gets immediately copied. The success of programs like *Who Wants to Be a Millionaire?* and *Survivor* ignited a boom in primetime game shows and reality programming in the late 1990s.

The same thing happens in broadcast news, where successful methods and formats are copied with regularity. When the "Action News" format (emphasizing shorter stories, more video, and lots of action) emerged in the 1970s, it became a staple at newsrooms all across the country. Given the high stakes of today's television news, stations often prefer to stick with proven styles they know will work. In 2003, CBS News President Andrew Heyward said, "I don't think there are vast philosophical differences [between the network newscasts]. All three were a little too similar, given how competitive the marketplace is" (de Moraes, 2003).

Table 2.3   Use of Technology in Television Newsrooms

Type of Technology	Percentage of All Stations Using
Digital field cameras	58
Computer-assisted reporting	54
Digital editing	46
Digital studio cameras	20
Virtual (computer)-generated news set	5

SOURCE: Papper and Gerhard (2001).

The upshot is that producers face many of the same challenges, whether they are at the network level or producing for a local station. In its Journalism and Ethics Integrity Project, the Radio and Television News Directors Foundation (RTNDF, 1998) noted that most Americans are satisfied with the state of broadcast news, but "both news directors and the public agree that the desire to increase television ratings and the desire to make a profit can improperly influence local television news" (p. 5).

Local producers must deal with financial accountability, the rise of entertainment in news programming, and the role of technology in the newscast. For example, consider how local producers must deal with technology. It should be obvious that stations want to produce the most sophisticated and visually compelling newscasts possible, but it is also clear that sometimes this effort focuses too much on the presentation of the news and not enough on the content. Aside from that issue, many of today's producers see technology as more of a benefit when it comes to putting together a newscast (see Table 2.3). According to Matt Ellis, news director at WBZ-TV in Boston and former producer,

> Technology is a tool. Live shots give a newscast an infusion of energy over taped reports and graphics help illustrate facts and explain complex information. That said, some television stations lean more heavily on graphics, live shots and music to jazz up their product. A good producer knows how to use the tools to enhance the basics: stories that are important to the community, stories that are told well and teases that keep viewers watching. (Personal communication, April 2003)

News director Rick Hadley of WBAP-FM in Dallas agrees that technology can make a tremendous difference in helping a producer gather, organize, and present information.

Figure 2.1   How Much Technology Is Too Much, Especially When It Comes to Weather?

In the time since I was producing WBAP's morning show nearly ten years ago, the availability of information has changed greatly. Ten years ago I barely knew of the Internet. Today it's one of the most valuable tools for the radio producer. You can find the answer to almost any question on the Internet. Need an expert to interview? Fire up your search engine and seconds later you have the names and phone numbers of dozens of experts at your disposal. Another area where technology has made the producer's job easier is moving from an analog tape-based recording format to digital, computer based recording. Now we can capture audio and edit it much more efficiently and creatively, enabling us to get better-produced sound on the air in a timelier manner. (Personal communication, April 2003)

No part of the newscast is more dependent on technology than weather, which serves as an example of how some stations have gone into technology overload. A lot of current thinking suggests that the more weather technology a station has, the better its presentation. Oftentimes, however, audiences cannot cut through the clutter of today's sophisticated weather graphics to get the only information they really want—what is the weather doing, and what will it do tomorrow?

Jeff Lyons, the chief meteorologist at WFIE-TV in Evansville, Indiana, uses as much current weather technology as anyone else. "The technology is terrific, and we have become adept at presenting the viewer with many, many different ways of seeing what the weather is doing," he said. But he also sounded a warning that producers of news and weather should consider:

I think we are probably at a point of near-technology overload. I would look for the pendulum to swing back the other way for a time and we will again see weathercasters in front of real maps with magic markers and magnetic numbers. As long as the technology is relevant to what the viewer needs to know, it will usually be accepted by the public. Technology for technology's sake is usually an annoyance and adds to the clutter in getting the message out. (Personal interview, March 2003)

Producers at both the network and local levels are struggling with these issues. How much does technology influence a newscast? How can we create an effective newscast, given limited resources? How important should the anchor be in the news presentation? For the most part, the answers to these questions will come on a case-by-case, station-by-station basis. But whoever can come up with the most effective solutions, you can be assured that it will not stay secret for long.

Thinking More About It

Professional media researchers and those in academics often try to learn more about broadcast news through what is called a *content analysis*. A content analysis is simply a detailed look at media content, whether it is magazine photographs, newspaper advertising copy, or broadcast stories. The easiest way to conduct a content analysis for broadcast news is to tape a series of shows (usually chosen at random) and then carefully look at the content of the stories for important trends. Tape a series of newscasts for both network and local television news and consider the following:

1. How much of the news is influenced by "entertainment?" How many stories are related to celebrities, pop culture, or "lighter" news?

2. How important are the anchors to the newscast? Of all the time devoted to news, how much is given to the anchors? If the show has two news anchors, does one seem to have more time or receive more attention?

3. How important is technology in the newscast? Do fancy graphics and sophisticated presentation seem more important than the stories?

4. Do the national newscasts seem drastically different from the local newscasts? Is one more "entertaining" than another? Does one put more emphasis on the personality of the anchor? On technology?

For a more detailed analysis of network news, Vanderbilt University in Nashville, Tennessee, has a complete library of every network television newscast dating back to 1968. This can help students see how the networks covered important stories and help track the important changes in network news over the decades. For more information on how to access the material, go to http://tvnews.vanderbilt.edu/

The Producing Process 3

By now, you have a pretty good idea of what a producer does to get a newscast on the air. So far, we have only talked about these duties in the abstract sense. It is now time to take a closer look at the step-by-step process of putting a show together.

Story Ideas and News Value

A newscast starts with a series of story ideas, which are nothing more than potential ideas that could eventually end up in the show. Story ideas come from a variety of sources, and the good producer will often come to work with several story ideas already formulated. These may come from other media, be follow-ups from stories done the previous day, or be a consequence of personal observation (see Table 3.1 for examples).

Producers like their reporters to come to work with story ideas, and reporters should have some concrete suggestions for stories, even if these ideas never pan out. Too many reporters show up with the expectation that producers will have a story already assigned to them. This can waste a lot of precious news time as reporters scramble to try and set up a story or contact news sources.

Producers and reporters will suggest their story ideas at the editorial meeting, where they and the news director will discuss events going on in the area. The purpose of the meeting is to consider all possible story ideas and narrow them down to a list of stories that will go in the newscast. Some stories are included for obvious reasons—they involve important breaking news or have a special significance in the community. If the area

Table 3.1   Examples of Sources for Story Ideas

Source	Comment
Other media	Getting story ideas from the newspaper or other stations is fine, but avoid simply following what they are doing. Try to take a simple idea and expand it into something new. Competing stations should always be monitored but not necessarily copied.
News wires	News services like the Associated Press (AP) provide producers with hundreds of stories every day. Some of these stories can be run as items of national or regional interest. Others can be localized to the station's community. For example, if AP reports that binge drinking has increased on college campuses, the station can investigate the situation at the local school.
Beat system	If the station has enough resources, it can assign reporters to "beats"—covering the same story or issue every day (such as city hall or health). The problem is that most broadcast outlets do not have enough reporters to assign them to beats. Most have to be general assignment reporters, covering different stories every day.
News releases	Stations receive dozens, maybe even hundreds of news releases every day, and it is up to the producer to determine their news value. Some are simply notices of meetings, organizational happenings, etc. Others might have items of genuine interest. It is important for the producer to realize that all of these releases are essentially public relations tools, and the people that send them have a specific agenda. The governor wants you to attend his news conference so he can talk about a new initiative, not to ask him questions that might generate negative coverage. When using news releases to shape story coverage, producers should always be aware of the agenda behind them.
News tips	One thing you will learn about working in the news business: There is never a shortage of people willing to give their opinion. People constantly call the newsroom with story ideas or tips, most of which never amount to anything. However, you should never automatically dismiss any tip. Not only does it make the caller mad, but you might actually miss out on a good story. This is especially true in an age when most people have cell phones and can call stations from the scene of breaking news. If possible, always double check the information before committing news resources.
Recycling old stories	Many stories have a long shelf life and can be brought back at appropriate times, such as anniversaries. One-year, 5-year, and 10-year stories are extremely popular, as are stories that observe the anniversary date of a particular event.
Personal observation	Some of the best story ideas come from simple observation or individual ingenuity. You may notice something new on the way to work or read a small announcement in the paper that could lead to a big story. Producers and reporters should always keep their eyes open in the community and be on the lookout for story ideas.

is threatened by severe weather, for example, the station will make sure to emphasize that story in its news coverage.

The most obvious consideration in selecting story ideas for the show is news value (Table 3.2). Certain elements of a story idea make it more attractive to the audience, such as geographical proximity or timeliness. Just as important, some elements of a story idea make it unattractive, such as stories that simply fill air time, are done because they're expedient, or are considered overly superficial or sensational.

Not all story ideas are accepted or rejected based on news merit. The resources a station has often dictates how and if it will cover a certain story. For example, the big story of the day might be a court case involving a prominent local citizen. If the trial takes place several hours from the station, however, that will affect the station's coverage. The news director might ideally want live coverage of the story, but a live shot might be technically impossible given the distance involved. Therefore, some alternative form of coverage will have to be considered.

Thus not only do stations decide what stories to cover but how to cover them (Table 3.3). Generally, the more important stories are given live coverage or extended time by reporters. Stories not considered important can be read on the desk by the anchors or handled with a short interview. But again, this is not always determined by news value. Available resources play a part, as does the news deadline. Reporters need additional time to put together extended stories; engineers also need more time to set up live coverage. Distance between the story and the station is also a factor, as drive time to and from stories must be considered.

During the editorial meeting, the news staff will decide on the nature and format of many of the stories in the show. Reporters and producers will get their assignments, and they will be responsible for putting together stories of a predetermined length. Live shots often run in excess of 2 minutes because they include so many unpredictable elements. Almost every station has a story about a live shot that was accidentally knocked off the air or disturbed in some other fashion. Packages typically run in the range of 1½ minutes; a reader or SOT might go anywhere from 15 to 45 seconds.

Of course, this depends on the nature of the story involved. For an extremely important story, reporters will get extra time. In some cases, the producer will decide to use "team coverage" and have different reporters work on different aspects of the story. For example, in the case of severe weather, one reporter might report on the traffic situation, another on the damage to homes and property, another on school closings, and so on.

Rundowns

Once a producer has a list of stories and their formats, the task of actually putting the show together begins.

Table 3.2   What Gives a Story News Value?

Quality	Comment
Timeliness	This is especially important in the age of the Internet and cable news, where people can get news any time of day or night. The news cycle continues to shrink, and people want their information now—not hours or even minutes from now.
Relevance	How does the story affect the lives of the audience? Why should the people watching or listening at home care about this story? These are the questions producers should ask about all story ideas. If it does not affect a large number of people in the audience in some way, it has little news value.
Proximity (geographic and emotional)	Certainly geographic proximity plays a role in news value. If something important happens close to home, that makes a big difference to the local audience. But there is also news value in emotional proximity. This is the kind of story that touches a common emotional chord in the audience, regardless of where it takes place. In fall 2002, the nation was gripped by the daring rescue of nine Pennsylvania coal miners trapped underground. The emotions of the story—anger, sadness, fear, and ultimately happiness and pride— gave it audience appeal far beyond the local region where the rescue took place.
Prominence	When something happens to someone famous, it makes news. A car accident involving two private citizens might rate a bare mention on the news, but if the mayor was involved, the story gets much more attention. Unfortunately, much of news is now focused on the famous and those with "celebrity," even if they are not making news. Producers have to be careful not to let their coverage of viable news stories drift into the sensational.
Conflict	Politics, law, government, sports, and even the weather can be reduced to issues of conflict, whether it is one person against another or someone struggling against other obstacles. Ultimately, most of journalism is about reporting on how specific conflicts affect the audience. However, there is a danger in simply reporting the "he said, she said," part of conflict. Good stories go beyond the conflict and examine the underlying issues.
Novelty	Every day in this country, thousands of people are victims of domestic abuse. So why do we remember the name of John Wayne Bobbitt? Because of the unusual circumstances surrounding the incident. The novel or unusual always has an interest for an audience. The problem is that with so many channels now available, and so many shows pushing the moral envelope, it is getting harder and harder to see something unique. Producers should avoid running novelty material just for the sake of sensationalism or titillation.

Table 3.3   Story Formats

Story Format	Description	Comment
Live	Reporter goes live from scene, or a camera is set up to show events as they are happening.	Usually for the more important stories, and often done in combination with a packaged report. The use of live reporting often depends on the reliability of the live signal back to the station.
Package	A self-contained taped report put together by a reporter or anchor. Includes all the elements of a report (sound, video, etc.) in a complete "package."	Again, for the more important stories. Can be used in combination with a live report, introduced by the reporter from the news desk, or as a stand-alone story.
Interview	Also called SOT (sound on tape), sound bite, bite, or actuality (radio term). Usually a 10- to 20-second interview segment with a person connected to the story. Can be used alone or in conjunction with video.	When the story is not as important, or when the deadline is such that reporters do not have time to put together a package. Can also be introduced by the reporter from the news desk or from a live shot.
Phoner	A live report phoned in by the reporter (or some other person) at the scene of a story. Often used for breaking news.	Extremely common in radio news, especially with the advent of cell phones. Not used as much in television because of lack of visuals, but is appropriate for breaking news, short deadlines, or where it is impossible to provide video.
Reader	The news anchor reads a story on air, with no supporting audio or video elements.	Usually reserved for the least important stories or for breaking news reported at the last minute. Producers do not like to fill up their shows with readers because the stories often do not engage or interest the audience.

Every show has a *rundown,* one of the most important tools a producer uses. The rundown is simply an outline that allows the producer to create, edit, switch, or eliminate stories within the newscast. The key to a rundown is flexibility, because producers will constantly make changes in stories right up to news time and even into the show. For example, if

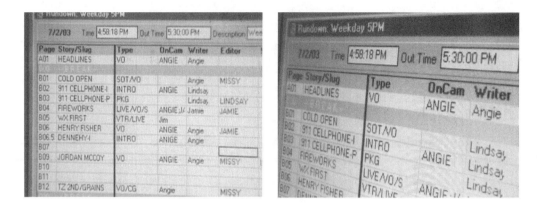

Figure 3.1   Two Views of a Newscast Rundown

SOURCE: Photographs by Mary Lou Sheffer. Printed by permission.

breaking news happens during the newscast, the producer will have to insert it into the rundown in the appropriate place.

All newsroom personnel—the news director, producers, reporters, photographers, technical directors, control room operators, and anchors—work off the same rundown. Each person uses the rundown for a different reason. Technical directors want to know what tapes to run and in what order. Anchors want to know who will be reading what stories, and audio people need to know when to open (turn on) and close (shut off) microphones. Given all this, the rundown is probably the single most important resource in the newscast.

Each station uses a particular rundown style, but almost every rundown contains the same important information.

Table 3.4 shows an example of how a small segment of the rundown might look. A more complete version will be displayed later, but the important thing right now is the headings at the top of the rundown. All rundowns indicate the *story slug,* or the name of the story. Usually, this is an abbreviated one- or two-word description of the story. All newsroom personnel will refer to the story by this name, and it is in all capital letters for easy identification.

Talent refers to which anchor will read the story on the air. This can be indicated in several ways, including the initials of the anchor (BES), the camera number, or some other reference to the talent (Wx is a standard broadcasting abbreviation for weather). In the "STORM" story row, 2-SHT in this case refers to the fact that two anchors will both be reading. Their exact reading assignments will be detailed on the story script, which will be described later in this chapter.

The *format* refers to how the story will be presented on the air. In our example, the "STORM" story will be a live report, "SCHOOL" will have the anchor introduce a reporter package, and "WRECK" will have an anchor

Table 3.4   Segment of a Typical Television News Rundown

Slug	Talent	Format	Tape No.	ERT	Tape	Total	Runtime	Backtime
STORM	2-SHT	Live	——	2:00	——	2:00	5:32:00	0:00
SCHOOL	BES	PKG	101	:20	1:40	2:00	5:34:00	+:10
WRECK	DFS	V/O	102	:20	——	:20	5:34:20	−:05
FORECAST	Wx	Live	——	1:00	——	1:00	5:35:20	0:00

Note: BES and DFS indicate the initials of the on-air talent; ERT, estimated running time; PKG, package; 2-SHT, two-shot (two anchors); V/O, voiceover; Wx, weather. Numbers in the ERT, Tape, Total, Runtime, and Backtime columns indicate time in minutes and seconds.

read over (or "voiceover") video. In the "FORECAST" story, the weather person will deliver a live update on the forecast.

If there is a tape connected with the story, it must be assigned a *tape number*. This is essential information for the technical director and control room people, who need to know what tape is rolled at what point in the newscast. Tapes are usually assigned numbers or other designations to make this process easier, but the possibility of error or mix-up remains high. Tapes are often mislabeled, misplaced, or run at the wrong time in the show. More and more stations are converting to digital technology and putting stories on computer files rather than tape. Still, human error remains a constant problem.

ERT refers to the estimated running time of the story, which gives the producer an idea of how long the story will run. If there's no tape involved, the ERT is simply a measure of how long it will take the anchors to read the story. In the days before newsroom computers, reading speed was often difficult to gauge, and producers usually had to guess based on the number of lines of copy on the script. Today's producing software automatically calculates ERT based on the anchor's own distinct reading speed.

If there is a tape involved, that time is indicated in the *tape* column. This indicates how long the taped piece in the story will run, generally around 15 seconds for a SOT and about 1½ minutes for a package. Producers expect reporters to keep their packages within a certain time framework. If the story comes in much heavier or lighter than projected, changes will have to be made elsewhere in the rundown, another reason that communication between producer and reporter is so important. It is possible to know exactly how long a taped segment lasts, unless the story is still being edited when the newscast starts.

The combination of the ERT and the tape gives the *total time* for the story. This lets the producer know exactly how much time each story will take and allows the producer to easily make changes to the newscast when

Figure 3.2   Producers Make Constant Changes to the Rundown, Even During the Show
SOURCE: Photograph by Mary Lou Sheffer. Printed by permission.

necessary. If the show is very slow and taking too long ("running heavy"), the producer can glance at the rundown and perhaps eliminate stories of a certain length. If the show seems to be moving quickly and under the allotted time ("running light"), the producer can add stories or let the anchors know to adjust their reading speed.

Many rundowns will indicate a *runtime*, which helps the producer gauge how the show is timing out. This is the clock time when the story is scheduled to run. In our example, the "WRECK" story is supposed to run at 5:34:20. If it runs much earlier or later, producers will have to adjust their newscast accordingly.

A better indication of how the show is timing out is called *backtiming*. This is a function built in to most producing software that allows the producer to know if the show is running heavy or light. After each story, the backtiming column will indicate a certain amount of time. If the time is followed by a plus sign (+), the show is running light by that amount of time. In our "SCHOOL" example, after the story runs, the show is 10 seconds light, and that time will have to be accounted for somewhere else in the newscast. When the time is followed by a minus (−) sign, the show is running heavy by that amount of time. (Note: There is no set standard for these designations. Depending on the software, running heavy and running light could be indicated in different ways.)

In most circumstances, it's important to end a newscast at a specific time, with no margin for error. Many newscasts lead into network programming, which cannot be missed. Ideally, the producer wants to end the show with 0:00 showing in the backtiming column. This can get very tricky, considering all the changes the producer has to make to the newscast. Many producers prefer to go in with a "light" rundown (one with a smaller news hole), with the expectation that things will go wrong and slow things down. It's also easier to add material to a newscast (or ask the anchors to slow down) than it is to drop things or speed up. In any event, backtiming allows the producer to know the exact time of the show as it progresses.

Our discussion of the rundown has assumed that you as a producer will have access to production software. Most commercial stations around the country have such software, although it is not as common on college campuses. Even without a software program, you can create a rundown using an application like Microsoft Excel. If you are producing a show completely without the aid of a computer, it certainly makes things more difficult. Everything has to be done by hand (or typewriter), and the timing must be done with a stopwatch or some other clock with a second hand. The same basic principles of the rundown apply whether you're producing with or without a computer; the main difference is flexibility and the ability to make quick changes.

SKELETON RUNDOWNS

Most stations use the same rundown format for each of their shows. There are certain elements that appear in the same place in the show every day—things like the opening sequence (the "show open"), weather and sports, and the closing sequence (the "show close"). This creates some consistency for the audience and makes the job of the producer much easier.

When the producer first sits down to work on the show, many of these elements are already in place. The producer uses some form of the skeleton rundown shown in Table 3.5 to start every show.

Table 3.5 clearly shows the elements that will stay the same in every newscast. For this particular station, the show opens with the anchors doing headlines, a short description of the top stories of the day. The show open and close are preproduced by the production department and rarely change. Only when a station wants to reshape its image will it change its open or close, as consistency helps create brand identity with the audience. The producer does not actively deal with these segments, other than to make sure they're accounted for in the rundown.

Weather and sports are usually given the same amount of time in each show, although this could change depending on the needs of the news department. Both are areas in which the producer has some flexibility to

Table 3.5   Typical Skeleton Rundown

Slug	Talent	Format	Tape No.	ERT	Tape	Total	Runtime	Backtime
HEADLINE	2-SH	V/O	101	:15		:15	5:30:00	+14:20
OPEN	VTR	VTR		:15		:15	5:30:15	
BREAK	——	——	——	2:00	——	——		
BREAK	——	——	——	2:00	——	——		
WX INTRO	3-SH			:10				
WX	JPL			3:00				
WX OUT	3-SH			:10				
BREAK	——	——	——	2:00	——	——		
SPORTS IN	3-SH			:10				
SPORTS	JC			3:00				
SPRT OUT	3-SH			:10				
BREAK	——	——	——	2:00	——	——		
KICKER	2-SH	PKG		2:00				
CLOSE	4-SH	VTR		:30				

Note: ERT indicates estimated running time; JC and JPL, the initials of the on-air talent; PKG, package; SPRT, sports; 2-SH, 3-SH, and 4-SH, multiple anchors; V/O, voiceover; VTR, videotape recording; Wx, weather. Numbers in the ERT, Tape, Total, Runtime, and Backtime columns indicate time in minutes and seconds.

adjust show timing. Beyond assigning time, the producer does not generally worry about these segments but rather leaves them to the weather and sports directors. There might be some coordination between the departments if the situation warrants, such as in the case of severe weather or an important sports story. There is also time built into the show for the news people to introduce the weather and sports segments and for those segments to return to weather. These "pitches" are not usually scripted, but a producer must account for their time. Pitches are another good way of adjusting for timing problems in a newscast, as producers can request that anchors talk longer or shorter.

Most stations usually run a "kicker" at the end of their newscasts—a light-hearted feature story that leaves the audience with a good feeling. So much of the news is about crime, death, or other terrible things that stations want to give the audience something uplifting at the end, in the hope that it will get the audience to come back for the next newscast. The kicker doesn't always have to be a package; it can be a short voiceover or even a reader.

Not everyone agrees with the value of a kicker. Many news directors see it as a waste of valuable air time, especially if the story isn't local. Research also indicates that when a kicker is used in a newscast, viewers rate the earlier stories in the show as less important or severe. According to the authors of the study (Zillmann, 1984), "[This] raises ethical questions about using soft news in this capacity. Is such a practice in the public interest?" Despite such concerns, the use of kicker stories is extremely common.

You'll also notice that "break" times are already in the rundown. These refer to the commercial breaks built into each show. Typically, stations will have the same number of breaks and commercial time in each show, but it can vary. That's why it's important for producers to check the station log (usually found in the traffic department or master control) to find out how many breaks are in the show and how long they last. As we have discussed, the break times are sacred in a newscast and can't be skipped, shortened, or eliminated except under extraordinary circumstances. Many producers check the commercial breaks first and make sure they're in the right places.

The information we have so far figures in the runtime and backtime columns. The show is supposed to begin at 5:30 p.m., when the show open starts. Backtiming indicates that the show is 14:20 light (+14:20). The computer has determined that given the elements already in the rundown, the show still needs more than 14 minutes of material to fill a 30-minute newscast. Barring any other changes to the rundown, the producer knows that he or she has a news hole of 14:20 to fill. As elements are added to the newscast, the backtiming figure adjusts automatically—unless the producer is not using a computer, in which case the calculations must be done by hand.

Blocks and Stacking

Looking at our sample rundown, you can see two main areas that need to be filled. They include the segment immediately after the show open and the segment immediately before weather. These segments are generally referred to as "blocks" because they operate in much the same fashion as building blocks.

Just as the pieces in a building-block construction are all connected and support each other, the same holds true for news blocks. The idea is that the stories should be connected in some fashion and flow together logically. This means that the stories are often grouped together based on their topic, importance, or some other factor. For example, many stations make the first block of their newscast a "local news" block and the second block a "national news" block. Others might devote the entire first block to an important news topic or theme, such as a high-profile community event.

One popular blocking format is called "11 at 11," which refers to 11 minutes of news at 11:00 p.m. These stations produce a mini newscast in the first 11 minutes of the show, complete with weather and sports. Variants include "10 at 10" and "9 at 9," depending on when the news show begins. The idea is that the audience can get all its important information in a shorter period of time.

For the sake of our example, let's assume that the station prefers a local news block followed by a national news block. The producer can use this framework to start putting stories in a certain order, a process called "stacking." Interestingly, most research indicates little or no relationship between segment placement and the level of viewer interest in general. That is, audience attention does not necessarily depend on the order of the stories. Even so, producers try to stack shows in the most logical, coherent, and reasonable format possible.

There are no written rules for stacking a newscast, but producers do follow certain accepted guidelines.

The Most Important Stories
Go First, Followed by Less Important Stories

This guideline is a broadcast version of the newspaper "inverted pyramid," in which stories are written with the most important information at the beginning. It is only logical that stations want to lead their newscasts with what they perceive as the most important stories of the day. This is especially important for broadcast stations, which face the growing threat of audience members switching channels if they don't find the top story interesting.

It's also why many stations incorporate live shots or packaged reports right at the top of the newscast. This type of coverage sends a signal to the audience that the story is important and bears following. Typically, a reporter will do a live report "on location" from the scene of the story. The reporter can give a live report, introduce a taped story, or simply conduct a live interview, depending on the needs of the producer. In some situations, especially when reporters aren't available or in the case of breaking news, a photographer might set up a live shot that simply lets the audience see what's happening at the scene. Someone involved with the story might be asked to answer questions from the anchors on the news desk.

Another currently popular format is to have the reporter go live from the newsroom, which carries the symbolic significance of a live shot without the technical risks of having to go on location. In reality, the reporter may be only a few feet away from the anchor desk. This raises the question of stations overusing live reporting and doing live reports even if the story itself doesn't necessarily warrant live coverage. In fact, some news directors have a standing order that every show must have some form of live report. There is great debate in the broadcast journalism community over live shots and what exactly constitutes good live coverage (see chapter 9). But its use continues to grow, especially as technology improves.

There are other ways to emphasize the importance of the first story without using a live report. Most lead stories involve reporter packages, and in some cases the reporter will introduce his or her own story from the news desk. A phoner might be appropriate, but again this falls into the area of live coverage. Phoners are extremely common in radio and are sometimes used by television stations when live shots aren't available.

The idea of *team coverage* has also become very popular across the country. This simply means extending the lead story by assigning more than one reporter to it. The stories all revolve around different aspects of a single topic, which ties the block together. Team coverage of a major fire in town might include stories on the fire details, the actions of the fire-fighters, the status of the victims, and so on. Team coverage is a good way of tying stories together, but it runs the risk of boring the audience. If the audience doesn't have an immediate interest in the story, it probably won't stay though the entire news block.

Even in the case of team coverage, stories can still be stacked from high importance to low importance. In the case of our fire, the story about the details of the fire would go first. In such situations, the immediate concern of the audience is to find out what happened, how it happened, and who's involved. The next logical story would probably be an update on the victims or something about the damage involved. The actions of the fire-fighters, although important, is not considered the single most important story of the block.

In our example, we're only going to devote one story to the fire and not try any team coverage. Many stations simply don't have enough reporters to devote them all to a single story, and others just don't like the concept of team coverage. A live shot might be appropriate, but there are logistical and other considerations. Can a station get a live signal from the scene of the fire? Will the fire still be going on at newstime, or will anything be happening to provide context and background for the live shot? Too many stations do live shots without consideration for what's going on behind the reporter. The result is often that the background does not help the audience understand what's going on in the story. A perfect example is a live shot done at night, where the reporter is standing in front of total darkness.

Let's assume that our fire will still be going, so the producer decides to have a live report. The reporter will be live on the scene and then introduce a package that tells the audience the important facts about the fire. The reporter can also provide updates, if information becomes available. Now we can add the first story to the first block of our rundown (Table 3.6).

Table 3.6   First Block of Rundown

Slug	Talent	Format	Tape No.	ERT	Tape	Total	Runtime	Backtime
HEADLINE	2-SH	V/O	101	:15		:15	5:30:00	+11:50
OPEN	VTR	VTR		:15		:15	5:30:15	
FIRE	2-SH	LIVE	102	1:00	1:30	2:30	5:30:30	
BREAK	—	—	—	2:00	—	—		

Note: ERT indicates estimated running time; 2-SH, two-shot (two anchors); VTR, videotape recording. Numbers in the ERT, Tape, Total, Runtime, and Backtime columns indicate time in minutes and seconds.

The producer will have to add the appropriate information for the new story. The slug is "FIRE," and it will be introduced by two anchors from the news desk. It is a live shot that also includes a taped package (tape no. 102). The time that the anchors talk and the reporter is actually reporting live is about 1 minute. This is a time figure that could easily change, especially if the anchors ask questions of the reporter on location, so the producer needs to try and keep it under control. The taped package runs 1:30, so the total time for the story is about 2:30.

Notice also that the story is scheduled to start at 5:30:30, so our back-timing figure has changed again. The addition of 2:30 for the "FIRE" story has reduced our news hole to +11:50, which means the producer still has to come up with almost 12 minutes of news material.

The Stories After the Lead Should Follow in a Logical, Coherent, and Consistent Manner

There should be some relationship between stories, which means that in this case the next story should have a logical connection to the fire story. That doesn't mean that it has to be a story about another fire or even about tragedy. But the fire story has set the tone for the rest of the block—stories should be serious and important. Even if team coverage is not used, it is probably serious enough to warrant at least one related story. For example, if the fire started in an old abandoned warehouse, city safety codes might be an issue. It might be possible to get an interview with the city inspector or the person in charge of the codes.

Depending on the deadlines, the interview could be handled in a variety of ways. Let's assume that our deadline is fairly short, and we don't have time for a taped interview. The best solution might be to have the person come in for a live interview with the news anchors on the set. We can now stack another story in our first block (Table 3.7).

Table 3.7   First Block of Rundown

Slug	Talent	Format	Tape No.	ERT	Tape	Total	Runtime	Backtime
HEADLINE	2-SH	V/O	101	:15		:15	5:30:00	+10:20
OPEN	VTR	VTR		:15		:15	5:30:15	
FIRE	2-SH	LIVE	102	1:00	1:30	2:30	5:30:30	
CODES	2-SH	SET		1:30		1:30	5:33:00	
BREAK	——	——	——	2:00	——	——		

Note: ERT indicates estimated running time; 2-SH, two-shot (two anchors); V/O, voiceover; VTR, videotape recording. Numbers in the ERT, Tape, Total, Runtime, and Backtime columns indicate time in minutes and seconds.

The story is slugged "CODES," and it is a live interview from the news set that will take place on a two-shot with one of the anchors. There is no tape involved, and the producer has assigned a total of 1:30 for the interview. With the additional time, our backtime has changed to +10:20, indicating that we are still more than 10 minutes light. It may be that these two stories are all the resources we want to devote to this story in the newscast. There may be the potential for updates or sidebar stories in other newscasts.

Later Stories in the Block Should Be of Similar Nature But Not Be Treated the Same Way

You can see that our station has devoted a lot of resources to the coverage of the first few stories. Live shots require engineers, reporters, photographers, and other support personnel. Except in unusual circumstances, stations can fully commit these resources to only one or two stories per newscast. That means that other stories must receive lesser treatment, using formats such as voiceovers, sound bites, or readers. These other stories must still be similar in nature to the lead stories but not treated with the same amount of depth or commitment of resources.

Depending on what other story ideas came out of the editorial meeting, the producer can go ahead and fill out the rest of the first block (Table 3.8).

The next story on the rundown is slugged "BURGLAR" and is about a burglary that took place in the area. Photographers have video footage of the scene, but the story really doesn't warrant much more coverage than that, unless of course there are serious injuries or damages involved. "TUITION" refers to proposed tuition hike at the local college. This could be considered an important story, but, given the fire, it is downplayed in the

Table 3.8   First Block of Rundown

Slug	Talent	Format	Tape No.	ERT	Tape	Total	Runtime	Backtime
HEADLINE	2-SH	V/O	101	:15		:15	5:30:00	+6:25
OPEN	VTR	VTR		:15		:15	5:30:15	
FIRE	2-SH	LIVE	102	1:00	1:30	2:30	5:30:30	
CODES	2-SH	SET		1:30		1:30	5:33:00	
BURGLAR	AGW	V/O	103	:30		:30	5:34:30	
TUITION	BES	VO/SOT	104	:25	:20	:45	5:35:00	
ROADS	2-SH	PKG	105	:20	1:40	2:00	5:35:45	
MAP	AGW	R/G		:25		:25	5:37:45	
TEASE-1	2-SH	V/O	106	:15		:15	5:38:10	
BREAK	——	——	——	2:00	——	——	5:39:25	

Note: AGW and BES indicate the talent's initials; ERT, estimated running time; R/G, reader-graphic; SOT, sound on tape; 2-SH, two-shot (two anchors); V/O, voiceover; VTR, videotape recording. Numbers in the ERT, Tape, Total, Runtime, and Backtime columns indicate time in minutes and seconds.

newscast. VO/SOT stands for voiceover and sound on tape, a common television news format. The anchor reads while video is running, then he or she stops for a short interview segment. At the end of the interview segment, the anchor usually concludes with a sentence or two. In this case, the interview might be with students or the dean of the college.

"ROADS" refers to a story on local road construction. This might be important to an audience for a variety of reasons, and the station has decided to run it as a package. Coming out of the package, one of the anchors will give information about specific road construction sites. R/G means "reader-graphic," an indication that the information read by the anchor will be supplemented by some sort of graphics. In this case, it's a map of road construction going on in the area. The story could be presented as a simple reader, but graphics often help audiences understand story details better.

Don't Lose Your Audience at the End of a Block

Your newscast is competing against a multitude of other news and information programs on radio, television, and the Internet. Technology has not only increased news options, it has made it easier for audiences to avoid commercial breaks. Sophisticated home recording options such as TiVo allow audiences to record programming with no commercials at all.

Even without such sophistication, everyone has a remote control handy to click to another channel when commercials start to come on.

As the news block begins to give way to commercials, the audience has a strong temptation to change channels. This is a challenge for producers, who realize that once people click away, it's very difficult to get them to click back. The trick is to get people interested enough in the news to stay with the channel through the commercial breaks. It's also a major concern for the sales department, which is selling this air time to advertisers.

The most common solution is the news "tease," now used by almost every station in the country. Right before the commercial break, the news anchors will say a few enticing words about the upcoming stories in hopes that the audience will become interested and not change channels. These teases are usually short (in the range of 5 to 10 seconds) and try to do nothing more than pique the interest of the audience.

Writing teases (which usually falls to the producer) takes some practice. The producer should try not to give away too much information in a tease, much like a movie preview should not give away too much of the plot. If the audience learns everything it needs to know in the preview, why go see the movie? In the same way, why stick through the commercials to see a story you know everything about? On the other hand, many teases suffer from not enough information, and the audience is left with only a vague notion of what's coming up next.

Instead, teases should give enough information to arouse curiosity, which can be done in several ways. The combination of words and video can suggest certain images to the audience or play on common phrases. For example, the sports segment might include a story about how golfer Tiger Woods broke a scoring record at a certain tournament. An appropriate tease might be, "Tiger Woods keeps smashing records . . . that story coming up in sports." The tease interests the audience and creates a desire to know more information, without giving away details about the record itself.

Teases should reflect the tone of the story. That is, don't try to come up with funny, cute, or flippant teases for serious stories. Hard news stories should generally have very straightforward teases that get right to the point. A student reporter one time tried to tease the story about a fatal car-train wreck by saying, "We'll tell you about a race between a car and a train last night that ended in a tie." That is obviously inappropriate, but even when the story itself is lighter or humorous, producers should take caution— not everyone has the same sense of humor.

There is plenty of debate about the use of teases in a newscast. Some news directors think they are a waste of valuable air time and actually hurt audience retention. Most teases are accompanied by music and the phrase, "coming up," which are powerful cues to the audience that a commercial break is upcoming. However, research seems to confirm the value of news teases. Studies by Chang (1998) and Schleuder, White, and Cameron (1993) found that teases helped increase recall and comprehension of the story being teased. Apparently, it makes no difference whether the tease is visual, verbal, or a combination of both.

Know What Your Audience Wants

Several studies have been conducted to determine what audiences want from a newscast, and in a general sense there are certain elements of the newscast that are more appealing. Periodically, the RTNDF surveys audience members to find out this information (Table 3.9).

On the whole, you can see that audiences have a tremendous interest in such elements as weather, local crime, and the community. There is obviously less interest in such things as sports and religion. "The appetite [for sports] is 10 miles deep and a centimeter wide," says Alan Bell, president of Freedom Broadcasting (Greppi, 2002). That's an interesting way of saying that television sports fans are extremely passionate but few in numbers.

Does that mean that producers should drop or severely reduce the amount of sports coverage? Some stations have taken that extreme position, but it's more important for producers to know what's going on in their local markets. It would be foolish to reduce sports coverage in areas where sports are an important part of the local community. Stations

Table 3.9   Interest in Local Television Elements

Element	Viewers Expressing Interest (%)
Weather	94
Local crime	91
Community events	91
Education	91
World news	88
Local government	86
Environment	86
Health and fitness	83
Sports	63
Religion	58

SOURCE: RTNDF American Radio News Audience Survey, 2000. Reprinted with permission.

in Indiana devote almost the entire month of May to coverage of the Indianapolis 500, and the Green Bay, Wisconsin, market is completely committed to the NFL's Packers. The tastes and interests of audiences vary widely from market to market, based on a variety of factors.

One such factor is geography. Different geographic regions have different interests, based on such things as topography, local industry, and the economy. Audiences in western Iowa, for example, are extremely interested in agriculture and farming, and anything that would affect these activities would be of vital interest. The Detroit area certainly has a great interest in the automotive industry, but neighboring Toledo is more concerned with the glass industry. Almost every broadcast market in the country has something to which it pays particular interest.

Interest also varies according to the time of day the newscast airs. Newscasts now run almost throughout the entire day, but the same people don't sit down to watch all of them. Each newscast has a different audience that has different interests (see Table 3.10).

Morning shows (those from 6:00 a.m. to 9:00 a.m.) have a very specific audience—mainly men and women on their way to work, the stay-at-homes, and the elderly. Most of them have just awakened and are getting their first look at the news of the day. As a result, the news in this show needs to be reassuring and nonthreatening. People do not want death and destruction shoved in their face over their morning cornflakes.

Table 3.10   Producing Strategies, Based on Time of Show

Show	Audience	Strategies	Types
Morning	Going to work Just woke up	Reassure Don't scare	Anchor driven Low story count "Soft news"
5:00 p.m.	Women	Use more features Less hard news	Anchor driven Longer, PKG Features Graphics
6:00 p.m.	Mass, men	Hard news Breaking news Information	Story driven Live, team coverage High story count
9:00, 10:00, 11:00 p.m.	All; older Going to bed	Updates Recapitulate, summarize Don't repeat	Anchor driven PKG, live

There are certainly situations in which the morning news shows have to deliver unhappy news, such as the terrorist bombings of September 11, 2001. But for the most part, producers of these shows try to keep things light, happy, and cheerful. Many audience members are women, and the news is often designed to appeal directly to them. This includes "softer" news stories focusing on health, self-improvement, exercise, and cooking.

Many of these programs are also "anchor driven," in the sense that the news itself is not as important as the people delivering it. People will stick with these programs because of the anchors and their personalities and not so much for the story content. That's a big reason morning news anchors like Katie Couric and Matt Lauer of NBC can command multimillion-dollar salaries. Producers tend to focus on the anchors and don't try to cram too many stories into the show. *Story count* refers to the number of stories in a newscast, and morning programs tend to have lower story counts.

The 5:00 p.m. (or early afternoon) newscast is much like the morning shows, although more hard news is included. Again, the audience is primarily stay-at-home and especially female. More attention is focused on stories and issues that appeal to women, like those covered by the morning shows. The lead-in to the show also plays a part in this process. Many early afternoon news programs are directly preceded by woman-oriented shows, such as *Oprah!* or *Maury*. Thus the news in this time slot is designed to cater to the primarily female audience left over from the other shows. Oftentimes, an early afternoon newscast will pay particular attention to an issue covered in its lead-in. If *Oprah!* spends an hour talking about teenage eating disorders, the newscast might devote time to that issue on the local level.

This is not to say that these shows are devoid of hard news material; there is plenty of information presented. But in general, an early afternoon newscast is much lighter and "featurey" than other newscasts.

The 6:00 p.m. newscast is really the signature show for most stations and has the most information and hard news. Most workers have returned home by that time and are anxious to know what's going on in their community. It's the biggest "mass" audience for the local newscast, in the sense that it involves a wide variety of demographic groups. As a result, this newscast is more "story driven" than other shows and has a high story count. The emphasis is on information and catching people up on what they have missed during the day. The news itself is much harder and more serious.

The 6:00 p.m. show used to be the pivotal newscast of the entire day. It was "appointment" television for people interested in news. With the advent of the Internet and 24-hour cable news networks, that's not as true anymore. People can easily find out the big stories of the day before they ever get home from work. But at least for now, this show remains the centerpiece for most broadcast stations.

The late newscast (9:00, 10:00, or 11:00 p.m., depending on the market) is more of a summary or wrap-up of what's happened during the day. Audiences don't really expect any new information, unless there's a breaking story, and simply want to get the latest information before they go to bed. Updates play a big part of this newscast, and stations also make a strong effort to offer something "new" or not seen on earlier shows. It's very important not to repeat the same stories from before, but producers simply don't have the resources to go with all new stories.

To solve this problem, most stations simply run the same stories in different formats. The fire story that was a live shot at 6:00 p.m. may be a package at 10:00 p.m. The story on road conditions that was a package at 6:00 p.m. may be cut down to a VO/SOT for the late news. In this way, producers can use much of the same material from earlier shows but present it in a slightly different version. Reporters understand that their story from the early news will have to be recut into a different version for the late news.

Even with different formats, much of the material in the late show is the same as in earlier shows. There are typically only one or two completely new packages for the late news, depending on the size of the station and its news resources. Because the audience already knows much of the information in the show, late newscasts are often anchor driven, and many times people will watch simply for the anchors. This is especially true in markets where there is little differentiation between stations in terms of news product, and it is another reason why producers should work to give the show a different feel and appearance and not make the audience feel as if the stories are simply recycled.

Emphasize Localism

In the old days of broadcasting, most stations had captive audiences because there weren't that many news options. Those who wanted to watch television typically had three or four local channels to choose from, and local stations became important sources for local, regional, and national news. Many people got all their news from the local station.

The situation is obviously much different today. Cable, Internet, and satellite news channels make news available on a 24-hour-a-day basis. Newspaper websites can also provide audiences with important local and regional happenings. In a very practical sense, audiences don't need broadcast stations to keep up with what's going on.

That's why it's so important for local stations to emphasize local news. In many markets, a national newscast will immediately precede local news, not only giving audiences plenty of national coverage but doing it better than a local newscast could. Local stations must give local audiences a reason to tune in, and that means focusing on stories and issues important in the community. This doesn't mean that there can't be national news material in a local newscast, and audiences do expect stations to update them on important stories outside their market. But on the whole, producers cannot make national material the focus of local news programming and expect audiences to pay attention.

Make Your Show Interactive

One way of emphasizing localism is to make your newscast more interactive. Broadcasting has traditionally been a one-way communication process, in which the station sends out information and the audience passively receives it. But developments in technology have now allowed the audience to take a more active role in news.

Many stations have experimented with getting their audiences more involved through such things as viewer polls, contests, and other lines of feedback. The growth of cell phone use has made it possible for stations to put listeners at the scene of breaking news directly on the air. The Internet has been very useful in making news more interactive in a variety of ways. The most obvious is that audiences can now directly e-mail stations with story ideas, feedback on stories, and suggestions. Most news organizations now have websites that update audiences on important news and give them an opportunity to contribute their opinions. How much of this has any direct impact on the station's news product is unknown, but it does give the audience more of a stake in the newscast (for more on producing news for the Internet, see chapter 7).

Push the Envelope, But Realize Your Limitations

We have discussed the fact that news coverage depends largely on the station's resources. These resources can be technical, such as cameras, microphones and live trucks, or they can be human resources, such as reporters, photographers, editors, and the like. One of the primary jobs of a producer is to use these resources to put together the best possible newscast.

"Pushing the envelope" means nothing more than maximizing the available resources to cover the most news. Too many times, producers prefer to play it safe and do things the easy way. However, playing it safe does not always work in an era of increased competition and more news options. Chances are, other stations are trying to do things bigger and better and take away your audience.

How does a producer maximize resources? In a number of ways. If a reporter and photographer have to make a long drive out of town to cover a story, could they possibly pick up any other news in that area? Is there another story close by that they could get? Maybe the sports department is covering a game in that area, and a sports person could pick up the news story. In this way, producers have additional resources to use somewhere else.

Are there other news outlets that could help in story coverage? Many stations use stringers or interns for this purpose, although their contribution is usually limited. But stations often enlist the help of other stations (although not competing stations in their own market) in covering stories. Each station might contribute something to a joint effort that allows both stations to have better coverage than they would have had alone. For example, when a school shooting rocked Paducah, Kentucky, in 1997, stations from all across the Midwest converged on the city. Local stations affiliated with the same network worked together in coordinated coverage, and their "pooling" of resources allowed them to cover the story in much greater depth.

However, there is a danger in pushing the envelope too far. All resources, whether technical or human, have limits. It would be foolish, for example, to count on a live shot if the distance or weather conditions involved are prohibitive. Reporters aren't just resources to be moved around at will; they're also human beings who can suffer from overwork, fatigue, and frustration. It would not be very productive to take a reporter who has been working all day on a difficult story and reassign him or her to a completely different story later in the afternoon. Sometimes these things must happen, such as in the case of breaking news, but they should not be done on a consistent basis. A good producer realizes the limitations of the available resources and plans the show accordingly.

Think "Big Picture"

There's no doubt that blocking, stacking, rundowns, and story formats are important considerations for producers, but sometimes it's easy to miss the forest for the trees. A producer who gets wrapped up in the little details of producing may miss the bigger picture: producing an effective and engaging newscast.

A well-produced newscast is more than just the sum of its technical parts; it involves teamwork, coordination, critical decision making, and flexibility. Good blocking and stacking are important, but by themselves they do not make for a successful show. Some of the most interesting newscasts are done "by the seat of the pants" and seem to come together only at the last minute. By contrast, many shows that are blocked and stacked well fall flat with the audience.

Things Viewers Never, Ever Say

Steve Safran is the executive producer of New England Cable News and contributes to *Lost Remote* (http://www.lostremote.com). He says that many of the things producers get in arguments about—sometimes very heated arguments—are just stupid because the audience never even considers them. Safran says the following list of what "viewers never, ever say" illustrates how producers need to reconnect with their audiences.

- "They went: package, VO, package, SOT. Wouldn't it have been so much better if they had gone: package, VO, SOT package?"

- "Margaret! They're going to give me the details of that man wanted in the downtown robbery. Get me a pen!"

- "The police want *my* help in solving this crime? Cool!"

- "One person was slightly injured in that accident? Good thing they had a helicopter there."

- "That thing that happened half a world away? I hope this local newscast tells me if it could happen here."

- "Good thing they ran that voiceover of people putting on seatbelts during that seatbelt law story. I had no idea what seatbelts looked like."

- "They're leading with the same story at 5:30 as they did at 5? Booooooring!"

- "Oh, they're *live* at the State House. There was no way I was going to believe a prepackaged story about the budget."

- "No, I *hadn't* recalled that *Action News* first told me about this story last week. Thanks for the reminder!"

- "It's gonna snow/be hot/be very cold? I sure hope they'll tell me what to do with my pets and older relatives. I have no idea."

- "Wait! Wait! What happened to the anchor I'm used to watching? He's not there tonight! Is he dead? Oh, thank God . . . he's on assignment."

- "*Team* coverage? Now I'm watching!"

SOURCE: Safran (2003).

Finishing Strong

Let's keep these things in mind as we go ahead and fill out our example rundown (Table 3.11). We still have to finish the national news block, which, obviously, depends on the important stories of the day and what

Table 3.11   Completed News Rundown

Slug	Talent	Format	Tape No.	ERT	Tape	Total	Runtime	Backtime
HEADLINE	2-SH	V/O	101	:15		:15	5:30:00	+0:20
OPEN	VTR	VTR		:15		:15	5:30:15	
FIRE	2-SH	LIVE	102	1:00	1:30	2:30	5:30:30	
CODES	2-SH	SET		1:30		1:30	5:33:00	
BURGLAR	AGW	V/O	103	:30		:30	5:34:30	
TUITION	BES	VO/SOT	104	:25	:20	:45	5:35:00	
ROADS	2-SH	PKG	105	:20	1:40	2:00	5:35:45	
MAP	AGW	R/G		:25		:25	5:37:45	
TEASE-1	2-SH	V/O	106	:15		:15	5:38:10	
BREAK	——	——	——	2:00	——	——	5:38:25	
IRAQ	2-SH	PKG	107	:15	1:30	1:45	5:40:25	
N KOREA	AGW	VO/SOT	108	:30	:20	:50	5:42:10	
CRASH	BES	V/O	109	:25		:25	5:43:00	
ELECTION	BES	SOT	110	:15	:15	:30	5:43:25	
ECONOMY	AGW	R/G		:20		:20	5:43:55	
TEASE-2	2-SH	V/O	111	:15		:15	5:44:15	
BREAK	——	——	——	2:00	——	——	5:44:30	
WX INTRO	3-SH			:10		:10	5:46:30	
WX	JPL			3:00		3:00	5:46:40	
WX OUT	3-SH			:10		:10	5:49:40	
TEASE-3	BES			:15		:15	5:49:50	
BREAK	——	——	——	2:00	——	——	5:50:05	
SPORTS IN	3-SH			:10		:10	5:52:05	
SPORTS	JC			3:00		3:00	5:52:15	
SPRT OUT	3-SH			:10		:10	5:55:15	
TEASE-4	AGW			:15		:15	5:55:25	
BREAK	——	——	——	2:00	——	——	5:55:40	
KICKER	2-SH	PKG	112	:15	1:15	1:30	5:57:40	
CLOSE	4-SH	VTR		:30		:30	5:59:10	

Note: AGW, BES, JC, and JPL indicate the talent's initials; ERT, estimated running time; R/G, reader-graphic; SOT, sound on tape; SPRT, sports; 2-SH, 3-SH, and 4-SH, multiple anchors; VO and V/O, voiceover; VTR, videotape recording. Numbers in the ERT, Tape, Total, Runtime, and Backtime columns indicate time in minutes and seconds.

material we're getting from our national newsfeeds. Almost all national news material will come from the wires and network newsfeeds. Many stations subscribe to more than one newsfeed, usually their own network's feed and that of some other independent news provider.

We've filled out our rundown with national stories on Iraq, North Korea, an election, and the economy. The economy story is a reader-graphic indicating the final business averages of the day and any stocks of local interest. We've also added our teases, which come at the end of each block, and the actual time of our kicker package. There's no sports or weather material yet, but those departments will take care of that. Because most weather segments are unscripted, that part usually stays as just one line in the rundown.

You can also see how our runtime columns are now all filled, indicating at what exact clock time each story in the show should air. It's important to realize that very few stories actually go on the air at their scheduled time, for a variety of reasons. Stories might not be ready, reporters might be running late, or a tape machine might break down. Producers will have to make adjustments for these problems during the show.

Notice also that our backtime figure is now +0:20, which means the show is 20 seconds light. As we've discussed, it's probably better for a producer to go into a show light rather than heavy because extra time allows for the problems that inevitably occur. It's much easier to add material to a show than to dump material, and producers can also have the anchors take up more time with "happy talk" on the set. Using credits (a graphic list of the news personnel who work on the show) is another device producers have to adjust for time. If the show runs light, the producer can have credits run at the end. If it's on time or running heavy, the credits can easily be dropped.

Obviously, not every news show will follow this rundown, and there are dozens of different formats available for a producer to use. Some will vary in the use of teases, and others may use an "11 at 11" format. Still, this rundown can give you an idea of how producers put shows together. Formats may differ, but the process of building a news show is fairly standard.

Scripting

Once a rundown has been completed (and sometimes even before), the producer can begin work on creating individual story scripts. The script has the actual words that will be read on the air, along with important information for the technical director. As with the rundown, everyone connected with the newscast needs a copy of every story script. This includes the producer, anchors, studio personnel, and technical crew. All of these people must be made aware of any changes to the script, which happens quite often.

There are two important parts to a television script. Think of it as a piece of paper with an imaginary line running down the center from top

Table 3.12   Sample Television Package Script

BES	STARTING NEXT YEAR, IT WILL COST A LOT
Cam-1	MORE TO GO TO SCHOOL AT STATE
	UNIVERSITY. JOHN SMITH REPORTS THAT
	TOUGH ECONOMIC TIMES HAVE LED THE
	STATE BOARD OF TRUSTEES TO RAISE
	TUITION RATES.
TAKE PKG	
Length: 1:30	
CG: State College/:02	
CG: Jim Johnson, Dean/:15	
CG: Stacy Jones, Student/:40	
CG: John Smith, Reporting/1:15	
OUTQ: Standard	

Note: BES indicates the talent's initials; Cam-1, camera 1; CG, character generator; OUTQ, outcue; TAKE PKG, roll tape. Numbers indicates times in minutes and seconds.

to bottom. All information on the left-hand side is for the technical director; all the information on the right-hand side is words the anchors will read on the air (see Table 3.12).

There is certain technical information that must be included on the left side of the script. In Table 3.12, "BES" refers to the anchor reading the story, and "Cam-1" indicates on which camera the anchor will appear. This tells the technical director who is reading the story and what camera is involved.

"TAKE PKG" lets the director know there is a tape involved with the story and when to roll it. Different stations use different notations for this, such as "roll," "take" or "cue," but the purpose is the same. The time listed (1:30) tells the director how long the tape lasts, so he or she knows when to go back to the anchor. "OUTQ" stands for "outcue" and refers to the last two or three words of the tape. This lets the director know exactly when to exit the story. In this case, the outcue is "standard," which means the reporter will end the story with a standard phrase like, "This is John Smith reporting for News 12."

It's especially important to let the director know when the outcue is nonstandard. Another problem can arise if the last few words of a non-standard outcue are repeated, such as in the case of a SOT that ends with, "The damage caused by the fire is terrible, just terrible." If the outcue is listed as "terrible," the director might be tempted to cut out of the story after he hears the first mention of the word. Most stations get around this problem by writing "FALSE OUTQ," which lets the director know to wait until he or she hears the outcue a second time.

"CG" stands for character generator, which refers to any printed material on the screen. It may also be referred to as *chyrons* or *supers*. Typically, this is graphic information that shows someone's name or identifies a certain location. In this example, there are four CGs that need to be used in the story. The producer will have to indicate the exact CGs and the times they appear in the story.

Traditionally, CG information has been loaded into the show by a graphics specialist. A producer might give a list of all the CGs that appear in the newscast to the chyron operator, who then types them on separate pages. At appropriate times during the show, the director will call for the chyron operator to display the right CG. However, new computer software has made the CG process much easier. Some programs allow the producer or reporter to directly type their chyrons right into the script, eliminating the need for a CG operator. In either event, careful attention must be paid to CG spellings and times.

Even when stories vary by format, the information the technical director needs rarely changes. The director certainly wants to know if a story requires some sort of special technical direction. But whether the story is a live shot, package, interview, or something else, the director must have certain basic information on each script, as shown in Tables 3.13 and 3.14.

The right side of the script deals strictly with material that will be read on the air, and it is, obviously, the part that interests the anchors and news readers the most. You may have noticed that scripts are usually typed in all capitals and double spaced. This keeps the anchors from losing their place and makes it easier for them to see the words in the teleprompter.

The teleprompter is a device, usually attached to the studio camera, which allows anchors to read the scripts. When the anchors look into the camera, they're actually looking at the scripts. The scripts roll by at a certain speed, either determined by the anchor or by someone running a teleprompter machine. Years ago, stations had to use teleprompter machines in which the scripts were taped together and then rolled on a conveyor belt. Modern technology has virtually eliminated this process by attaching the teleprompter to a computer. Many anchors can now control the teleprompter themselves, by using a foot pedal that feeds the scripts at an appropriate speed.

In addition to double spacing and typing in capitals, there are other ways producers can help make the anchors' jobs easier. Words that are hard to pronounce should be written phonetically, and producers should point them out in advance. Some common print conventions, such as decimal points and figures, should be written out. For example, instead of "THE BUDGET INCREASED TO \$2.5 MILLION," the broadcast script should read, "THE BUDGET INCREASED TO 2-POINT-5 MILLION DOLLARS." Producers should always remember that everything they write will have to be read on the air.

Table 3.13   Sample Television Voiceover Script

BES Cam-1	STARTING NEXT YEAR, IT WILL COST A LOT MORE TO GO TO SCHOOL AT STATE UNIVERSITY.
TAKE V/O CG: State College/:02	TODAY, THE STATE BOARD OF TRUSTEES ANNOUNCED A TUITION HIKE OF THREE PERCENT. THAT WILL COST THE AVERAGE STUDENT AN EXTRA ONE HUNDRED DOLLARS PER SEMESTER. UNIVERSITY DEAN JIM JOHNSON SAID A POOR STATE ECONOMY AND DECLINING ENROLLMENT FORCED THE DECISION. THE TUITION INCREASE WILL GO INTO EFFECT FOR THE FALL SEMESTER.

Note: BES indicates the talent's initials; Cam-1, camera 1; CG, character generator; TAKE V/O, roll tape for voiceover. Number indicates time in seconds.

Producers should also be ready to change a script at a moment's notice. This includes not only the content of the script but the show order. Computing software has made it possible to make changes that instantly appear in the rundown. For example, if a breaking news story needs to be inserted into a newscast, the producer can quickly write it and then add it in the appropriate place. The other stories will automatically drop down behind it, and the computer will adjust the time. Anchors will then be able to read the story on the air, although they may not have the luxury of having seen it before or having a paper copy of the script.

Much of the challenge of producing lies in these types of changes, because each newscast will probably go through numerous revisions and updates. Producers must be flexible enough to handle change on short notice and incorporate it into the show. Many of these changes take place in a matter of minutes while the show is already on the air.

Table 3.14   Sample Television Voiceover and Sound on Tape Script

BES Cam-1	STARTING NEXT YEAR, IT WILL COST A LOT MORE TO GO TO SCHOOL AT STATE UNIVERSITY.
TAKE V/O CG: State College/:02	TODAY, THE STATE BOARD OF TRUSTEES ANNOUNCED A TUITION HIKE OF THREE PERCENT. THAT WILL COST THE AVERAGE STUDENT AN EXTRA ONE HUNDRED DOLLARS PER SEMESTER. UNIVERSITY DEAN JIM JOHNSON SAID A POOR STATE ECONOMY AND DECLINING ENROLLMENT FORCED THE DECISION.
SOT Length: 16 CG: Jim Johnson/:15 OUTQ: "tough decision" BACK TO V/O	THE TUITION INCREASE WILL GO INTO EFFECT FOR THE FALL SEMESTER

Note: BES indicates the talent's initials; Cam-1, camera 1; CG, character generator; OutQ, outcue; SOT, sound on tape; TAKE V/O, roll tape for voiceover. Numbers indicate time in minutes and seconds.

In the Control Room

For several reasons, the producer watches the newscast from the control room. It gives the producer direct access to the director and other control room personnel, which makes quick changes to the show possible. If a story needs to be dropped, moved, or changed, the producer can immediately notify the director. Watching from the control room also helps the producer look for potential problems. If a tape is late coming in or a machine breaks down, the producer can instantly make a decision about what to do next.

Figure 3.3 Producers Watch the Newscast From the Control Room

To make quick changes and decisions, producers remain in the control room during the newscast. They usually sit or stand behind the technical director, with whom they keep in constant contact.

SOURCE: Photo by Brad Schultz.

Making these kinds of critical decisions on the fly is the main priority of the producer during the newscast. Sometimes producers have only seconds to adjust a newscast when problems arise. Suppose a reporter calls in from a live shot to let the producer know that the interview subject hasn't shown up yet. Does the producer drop the live shot to later in the show or keep it in the same place in the hope that the person will get there on time? Is there someone else at the scene who could speak instead, or should the reporter forget the interview and do the live shot alone? A producer may make dozens of these decisions during the course of a newscast, and there's really no way to determine a right or wrong decision ahead of time. In such situations, producers base their decisions on a variety of factors, most notably experience and news judgment.

You can see that during the show, producers have to keep in constant communication with other members of the newscast. The producer has direct access to the director and other control room personnel but must also indicate any changes to anchors and studio workers. These people are usually hooked up to an interruptible frequency broadcast (IFB), which allows the producer to talk to them at any point during the show. Anchors wear custom-made earpieces that connect them to the IFB, and studio personnel usually listen on headsets. The IFB allows the producer to announce changes to all the affected people, sometimes even as the changes are happening.

The producer's other main job during the newscast is timing. Producers should keep fairly tight control over the timing of a newscast and try to stick to the rundown. When problems do arise, or the show's timing falls off schedule for some other reason, the producer makes adjustments to keep the show on track. As previously noted, this is most often done by lengthening or shortening certain segments within the newscast, dropping or adding news material, or telling the anchors to speed up or slow down. Some producers build in a certain amount of time for "happy talk," where the anchors simply chit-chat with each other. This is an obvious place to modify the timing of the show, if necessary.

The producer usually has to make sure that the newscast ends at a specific time. Once the show is over, many stations will bring all the newscast crew together for a critique. This provides immediate feedback about what worked, what went wrong, and what needs changing in upcoming shows. Generally, the critique is done at the discretion of the news director, who may do it in person or post a written version. Unfortunately, many stations do not spend much time on critiques. Once the newscast ends, all energy is focused toward getting ready for the next show—that's the nature of the news business.

News Producing: Matt Ellis

Matt Ellis has spent nearly 20 years in television news, much of that time as a newscast producer. He started as a reporter at WVVA in Bluefield, West Virginia, but eventually moved over to producing. After stops in Buffalo, Tampa, Boston, and Providence, he landed in New York—first as executive producer for WCBS and eventually as head writer for ABC's *Good Morning America*. He's now the news director at WBZ-TV in Boston.

Q: What are the duties of a news producer?

A: A news producer for a local television station is the architect of the program. He or she is responsible for choosing the content, slotting the stories, and writing much of the copy. The producer also oversees the

Matt Ellis, News Director,
WBZ-TV, Boston

presentation of the broadcast from the control room. News producers possess a number of skills. Chief among them is the ability to take the facts of an incident and turn them into a story that is clear, concise, and compelling. News producers are constantly making decisions, and their judgment is regularly tested. Any good producer is organized, smart, and well read. It is also helpful to know the community and its history.

Q: What are the difficulties associated with producing in today's environment?

A: As television stations continue to struggle with finite resources, cable competition, and a loyal viewer base that is continually aging, producers are under more and more pressure to jazz up the news. Any news director will tell you that accuracy can never be sacrificed, but a newscast devoid of style is a failure. In recent years, the use of splashy electronic graphics has enhanced the packaging and promotion of the news. Indeed, news promotion is now seen as a critical component of any successful operation. Many news managers will joke that it doesn't matter how great a story or a broadcast is if the viewers aren't watching. With remote controls within every viewer's grasp, managers make sure producers are including stories that have promotional value and marketing them properly. Any good news producer is also a good tease writer.

Q: What is the main satisfaction you get from producing?

A: Producers spend many hours planning and creating their newscast, and few things offer the satisfaction of a well-timed, well-executed broadcast. There is a definite adrenaline rush a producer feels in the control room when the show hits on all cylinders. A good newscast has a rhythm; it feels good. And while it is truly a team effort, it is the producer who is the team captain, pulling together the elements and creating the game plan that ultimately transforms raw information into a polished product. That said, it is worth noting that some of the best newscasts are the ones where the script and rundown get tossed aside and the team responds to breaking news. That is perhaps the best adrenaline rush of all, producing on the go and knowing that you have tested the limits of yourself and your team to win the big story.

SOURCE: Matt Ellis (personal communication, April 2003)

Thinking More About It

Consider taping a series of local newscasts for a content analysis (for more information on content analysis, see "Thinking More About It" at the end of chapter 2). Analyze the newscasts and consider the following:

1. How are the shows blocked and stacked? Did the blocking and stacking affect your perception of the show? Were the shows that you considered well blocked and stacked "good" newscasts? Why or why not?

2. What type of organization or order is used that holds the show together? Did the show seem to flow together well, or did it seem disjointed? Over a series of nights, did the newscast have the same general order and structure?

3. What formats are most commonly used to cover the most important stories? How much time was allotted to the most important stories?

4. How does the newscast at one station compare to another local station? Did the shows look the same? Did they generally cover the same stories? If so, did they use the same formats or give the stories a different treatment?

5. Could you detect any places in the show where it looked like late changes had been made (for example, to insert breaking news)? Did the change cause any on-air problems?

6. How often do anchors read off their scripts compared to using the teleprompter?

Writing 4

Many producers tend to think of producing and writing as two different things. In their minds, producers produce and reporters write. In actuality, producers often spend the majority of their time either writing or rewriting news material. Producers must know the basic journalistic skills of creating a compelling lead, using good grammar, writing in active voice, and all of the other things that go into the creation of a good broadcast news story.

Before we get that far, it's helpful to rethink the entire writing process. Actually, it's a communication process, because what you're trying to do with a broadcast story depends more on communication than simply on writing words. Think of each story you write as a three-step process: (a) Communicate a simple idea, theme, or message (b) using the available story elements in the best possible way, (c) leading to audience understanding and comprehension.

COMMUNICATING AN IDEA

Communicating an idea, theme, or message means that you should center your story around a simple concept. Even the most complex stories can essentially be reduced to one sentence. The nasty political fight between the mayor, city council, and citizens groups may have a lot of different components to it, but in a broad sense, it still has a simple theme: The mayor, council, and citizens are fighting about something.

That may sound like a gross oversimplification, but it's really just a starting point for the story. You can then add details that support the basic theme or message of the story. The key thing is not to add too many details or facts that detract from the message you're trying to communicate. People only get one shot when watching or listening to a broadcast story, and unlike with print, they don't have the opportunity to go back and read over what they don't understand. That means not going overboard with facts, figures, and other details that can cause confusion by creating information overload. The point of a good broadcast story is not to cram in as many facts as possible, it's to communicate an effective story.

Communicating an idea also means good organization. Your stories should be well organized, beyond the obvious requirements of beginning, middle, and end. Organization includes such things as fact selection and fact ordering. Fact selection is the process of picking out the most important and relevant facts to include in the story. We know we don't want to overwhelm the audience with too much information, but even if you could use every fact, you wouldn't want to. Some are simply incidental, irrelevant, or extraneous. Use only those facts and details most important to the audience in terms of explaining the theme or message of the story.

Fact ordering is putting the information in the proper order, given the nature of the story. A serious or hard news story generally orders facts in the inverted pyramid style, in which the story starts with the most important facts and works down to the least important. A less serious or feature story might start with a relatively unimportant detail, then use it to introduce the main theme.

It's also common to start a story by focusing on an individual. A story that starts in this fashion can then use the person to introduce the main theme or message. For example, a story might start by talking about someone who has the flu and all the problems this person has had because of the illness. That can lead to the broader issue or topic of the story—a flu epidemic in the local community. A local doctor might then talk about how widespread the problem is and what people can do about it. Often, these stories are circular, in that they end with the same person shown in the beginning as a way of tying everything together.

This circularity is an effective technique for personalizing stories or telling stories through people. A producer or writer should always realize that ultimately, all stories are about people. City council meetings, crop failures, and automobile recalls are only significant to the degree that they affect people. If a plane falls out of the sky with no one in it and no one gets hurt, it might rate a short mention on the news. But if the same plane falls and kills hundreds of people, then it becomes a major news story.

This is just another way of saying that you should write news that is relevant and important to people's lives. Write in such a way that the audience will care about your message. The audience may yawn about a new technical process developed by the local power plant, but what if people knew it would significantly cut their electric bills? Most people in your audience might not care about an earthquake in South America, but they would be interested to know if local people are involved in the rescue or rebuilding efforts. Find a way to put the news in the proper context and perspective that makes your message relevant to the audience.

USING AVAILABLE ELEMENTS

Stories are most effectively communicated when the available elements of the story are used in the best possible way. Think of the "available elements" as all the things that go into a story: written words, video and visual images, interviews (sound bites), and natural sound (the background sound that occurs naturally at the scene of the story). Too often, young producers and writers feel like they have to write a lot to create an effective story. It may be, however, that words are not the most effective way to tell the story. If you were telling a story about a beautiful sunset, would it be better to try and describe it with words or simply show someone a good picture?

In other words, consider your best elements and give them the most use in the story. If you have good video and natural sound, focus on those elements to tell the story, and don't worry so much about the words and sound bites. If you have dynamite sound bites, don't be afraid to let them run long, even if it means cutting short the words, pictures, or natural sound. When the story doesn't have much in the way of video, sound bites, or natural sound, that's when the producer has to work harder at writing to effectively communicate.

All of this seems like fairly common sense, but many times a producer or writer will try to make a story fit a particular preconceived formula: so many words or sentences, so many sound bites, and so many pictures. Every story is different, and so are the elements that you use to create it. It sounds corny, but think of each story as a recipe. The final product depends on the quality and quantity of each ingredient, which can obviously vary each time you cook.

AUDIENCE UNDERSTANDING

If you're cooking a meal, the end result should be that the people eating it like it and think it tastes good. With a story, the end result is that elements you used worked together properly and the audience understands the message you tried to communicate. The audience should walk away from the story completely understanding the idea or theme you started with. Stories can fail for all kinds of reasons. Maybe you put in too much information, which overwhelmed and confused the audience. Maybe the elements weren't used in the right way, and the audience got sidetracked. Instead of thinking about the message, people were thinking that the interview was too long, or they wondered why the pictures didn't match the words. If the audience doesn't understand the message, you've failed to properly communicate the story, no matter how pretty the pictures, no matter how dramatic the sound bites, no matter how strong the writing.

Notice also that we're talking about audience *understanding*, not *agreement*. Journalists are not in the business of doing stories so everyone can feel good or happy. Many times, listeners or viewers will get upset with stories, even to the point of strenuous complaint. But as long as they understand the story, you've done your job.

TEN SUGGESTIONS FOR BETTER BROADCAST NEWSWRITING

Up to this point, we've concentrated mainly on the "big picture" part of writing, such as communicating a message, context, relevance, and audience understanding. Now let's get to the nuts and bolts of better writing—specific ways of improving your writing and helping you produce effective stories.

1. Use Active Voice, Not Passive Voice

This is one of the basic commandments of broadcast writing but one of the most ignored. Passive voice is a sentence construction in which something is being "acted upon" rather than a construction in which something is doing the acting. Beware of the verb *to be*, which usually indicates the passive voice. You should always try to write "the police caught the suspect" rather than "the suspect *was* caught by police." Active voice is shorter, more conversational, and more ideally suited to broadcast. Writing in active voice isn't difficult, but it is often ignored because we usually think and talk in passive voice. However, active voice makes the broadcast writing more interesting, emphatic, and understandable.

The presence of *to be* doesn't always mean the sentence is passive; it can be used to indicate things such as simple condition ("George Bush is president of the United States"). But even when it doesn't indicate the passive voice, *to be* is flat, uninspiring, and doesn't make for good broadcast writing. When you see a form of the verb *to be*, it should send up a red flag that the sentence could be improved by changing the structure. Also, keep in mind that the tense of the verb has nothing to do with passive or active voice. For example, consider the following sentences:

The ball is caught by the player. (present)

The ball was caught by the player. (past)

The ball will be caught by the player. (future)

The ball has been caught by the player (present perfect)

The ball would have been caught by the player (future conditional)

Each of the sentences is a different tense, but all contain the verb *to be*, and all are passive. The easiest way to convert to active voice is simply to turn the sentence around:

Passive: The storm was predicted by weather experts to hit at 10:00.

Active: Weather experts predicted the storm would hit at 10:00.

In situations where you can't turn the sentence around, you can change the verb:

Passive: The president was in Chicago today. . . .

Active: The president visited Chicago today. . . .

As in the next example, both these sentences are in the active voice, although the second sentence uses a more colorful and interesting verb. Although the passive voice invariably uses some form of *to be*, using a form of *to be* doesn't invariably make a sentence passive. In such situations, remember that changing the verb should not change the meaning of the sentence. For example, you wouldn't want to say the president "spoke" in Chicago, if in fact he did not make a public speech. Similarly, you might want to avoid "spent the night in," "toured," or other verbs, depending on the facts of the story.

For the most part, broadcast writing adheres to the same grammatical rules you learned in junior high school. But in some situations, it's permissible to bend the rules a little. A common broadcast convention is simply to drop the verb:

Standard: Firefighters were busy today in the forests of California. . . .

Broadcast version: Firefighters busy today in the forests of California. . . .

In some rare situations, it's simpler and easier to leave the passive alone, especially when trying to change it to active convolutes and confuses the meaning. This would be especially true for well-known sayings or phrases or in situations in which the person or thing being acted upon is the most important part of the story. Consider the case of political prisoners or hostages. It's probably better to write "The hostages have been freed," rather than "Today extremists released the hostages." But in most situations, using active voice makes for better, more memorable, and more conversational writing.

2. Use the Lead to Keep the Audience's Attention

No matter whether the producer is writing for a reader, V/O, VO/SOT, or package, all written stories start with a lead. The lead is the first few lines of the copy that set up the rest of the story. Most print journalists were taught to put some form of the five "Ws" in the lead: who, what, when, where, or why, and that form still works for newspaper writing. But in broadcasting, such writing would overwhelm the listener with too much information. Therefore, the main job of writing a broadcast lead is to create interest and compel the listener to stick with the story.

There are several different types of broadcast leads, each of which depends on the tone or style of the story involved. The hard lead is basically a summary of the story in a no-nonsense delivery and is usually reserved for the most serious or important stories.

Hard lead: A jury today convicted John Smith on three counts of first-degree murder.

The same story could also have a throwaway or umbrella lead, depending on the other facts of the story. In the throwaway lead, an innocuous line is used before the real story begins. An umbrella lead combines several different points of the same story.

Throwaway lead: A verdict tonight in the John Smith murder trial. A jury today. . . .

Umbrella lead: A guilty verdict in the John Smith murder trial has brought tears and relief to the victim's family.

By contrast, some leads would be completely inappropriate for this story. That would include the soft lead and the humor lead. These types of leads should only be used for softer, feature-type stories.

Soft lead: Compared to his recent battles with cancer, Jim Jones must look at his re-election campaign as a walk in the park.

Humorous lead: Who could have guessed before the tournament started that Tiger Woods could shoot a 15 on the final hole and still win the U.S. Open?

You can see how foolish it would be to use a soft lead for the murder story or a hard lead for the Woods story. The type of lead used for each story depends on the tone of the story involved.

There is one type of lead that should be used only in rare situations, if at all. The question lead is dangerous, because it could ask a question that turns off or loses the interest of the audience.

Question lead: Could anyone be happier tonight than the million-dollar lotto winner?

In this case, the audience could think "Yes" or, even worse, not have any interest in the answer. It's much better to rephrase the question as a statement:

New lead: The new lotto winner has a million reasons to smile tonight. . . .

No matter what type of story is involved, the lead should involve the *hook* of the story. The hook is simply the main or most interesting part of the story. Each story has several angles, but usually one sticks out as the central theme. This is the one that should be emphasized in the lead, if possible.

Poor lead: More than 15,000 people attended a pro-life rally today.

Better lead: Abortion opponents rallied today to call for new legislation protecting the unborn.

Unless the attendance figure is the central issue of the story, it doesn't belong up top. In some cases, extremely high or low attendance figures are important, but even then, they are rarely used in the lead.

All stories should be reducible to a single sentence. Think of what you would tell someone if he or she asked you about the story. How would you describe it in one sentence? The important part of our abortion story is not how many people showed up but what they did. Find out the most important thing in your story and work it into the lead. Remember that the main purpose of the lead is to keep people listening to the story. Too many producers fall into the trap of cramming too much information into a lead, which either overwhelms the listener or gives away too much of the story. Always remember that the lead exists mainly to compel attention, and save the details for the rest of the story.

Poor lead: After three days of deliberation, a jury has convicted John Smith on three counts of first-degree murder in the January beating death of 11-year-old Ashley Jones.

Better lead: Guilty on all three counts. Today a jury. . . .

In the second example, the lead indicates the most important point of the story—that a jury has returned a guilty verdict in the murder trial—and saves the details for the rest of the story. This lead is simple, interesting, and makes listeners want to stick with the story to find out more.

Another pitfall for producers is the plain or boring lead. The facts and information may be correct, but the lead fails to generate any interest or excitement.

Poor lead: The Board of Trustees met last night.

Better lead: The Board of Trustees voted last night to raise tuition at the university.

Even better: University students will have to brace for another tuition hike. Last night. . . .

Again, the point of the story is not that the board met, but what it did—raise tuition rates. The poor lead makes no reference to what's really important in the story. Although the second lead does this, it does not do as good a job of compelling interest as the third lead.

3. Use Proper Grammar

With a few minor exceptions, writing for broadcast news should follow the rules of basic grammar. That means proper sentence structure, style, and word usage. Some of the more common mistakes made by news writers include the following.

Pronoun Agreement. The pronoun must agree with the subject, which can cause a lot of confusion.

Wrong: The Board of Trustees said last night they would not support the tax measure.

Right: The Board of Trustees said last night *it* would not support the tax measure.

Always remember that *board, council,* and *group* are singular. The pronoun ("it") here refers to "board" not "trustees." Referring to board *members* would change the pronoun to "they."

Attribution. Attribution always goes first in broadcast writing, although newspaper writing puts it second. Because the listener or viewer only gets one chance to hear the information, it's important to know who's saying it.

Print: The United States is in no danger of nuclear attack, said president Bush.

Broadcast: President Bush says the U.S. faces no danger of nuclear attack.

In the first sentence, the listener can't immediately tell who has the opinion and might attribute it to the news anchor. Notice also that we changed the verb in the sentence, making it more interesting.

4. Use Simple Words and Numbers

Keep in mind that you're trying to communicate a story or idea. Using words the audience doesn't know or understand slows down and impedes the communication process. This isn't a call for simplistic or monosyllabic words, merely a reminder that your writing will really hit home when the audience knows exactly what you're trying to say.

Wrong: The dogs were euthanized by humane shelter staff.

Right: Humane shelter staff put the dogs to sleep.

You might know that *euthanized* means *put to sleep,* but it's still a difficult word that many audience members might not know. Don't take a chance on words that might be misunderstood. In this example, we also changed the sentence from passive to active.

Wrong: The new city budget is 1,335,412 dollars.

Right: The city will have a new budget of just over 1.3 million dollars.

Is it really important to know the exact city budget, or is it more likely that too many numbers and figures will simply confuse the audience? In some cases, such as with disaster death tolls, it's important to give the precise number. But more often, especially when big numbers are involved, a simple rounding or approximation gives the audience a much clearer picture of what's involved. When a story includes numbers, producers should consider how important it is for the audience to know the exact figure.

5. Keep Your Writing Clean and Simple

It's not just a matter of simple words but of using them in the right way. Too many writers try to get too complicated, with the result that the viewer suffers from information overload. William Faulkner was one of the greatest writers of the 20th century and famous for long, run-on sentences. But Faulkner's stream of consciousness approach would completely fail for broadcast writing, because the audience would get lost along the way. Better to think in terms of Ernest Hemingway, whose writing was characterized by short, simple sentences.

6. Be Well Read on a Variety of Subjects

A typical newscast will involve stories on a dozen or so different topics—international conflict, the economy, politics, law, and the like. Producers certainly can't be an expert in all these areas, but they can be expected to know enough to speak intelligently. At the very least, a variety of knowledge could save the producer from some embarrassing errors.

During John Glenn's famous return to space in 1998, a local news anchor in Illinois commented on the air that Glenn was the first person to land on the moon. If the producer had had only a basic knowledge of U.S. space flight, the error could have been prevented and Neil Armstrong would have received his proper credit as the moon's first visitor.

Former radio and television newsman Greg Byron complains that producers spend too much time in the newsroom and not enough in the community. "These people don't get out at all," says Byron (1997). "They are primarily re-writers and show strategists whose view of the world is from the newsroom. The main reason why television news around the country tends to look the same is because many of these people—often involuntarily—move from television market to market." Make an effort to get out of the newsroom and learn about what's going on in the world and in your community.

7. Don't Forget Creativity and Originality

As Byron suggested, many of today's problems with writing are due to a lack of effort on the part of the writer. It's much simpler and faster (especially when facing a deadline) to recycle old material than to come up with something new. That's one reason the audience hears so many old phrases and clichés (see Table 4.1 for a list).

Creativity does not necessarily mean going over the top. Some simple creative ideas include using more alliteration or remembering the "rule of threes." Which of the following sounds more appealing?

"The Cougars showed a lot of poise in their win over Central. . . ."

"The calm and collected Cougars showed a lot of poise. . . ."

There are literally hundreds of ways to make your writing more exciting and interesting. Just make sure that whatever you do fits in with the general mood and tone of the story. Certain types of writing are inappropriate for certain types of stories, such as taking a light-hearted approach to a very serious story. But in general, don't be afraid to experiment. Creative writing isn't limited to feature stories.

8. Humanize Your Writing

Let me repeat the point that all stories are essentially about people. Your writing should not only focus on the people involved, it should connect to the people in the audience. Why should the people sitting at home care

Table 4.1   News Clichés to Avoid

Cliché	Comments
"Only time will tell"	Probably the most overused cliché in broadcast news. Many reporters end their stories with this comment, despite that fact that it applies to almost every story. It is good to try and advance a story forward, but this ending doesn't do anything but tell the audience, "We don't have a good ending for this story."
"One thing's for certain"	Bad mainly from the standpoint that it's grammatically incorrect. You don't need to say something is "for certain," or "for sure." It's simply "certain" or "sure."
"Back to you"	Not a horrible crime, but it does point out many of the overused clichés of live reporting. "Back to you," or referring to people by name ("back to you, Jim") makes it sound like the anchors and reporters are just talking to themselves. The story should always be directed toward the audience, which may find all the inside references irritating.
"The greatest," "the biggest," etc.	Try to avoid referring to things in the superlative, such as "biggest disaster ever," "most devastating flood," unless there is factual basis to back up the claim. It is possible to verify, for example, whether a plane crash involves the worst loss of life in U.S. aviation history. The problem arises when producers start attaching subjective opinion to make the story sound more important. Constantly calling something the "worst," "best," "biggest," etc., leaves you no room when something really big does happen.

about this story? What does it mean to them? Write *about* the people behind the events, and write *for* the people watching at home.

9. Sometimes Less Is More

One of the most common mistakes young producers make is to write too much. They feel as if they have to describe every piece of video and explain every sound bite. Remember, in television and radio, the words are only one component of the overall presentation. Sometimes you need to use more words and other times hardly any at all.

In general, pictures and sounds have more impact than words. When you have very strong video and audio, keep your writing to a minimum and let the other elements tell the story. When your sound and pictures are poor, you'll have to write more to compensate. Consider a story on a local fire. If you have compelling sound or pictures from the scene, you don't have to write as much; let the video tell the story. If the sound and audio are unexciting, the story might need more help from your writing.

To repeat the recipe analogy, all the ingredients should come together to make an enticing final product. If you don't use the proper proportions of each, the end result can leave a bad taste in the viewer's mouth.

10. Incorporate Natural Sound Into Your Writing

Natural sound is simply the sound that occurs naturally at the scene of a story. For a football game, it could be the roaring crowds or marching bands. At a protest or strike, it's the people yelling on the picket line. Natural sound (or "nat sound") has become much more important over the years in broadcast news. In the early days of broadcasting, producers and reporters ignored natural sound and instead used canned music or just plain silence. Later generations of reporters and news directors realized that natural sound could make or break a story. The cheers of a crowd, the sounds of sirens screaming, and the gasp of a courtroom all contribute to the scene and the mood of a story. Modern-day storytelling involves taking occasional pauses to let the natural sound come up to full volume.

There is no right or wrong place to use natural sound, as long as it adds something to the story. Starting a story off with natural sound is particularly effective, as it helps the audience understand what is to follow. This is especially true in radio, where the producer does not have the additional support of video but has to create a picture in the listener's mind. Starting a radio piece with the natural sound of picketers chanting strongly suggests to the audience that the story will be about a strike of some sort.

Natural sound can also be used to break up long pieces of narration. If the story includes long stretches of reading, the audience can quickly lose interest. One way around this is to stop once or twice in a story and let the natural sound come up full. But be careful not to use too much natural sound in a story or to let it become distracting.

You should try to keep the natural sound fairly short, in the range of 3 to 6 seconds. After that, the audience may start to lose interest. This particularly applies to some types of natural sound that may not be that appealing. For example, if the story is about a new dental drill, you probably wouldn't want use that natural sound for very long.

Unless the natural sound is easily understood, it also needs to be supported with some explanation. Again, this is more common in radio, where the audience has no video to rely on:

Radio story: (Natural sound of picketers off top) The members of Union Local 204 spent the day walking a picket line outside the hospital. They asked for. . . .

Even for television, where the audience can see what's going on, such description helps the audience understand the story better.

One of the most important considerations of natural sound is that it usually must be planned out in advance. Producers should get reporters to think about the natural sound possibilities of a story before they go out. For example, if the story is about a local track meet, the reporter will need to work ahead of time to get the natural sound of the starter's gun. The key is to think about natural sound ahead of time, because thinking about it after the story has been done is often too late.

Writing for Packages, V/Os, and VO/SOTs

All forms of broadcast writing should have the same basic elements: beginning (lead), middle, and end. But writing for stories that include taped elements requires a little more effort and imagination than writing a reader.

VOICEOVER

The main focus of writing a V/O is to make sure the script matches closely with the video. Ideally, the writer should find a middle ground between writing too specifically for video (the script exactly matches the pictures) and writing too generally (the words and pictures have no relationship at all). Remember, when the viewer can see exactly what's happening, too much description is overkill.

> *Poor writing:* Here the workmen are making major repairs to the road. They're blasting holes in the road shoulder for future bridge abutments. They're also filling in potholes and making other road repairs. [Too specific]

> *Poor writing:* The state has appropriated nearly a million dollars for road repairs—part of the legislature's new campaign to improve the state's infrastructure. [Too general]

> *Better writing:* Workmen on Interstate 10 spent all day smoothing roads and fixing potholes—all part of a million-dollar state effort to improve the state's roadway system.

The first example, obviously, gives us too much detail, and although the second example is a little better, it doesn't relate the information to what's happening in the video. The third example is the best of both worlds: not too specific and not too general, with some added information for more depth. It also personalizes the story by referring to the workmen involved.

If this were a radio story that relied solely on the writing without the aid of any video, it would have to be more descriptive. In that case, the writer would have to add more details to set the scene for the audience and give it perspective.

Radio version: Workmen on Interstate 10 spent all day smoothing roads and fixing potholes—this crew worked to fill a big hole near the exit of Highway 6 at Keystone Crossing by dumping a mixture of hot tar and sand. It's all part of a million dollar state effort to. . . .

VOICEOVER–SOUND ON TAPE

The VO/SOT requires the same writing for video as the V/O and adds the element of a sound bite (taped interview). The main trick of writing for sound bites is the lead-in, or the words that come right before the sound bite. In radio, sound bites (actualities) have to be preceded by the name of the speaker for identification purposes.

Radio: According to Mayor Tim Thomas, city council has a rough road ahead. [Actuality]

In such situations, it's important to identify the speaker because the audience has no way of knowing who it is. No such restrictions apply in television, where the speaker is clearly identified by chyron or CG. Thus, television producers can be much more general in introducing a sound bite and can even omit reference to the name.

Television: And the city council has a tough road ahead. (Sound bite: Mayor Tim Thomas)

In the rare cases where the chyron malfunctions and no name appears on the screen, the anchor can identify the speaker once the sound bite ends.

Television: And the city council knows it has a tough road ahead. (Sound bite) By the way, that was mayor Tim Thomas.

In either television or radio, it's important not to introduce the sound bite by repeating what's in the interview.

Poor writing: Mayor Tim Thomas says city council will have a tough time deciding this issue (Sound bite: "City council will have a tough time deciding this issue. No one likes to see taxes raised, especially in a poor economy.")

In this case, the introduction to the sound bite simply duplicates what's on tape. Try to introduce the sound bite in a more general way, by leading into the interview or by adding new information.

Better writing: Mayor Tim Thomas knows what's in store for the council. (Sound bite: "City council will have a tough time deciding this issue. No one likes to see taxes raised, especially in a poor economy.")

PACKAGES

In most cases, reporters will write their own package introduction, which allows the intro and package to flow together more smoothly. Because the reporter has written the package, he or she usually knows the best way to introduce it.

In some cases, usually if the reporter doesn't have time or is doing a live report, the producer may have to take over this responsibility. It's important for the producer and reporter to communicate, so that the intro doesn't repeat the first few lines of the package. Other than that, writing a package intro is much like writing a good lead—it must be short, to the point, and compel people to keep listening. Typically, the reporter is introduced as the last thing before the package, but this is not always the case:

Intro 1: Guilty on all three counts. Today a local jury convicted John Smith in the beating death of young Ashley Jones. News 12 reporter Amanda Marcus has the story. . . .

Intro 2: It took three days for a local jury to reach a guilty verdict in the murder trial of John Smith. News 12 reporter Amanda Marcus has been following this story and has more on the verdict and the reaction from the victim's family. . . .

Sometimes a package will also have a *tag*, which is a written exit from the story read by the anchors. Again, tags are fairly short and should generally try to move the story forward—that is, tell the audience what happens next.

Tag: Smith will have a sentencing hearing in two weeks.

SUMMARY

Writing is a vital part of a producer's job. Reporters will contribute only a small fraction of material to the news hole; the remainder falls to the producer. In some cases, a producer might be responsible for writing the entire content of a newscast. A lot of attention today is focused on stacking a newscast, but much of the important work actually gets done when the producer sits down to write news stories.

Thinking More About It

Here are some exercises to help you with the topics discussed in this chapter. You can also get more practice by going to an Internet news site and rewriting the material into a better broadcast style.

1. Rewrite the following sentences to correct for passive voice, attribution, leads, and conversational broadcast style.
   a. A joint European-U.S. investigation has broken an international pedophile ring. The investigation was called operation "Hamlet," a 10-month probe that included the Justice Department and the Danish National Police. The ring abused and exploited at least 45 children, 37 of whom are citizens of the United States.
   b. Chrysler said Friday that it's recalling 464,315 2001 and 2002 Chrysler PT Cruisers, Reuters reported. The recall is being made to install a seal in a fuel pump. Chrysler introduced the PT Cruiser in 1998, and so far more than 6.5 million cars have been sold.
   c. A surgeon who left a patient anesthetized and with an open incision in his back while he went to a bank several blocks away has had his medical license suspended. The patient was not harmed, but Dr. Charles E. Pierce created an immediate threat when he left the patient at General Hospital in Cambridge to go to a bank in Harvard Square, the Massachusetts Board of Registration in Medicine said. His license was suspended indefinitely.
   d. Stocks were flat Friday afternoon, as investors were undecided after a 3-day rally that pushed the Dow Jones industrial average almost 700 points higher. At 1:30 p.m., the Dow was up 2.49 at 8,714.51, but moved closer to breakeven by midday. The Nasdaq composite lost 7.11 to 1,309.41.

SOURCE: Associated Press (August 2002).

2. Make all necessary changes in the following sentences.
   a. The Muscular Dystrophy Association says they will likely raise a million dollars this year.
   b. Critics of the police department say they have not handled the investigation properly.
   c. The new tuition increase will hurt enrollment at Jackson State, according to the faculty union.

    d. Auburn beat Florida to improve their record to 5-and-1.

    e. President Bush says the economy is likely headed for a strong rebound.

    f. NASA launched a Titan-4 multi-stage rocket today to put a new satellite into orbit.

    g. The president announced that the economy has grown at a rate of 2.9% over the past 6 months and the unemployment rate has dropped 1.8% over the same period.

    h. Show me the money! The newest lottery winner received his winnings today—nearly 5 million dollars.

    i. The senior class were honored last night by the teachers at Central High School.

    j. According to Stanford professor Erwin Jackson, the photo-phosphorous/ incandescent process should save consumers money on their electric bills.

3. Rewrite the following wire story in acceptable broadcast style.

> WASHINGTON (AP)–Parents who have struggled to strap in their children's car seats with safety belts are getting some reprieve— starting Sunday, all new vehicles and child safety seats must have attachments designed to make them fit together like a key in a lock.
>
> The new law can't prevent all child seat mistakes. Parents still need to research which seat is best for their child, make sure the seat fits tightly in the vehicle, and buckle the child in properly.
>
> But the National Highway Traffic Safety Administration (NHTSA) estimates the new system could prevent 36 to 50 deaths and 2,914 injuries annually.
>
> They say 80% of car seats are incorrectly installed, leading to 68 child deaths and another 874 injuries each year.
>
> The new system, called LATCH, which stands for Lower Anchors and Tethers for Children, is designed to make it easier to fit the child seat tightly in the vehicle.
>
> NHTSA kicks off a public education campaign about LATCH on Wednesday, but the agency still is stressing that old seats securely installed with seat belts work just as well as those equipped with LATCH.

SOURCE: Associated Press (August 2002).

4. Write two different kinds of appropriate leads for the following news stories.

    a. The IRS will begin using a new computer system. The system will allow the agency to collect an extra $7 billion in taxes. It will eliminate the need for about 34% of the IRS workforce, or about 40,000 jobs. The IRS employs about 115,000 people.

b. David Smith bought the winning lottery ticket worth $4 million. He bought it the day of the Super Lotto drawing on Monday. Later that night, Smith's wife washed his pants, with the winning lottery ticket still inside. The ticket has disintegrated. Lottery officials say without a winning ticket, Smith can't collect any money.

c. Accusations of sexual abuse of teens and children by Catholic priests have been surfacing for several years, but the volume of cases in recent months has stirred calls for stronger action by the Catholic Church. Over the weekend, some demonstrators called for the resignation of Boston's Cardinal Bernard Law, saying he failed to protect children from sexually abusive priests. Pope John Paul II has summoned U.S. Roman Catholic cardinals to the Vatican to address the sex abuse accusations involving priests. A source with the Catholic Church in Washington said the gathering would take place next week. There are 13 cardinals in the United States.

SOURCE: Associated Press (August 2002).

Producing
for Television 5

W e've already discussed several television news producing strategies, including stacking, blocking, and putting together a completed rundown (see chapter 3). These strategies are quite common for the 30-minute (Table 5.1) or 60-minute television newscast format that has become standard at most stations around the country.

The 30-minute news program has evolved over time into the television standard. In the early days of broadcasting, news lasted only 15 minutes, as getting news material was often difficult and expensive. In 1953, for example, the major networks faced significant obstacles in getting same-day coverage of the coronation of Queen Elizabeth in London. CBS and NBC chartered aircraft that returned to New York immediately after the ceremonies. While en route, technicians worked on specially installed machines to splice together and edit the film. Circumstances forced the planes to land in Boston and the edited film then had to be driven to network studios in New York.

By the 1960s and 1970s, technology had evolved to the point where news could expand to 30 minutes. Videotape replaced film, and satellite transmission made the distribution of news content much easier and faster. It also made television news a global enterprise, bringing viewers coverage of events in the far corners of the world. New developments in cable, home satellite signal receivers, and digital technology now enable viewers to know almost instantly when something of importance happens, as with the case of reporting during the 2003 war in Iraq.

This shortened news cycle puts tremendous pressure on news directors and producers, even at the local level. The growth of technology and alternative news outlets, such as the Internet, has led stations into a furious race to see who can provide the most news.

Table 5.1   Standard 30-Minute Television Newscast Format

Element	Time
Open	:30
First news block	6:00
(Break)	2:00
Second news block	5:00
(Break)	2:00
Weather	3:00
Health or news story	2:00
(Break)	2:00
Sports	3:00
(Break)	2:00
Kicker	2:00
Close	:30

Note: Stations will, obviously, tailor the news format to fit their particular circumstances, but most stations use some variant of this rundown. For a longer 1-hour show, stations often extend the length of the news blocks, add additional news blocks, or extend the time given to weather and sports. A 1-hour show might also include special segments on consumer news, politics, community interest, and so on.

Stations all across the country are increasing the hours they devote to local news content. Even in the smallest television markets (151+), nearly a third of all stations added more news between 1999 and 2000 (Table 5.2).

Obviously, not all of this additional news content comes in the form of the standard 30-minute news rundown. The rest of this chapter will focus on some alternative news formats and the strategies for producing them.

Alternative News Formats

Stations have several options when it comes to producing additional news programming and a variety of reasons for doing so. Sometimes, a station will want to give a topic extended treatment that doesn't easily fit into the

Table 5.2   Change in Amount of News Offered, 1999 to 2000 (%)

Type of station	Increased News	Decreased News	No Change
All local television	40	5	55
Markets 1-25	30	7	63
Markets 26-50	38	0	53
Markets 51-101	54	4	42
Markets 101-151	42	4	54
Markets 151+	27	7	66

SOURCE: Papper and Gerhard (2001).

standard 30-minute format. This could include things such as severe weather or breaking news. The station might also want to capitalize on a locally important topic or issue. These types of shows are especially common during election season, when stations hold debates or community forums.

An alternative news format might also be used to give the viewers a chance to make their voices heard, such as with a town meeting. Finally, there is a strictly pragmatic approach in which additional news is produced simply as a revenue source. Special news programs can be tailored to meet the needs of local advertisers. A special news program on breast cancer, for example, would be a very attractive advertising vehicle for local hospitals, pharmacies, and other health outlets.

There are several different formats for these special news programs, but generally they fall into one of six categories

LIVE

Many times, stations will do extended or special news programming live at a particular location. In many ways, the program will look like a regular newscast, in that there are anchors delivering the news and introducing taped segments, but going live on location gives the news a somewhat different look and feel. It sends a subtle message to the audience that this is special and not the routine newscast done every day in the studio.

The live show is typically produced in much the same way as a regular newscast. Producers will create a rundown, help put together scripts, and oversee the show from the control room. But the element of live

Figure 5.1   Producing a Live Show Has Many Advantages But Is Also
More Prone to Technical Difficulties and Other Problems

television adds an extra dimension of difficulty. With so much of the
news crew outside the studio environment, producers find communication more difficult. Stations usually assign a field producer to coordinate
activities on location and help the producer communicate with anchors
and technicians.

Any time a station goes live on location, it increases problems for the
producer. Technical problems can knock the signal off the air, guests can
fail to show up, anchors don't have teleprompters and can lose scripts, and
timing the show is much more difficult. Producers try to account for these
contingencies ahead of time, but no amount of planning can prevent the
occasional disaster. This type of show requires lots of communication and
flexibility, and producers should have backup plans in place. For example,
when a station decides to do its entire newscast on location, it will often
require additional anchors to sit at the news desk and be ready to go on in
the case of technical difficulties at the scene.

Despite these hazards, more and more stations are producing news
programs live on location. It could be as a way to highlight an event that's
happening in a particular area, such as some type of disaster. But it might

be nothing more than getting the news team out "on the road" so local audiences can see it. For example, KCRG-TV in Cedar Rapids, Iowa, has done a series of summer newscasts from different small towns in its viewing area. Doing the news from a fair or carnival or just in some small community is an effective public relations tool. Some viewers can become very attached to the local news, and they especially enjoy the opportunity of seeing their favorite anchors and reporters in person.

ROUNDTABLE

The roundtable gets its name from the fact that it usually involves people sitting around a table discussing a certain topic. Ideally, it is a discussion between a half-dozen or so prominent people on an important issue, but lately the format has become more argumentative. Shows like *Crossfire* and *The Capital Gang* on CNN have degenerated into shouting matches in an attempt to win more viewers.

This type of news program has several advantages, including the fact that it's relatively cheap to produce. Beyond getting a panel of people together, there's not much expense involved. The show is also fairly controllable, in that it usually takes place in the studio, is taped before airing, and can be edited. Of course, these conditions change if a station decides to do a roundtable show live on location, as ABC occasionally does with its *Viewpoint* program. This introduces all the problems of live news programming mentioned earlier.

The main drawback to a roundtable show is tedium. Like it or not, entertainment has become a big part of the news business, and audiences expect a sophisticated and engaging program. However, the roundtable is really nothing more than people sitting around having a discussion, and depending on the topic, that can get excruciatingly dull.

The producer's responsibility in these situations is to make the program as interesting as possible. Some consideration of personality and on-air presence should go into choosing participants, although this often is out of the hands of the producer. If the show is about the importance of the Federal Reserve Board, Alan Greenspan needs to be on it, whether or not he's an exciting speaker. Selecting an appropriate panel is the first duty of the producer in these situations.

The producer can try to increase interest by incorporating higher production values, such as music and graphics. Taped elements can also be used at various points in the show to offer a change from the discussion format. ABC's *Nightline* begins each of its discussion programs with an extended taped report introducing the topic.

No matter how the roundtable format is presented, the producer needs to be aware that simply watching "talking heads" for an hour or so is not an effective news presentation.

TOWN HALL MEETING

The town hall meeting is a good way for a station to gauge audience feedback on a certain news topic. Typically, the format is much like the roundtable, in that prominent newsmakers will discuss an important issue. But the emphasis in this show is more on audience input and interaction. Audience members will have the opportunity to give their opinions or make direct contributions to the show.

Given that so much of television news is now geared toward interactivity, this format can be a very effective way of engaging a news audience. The moderator can lead the discussion and also solicit feedback from the audience. Phil Donohue is credited with pioneering this format in the 1960s, and it has become quite popular. CNN's *TalkBack Live* is one example of the many variations of this format now on television.

The main problem with the town hall meeting is unpredictability. Not only does the producer face the difficulties of a roundtable discussion, he or she must constantly monitor audience feedback. Audience members can and will say almost anything on television, which reduces the control a producer has over the show. In some drastic cases, the entire format or content of the show might have to be changed. Again, these problems are lessened if the show is taped first and then edited for broadcast.

With this type of format, producers need both interesting guests and a topic that will generate good audience interaction. If the guest is unappealing, viewers at home will certainly tune out, and if there's little or no audience participation, guests often can't carry the show by themselves. Finding the right balance between guests and audience can make the town hall format very effective.

DEBATE

The debate is a format with limited use, in that it's generally restricted to political candidates running for office. But even though it's used only occasionally, it is still an extremely popular format during election season.

Most debates follow a very strict format, which usually includes a moderator. The moderator is the most important person in the debate, in that he or she controls the topic for discussion, who is speaking, and how much time the speaker has. The moderator must also keep control of the debate and not let participants shape the direction of the discussion.

One of the keys to producing a successful debate is finding a good moderator. In a sense, the moderator is like a producer, controlling such things as the time, content, and flow of the program. If the debate has a good moderator, the program producer actually does very little. The program itself is not scripted, except for a few introductory and closing remarks. The producer mainly keeps track of time and makes the moderator aware of things such as upcoming commercial breaks. Of course, the producer also must be ready to take control in the event of technical failure or other unforeseen problems.

Debates suffer from the same problem as roundtable discussions in that they can be very dull, but this is not the producer's responsibility. The format of most debates is usually fixed, so that each candidate will get an equal opportunity to speak. Audiences often tune in to see what the candidate has to say and how he or she reacts under pressure. They are forming important opinions about the candidates and don't need outside influences.

Even so, many stations extend their coverage to include postdebate analysis. Although not as tightly formatted as the debate itself, this coverage also usually follows a familiar pattern. Prominent people will comment on how the candidates fared, audience members might share their opinions, and the station might even convene a focus group to discuss the debate. Focus groups include a dozen or so audience members who represent different viewpoints. They will watch the debate together, and then a moderator (not the same as the debate moderator) will solicit their opinions.

In short, the entire debate format is usually tightly controlled, and producers don't have a lot of freedom. In addition, the general lack of interest in all nonpresidential debates and the fact that most debates are carried without commercials have caused stations to think hard about giving up valuable programming time. When a station does produce a debate, it is done more as a public service than as a means of profit.

ELECTION NIGHT

Most stations, no matter how big or small, put a lot of effort into election night. Viewers have a personal interest in elections and stations view their election coverage as an important public service.

There are many different ways of producing an election show, but one format in particular has emerged as extremely popular. Stations will have their main news anchors moderate election coverage from the news desk. The anchors update important elections results and introduce reporters who are covering races live from different locations and who will interview the candidates or other important election officials. Sometimes stations will have live reports from five or six different locations. Depending on the resources available, stations may not be able to do this kind of extensive coverage. But there are election-night producing strategies that apply to all stations, regardless of size.

Producers should understand that all elections eventually come down to winners and losers. Interviewing candidates and getting reaction is great, but viewers are primarily interested in results. Get as many race results as possible and present them to the audience in an understandable way. Many stations now use a "ticker," which shows election results at the bottom of the screen underneath the ongoing news program. Some tickers are so small or change so quickly that it's hard for viewers to keep up. How the results are presented isn't as important as that the audience gets the results in a timely and easy-to-understand fashion.

The presidential election of 2000 showed everyone in the news business the danger of getting tied up in predictions. Several major news organizations looked foolish for predicting a winner in a certain state, then having to retract the prediction. After the election, the Voter News Service (VNS) used to make predictions in elections was overhauled, then finally scrapped. Even before its demise, there were complaints that VNS would give predictions about races before the polls even closed. Hopefully, producers learned the lesson and will focus more on actual results.

It's also important for producers to have enough people on hand in the newsroom. Election night is the most labor-intensive night of the year for the news department, and people are needed to take phone calls, tabulate results, bring in food, and so on. Some of these positions can be filled on a volunteer basis, saving other news resources for more important work. The key is planning coverage ahead of time, knowing how many people you'll need, and defining their responsibilities.

Knowing the available staff and resources can help a producer determine how much election coverage to offer. There is now a great temptation for stations to go live from as many places as possible on election night, not only to surpass the competition but to show viewers that the station is "the place" for election night coverage. However, this type of all-out coverage makes little sense if the station doesn't have the resources to pull it off. There are simply too many races and issues to cover, and producers might be better off focusing on one or two key things. Know what's important in your area, and don't try to spread yourself too thin.

Remember, *all stories are about people*, and that applies to election night as well. Don't simply settle for campaign headquarters coverage; look for compelling stories to tell. How will the important issues affect people in your viewing area? For example, if there's a new gambling proposal up for a vote, what difference does that make in the lives of your viewers? Find people who have a direct stake in the outcome of elections (other than the candidates) and try to tell their stories.

THE CALL-IN SHOW

Although this format is much more common in radio, many television stations use it to some extent. A call-in show emphasizes the interactivity that has become so important in today's media environment and allows viewers to directly express their opinions. Generally, a moderator will lead discussion of a certain topic and then open the phone lines for feedback. Some stations will not even have a discussion but will simply fill the entire show with audience questions or concerns.

In terms of producing, this type of show is very similar to the round-table or town hall meeting. It's cheap and easy to put together but is extremely unpredictable and hard to control. Even with technology to delay or eliminate certain calls, almost every station in the country has a story about an obscene call that made it onto the air. There's also the danger that these types of shows are more suited to radio and are not enough to keep a television audience interested.

Given the growth of audience feedback and interaction through the Internet, these types of shows aren't very common on television today. Some producers have modified the format by replacing phone calls with e-mail. In Memphis, WPTY-TV airs a weekly show called *Law Line*, in which a panel of three lawyers responds to viewer questions submitted by mail and e-mail. In any event, producers should still be aware of the call-in show and know how to put one together.

How does a producer know which of these formats is most appropriate to use? That depends on several factors, including the issue or topic involved. Some topics are more naturally suited to certain formats, such as debate format for political candidates. Although the moderated debate works well for political discussion, it would not be as effective when issues such as school violence, escalating crime, or poverty are being discussed. Would a special news program on breast cancer awareness generate enough interest for a roundtable discussion or town hall meeting?

The producer must also consider the resources available for the program, including equipment and human resources. A debate or town hall meeting requires a tremendous resource commitment in terms of cameras, moderators, and finding a suitable venue. It may be that a station only has enough resources to effectively produce a roundtable discussion or live news event. It's often the case that the resources used to put these shows together may reduce the resources available for the regular newscast.

A final consideration should be the level of interest in the program, not only among the audience but among advertisers as well. Certainly, audience interest can influence what type of show to produce. If the show involves an important community topic with lots of public interest, a town hall meeting might be appropriate. If the pubic is uninterested or apathetic, it might be wiser to go with another format, such as a roundtable.

The station must also make an effort to gauge the interest of advertisers. If there is a strong advertising commitment, the show will have more flexibility in what it can do. More advertising means more dollars, which means the station might be able to afford a higher level of production. If there is little advertiser interest, the production will have to be scaled down accordingly. In the example of *Law Line*, the show itself served as an advertising vehicle for the law firm involved.

Alternative News Strategies

No matter what format is ultimately chosen, producers can rely on certain strategies for these alternative news programs.

Make the Show Interesting. Because many of these news programs deal with serious topics that can potentially bore audiences, the producer must look for ways to liven up the presentation. In some cases, such as debate, there's not much one can do. Many times, however, producers can help out a show with higher production values, such as music and graphics. It also helps to make the material relevant to the audience. Why should viewers care about this program? Personalizing or illustrating the topic with stories about real people can engage viewers in the show. Don't just give the facts and figures about breast cancer; tell a story about a woman who has fought it.

As mentioned, interactivity is always a good way to make the show more interesting because viewers care more about the news process when they feel they have a stake in it. There are probably other ways you can think of to engage the audience, but the bottom line is *do something different.* Give the show a different look or feel and let viewers know that this isn't just the same old news they see every day.

Plan Ahead and Prepare. Given all the things that can go wrong in these types of shows, it's almost impossible to prepare too much ahead of time. Good producers anticipate potential problems and work out backup plans for when things do go wrong. Nothing can prevent a show from experiencing problems, but good preparation will lessen their impact.

Coordinate. More than regular newscasts, these types of shows require coordination of staff within the station and people outside the station. Producers will need to make sure that all affected departments, including engineering, promotion, production, and sales, are aware of what's going on and what role they play in the show. Some of this coordination is done during the planning stages of the program and some needs to be done while the show is on the air.

Lots of red tape needs to be cut outside the station, especially when programs take place away from the station studio. This includes such things as making arrangements for an appropriate show venue, getting the required permission, finding locations from which to send back live signals, and lining up appropriate moderators and guests. Many shows have been changed or even dropped because a producer failed to go through appropriate channels.

Breaking News

In addition to these alternative programs, a station will occasionally produce unscheduled programming related to breaking news. It could be a fire, explosion, shooting, or whatever. But more and more stations offer special news programming in these situations, and they have a very short time to put it together. The very nature of breaking news is that it happens unexpectedly, and producers may have only a few minutes to get a show on the air.

Breaking into scheduled programming for these types of events has become a topic of debate in the broadcast journalism industry. No one would disagree that the events of September 11, 2001, warranted live and immediate coverage. But there's also a concern that too often, stations are sensationalizing their coverage of breaking news. This has become an important debate in Southern California, where stations often offer live coverage of high-speed freeway chases. For example, in 1998 viewers in Los Angeles watched as a car chase climaxed with a man's suicide. In 2003, city officials finally asked local stations to stop live coverage of car chases because they believed the coverage encouraged lawbreakers. But stations are reluctant to back off, given the tremendous audience interest. "I have to be honest, whenever I see a chase I just have to sit and watch," Los Angeles resident and chase fan Richard Trejo said ("Curb call," 2003).

Most of the time, the decision to break into scheduled programming will be made by a station manager, in consultation with the news director. They will consider some important issues related to the decision, including how the situation affects the viewing audience. There is certainly merit for breaking into programming if the news has a direct effect on a majority of the viewers, such as severe weather. A significant unexpected development, such as a major disaster or catastrophe, might also warrant special programming.

Once breaking news happens, all hell breaks loose in the newsroom, and staffers are running in a dozen different directions. That's why it's important for producers to have a producing plan already in place. This could include things such as important phone numbers and contacts, identifying potential interviews, preassigning staff to certain roles, and so on. Some producers even have enough foresight to have obituaries of prominent local citizens already done and ready to air in the event of a death.

A thousand different questions need to be answered once news starts to break. Is the live van ready to go? Are camera batteries charged? What crews will go out, and what particular part of the story will they cover? A producer can prevent a lot of problems by simply making sure these questions are handled ahead of time, if possible. Have a list of emergency contacts available, know how to contact your off-duty staff, and know the status of your ENG equipment. Knowing these things ahead of time allows the producer to concentrate more on getting news content on the air.

Obviously, planning and preparation will only go so far, and that's when the producer needs to focus on reorganizing and reprioritizing. All throughout a breaking news story, producers make decisions about the most effective way to get the story on the air. They must make immediate decisions about staffing, rundowns, and coverage formats. Who should cover the story? How should the story be covered? Do we need to call in additional resources or move people off from other stories?

The answers to these questions are constantly changing, depending not only on the resources available at the time but on the particulars of the story involved. Police may have blocked off access to a desirable live-shoot location or may have closed down an entire area related to the story. Many stations that wanted to use helicopters in the immediate aftermath of September 11 were prevented when the government instituted a no-fly zone around the scene of the terrorist attacks. Producers must constantly organize and reorganize coverage of a breaking news event.

If possible, producers should try to include as much live reporting as possible of breaking news events, assuming that the news justifies live coverage. Live television news can have a tremendous impact on the audience. The most unforgettable moment of the entire O. J. Simpson saga was the slow car chase down the freeway, watched by millions of viewers as it happened. People like to see news as it develops because this allows them to become part of the drama.

Again, stations face a great temptation to abuse this power, and certainly there are far too many television live shots. But in a justifiable news situation, nothing delivers the impact of breaking news like live coverage. Viewers can see what's going on, get instant information updates, and become drawn into the unfolding story. For stations without sophisticated technology for live reporting, phoners can be an effective alternative.

Even though so much of breaking news is chaotic, producers should strive for accuracy in all their newscasts. Too many times, accuracy is sacrificed for speed, as stations race to get information on the air first. This leads to a situation in which information is often put on the air without the requisite journalistic safety checks, such as with the 2000 presidential elections. Stations using a website to supplement their television news also face problems in this area. In recent years, both the *Wall Street Journal* and *Dallas Morning News* have had to apologize for erroneous material posted on their Internet news sites.

Producers should resist the temptation to air material simply because no one else has it. At the same time, they have to trust their reporters and photographers in the field because they're the ones with first-hand knowledge of what's going on. In many instances, there's simply no way for producers to check the accuracy of statements made during live coverage of breaking news, and mistakes will be made. Producers understand this, and the station will apologize on the air when necessary. But whenever possible, information should be checked thoroughly before it goes on the air.

SUMMARY

There is a lot more to news than the standard half-hour or hour-long newscast. Producers have a variety of options for putting news programs together, depending on the station's resources, the type of story involved, and the level of audience interest. Lots of planning goes into these shows, but sometimes much of it goes out the window when producers are faced with breaking news. In those situations, communication, coordination, and flexibility are the keys to good news production.

Thinking More About It

The following events are going on in your community (although not all at the same time):

- A special city council meeting is being held to discuss a proposed teenage curfew. The council is considering a 9:00 p.m. weekday curfew to help combat a rise in teenage crime. There is tremendous community interest in the proposal, both for and against, and a large crowd is expected to attend the meeting.

- One of the smaller towns in your viewing or listening area has won recognition as one of the best places to live in the country. The officials of the town, including the mayor, city council, and visitors bureau, are eager to promote the award; they see it as a way to help the town get some good publicity.

- Your city is celebrating the 50th anniversary of an important event—racial integration at the local university. The school has invited several important people back for the occasion, including the former university president and the first minority individual to attend the school. The university has several events planned during a week-long commemoration.

Your news director wants to create special programming around each event and has put you in charge as executive producer. In the process of putting together these shows, consider the following questions:

1. What format would you use to handle each situation? Why?

2. What specific advance planning would go into these shows? What other station departments would need to be in on the planning process?

3. What potential problems could make it difficult to produce these shows, and what steps can you take to address them?

4. What is the target audience for each of these shows? Given this audience, what specifically can you do to make the shows more attractive and interesting?

Weather and Sports 6

News producers have responsibility for everything that goes on during their newscasts, including the sports and weather segments. For the most part, producers do not directly involve themselves with content issues in these areas, leaving that for the sports and weather departments. But producers do have direct control over the time allotted for sports and weather and their placement in the show. Producers also often have to coordinate their own news coverage with what's going on in sports and weather. For these reasons and many others, it's important for news producers to know as much as possible about weather and sports production.

Weather

Many news directors and producers consider weather the single most important element in a newscast. Almost all research indicates that it is the one segment of the newscast that generates the most audience interest. People may not care about the lead news story or have much interest in sports, but the weather affects every single person in the audience.

For the most part, news producers give the weather department total freedom with its segments. Weather forecasting is a highly specialized skill, usually learned through years of study in meteorology or atmospheric science. It also depends on sophisticated equipment that requires special training. Weather forecasters use the latest computer technology for radar imaging, storm prediction and tracking, and long-range forecasting. The equipment is expensive and is usually contracted out to stations by companies that specialize in weather technology. Most producers simply do not have the educational background or the technical knowledge to offer any meaningful input into the content of the weather segment.

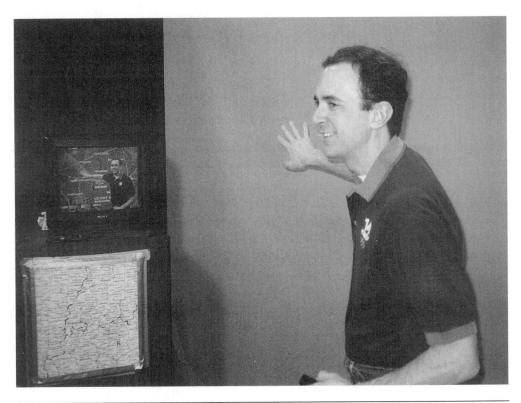

Figure 6.1   Modern Weather Forecasting Relies on Sophisticated Equipment That Usually Requires Specialized Training

It should be noted that some places, especially smaller markets and stations, do not have the money to invest in fancy weather equipment. Many, in fact, are not far removed from the days when weather maps consisted of magnets representing the sun, clouds, and thunderbolts. In these situations, weather segments are much less sophisticated, and producers can have much more input.

THE PRODUCER'S ROLE

In either event, producers do not simply sit by and let weather anchors do whatever they want. Primarily, producers assign a time for the weather segment. This time usually remains consistent for every show, assuming there are no unusual circumstances, such as severe weather. The time generally runs between 2 and 4 minutes, depending on the amount of audience interest in the weather segment, which can vary from market to market. In San Diego, for example, where it's sunny and 72 degrees almost every day, there's not much need for a lengthy weather segment. Audiences in Buffalo demand much more attention to weather during the winter months.

Aside from the time component, producers frequently use weather as a live segment within the newscast. These types of live segments are typically done in one of two ways. In the case of interesting or threatening weather, the producer can have a live weather segment from some outside location, often as the lead story in the newscast. This gives the audience the advantage of seeing the weather about which the forecaster is talking. In some cases, it might be as simple as having the weather anchor deliver the show from right outside the station. This is extremely simple to set up, does not strain the station's live resources, and gives the audience the impression that the weather department is on top of any breaking weather situation.

However, producers should exercise extreme caution when attempting a live shot during threatening weather. We've all seen television reports where some poor forecaster is almost blown away trying to describe an approaching hurricane. Live reporting during severe weather is not only technically difficult, it can be deadly. Live microwave transmission depends on a hydraulic mast that goes up to 80 feet in the air, which offers a perfect target for lightning. Scores of news people have been killed or seriously injured due to these lightning strikes or from getting the mast mixed up with electrical power lines. Producers should never schedule these types of live shots during thunderstorms or heavy winds.

The other type of live segment involves doing the weather from some particular location, business, or event. Carnivals, expositions, and bridal shows are just some of the places weather anchors might find themselves for a live report. Generally, the weather anchor will describe the event and what's going on at the location. After going through the weather presentation, he or she might also interview someone connected with the event.

It is believed that these types of live segments are good ways to involve the station in the outside community. The weather person has the opportunity to interact with the audience, increase station visibility, and create public goodwill. Many stations have now created specially designed live segments around their weather anchors. For example, one day each week in the summer, the weather segment could be done from a backyard barbecue at the home of a selected audience member. Most of these weather segments are considered more attractive for their public relations value than for their news value.

This points up the fact that many stations now expect weather personnel to do more than just deliver the weather. Even though weather is a specialized skill, modern technology makes it quick and easy to put a weather segment together. On most days, it takes the weather person only an hour or so to produce an entire segment, complete with fancy graphics and charts.

Given this, many smaller stations combine weather anchoring with some other duty, such as reporting or photography. For example, a person who does the weather forecasts on the weekend might also be expected to report news 3 days a week. In some cases, the weather person might report in the morning, then do weather later in the day. Combining duties in this way helps a smaller station stretch its resources. In larger markets, the weather person generally has no other duties but is expected to represent the station in the community. Because of weather's importance and interest, audience members often develop a strong attachment to the weather anchor, who fills a very important public relations role at the station.

SEVERE WEATHER

The single most important job for the weather department is during severe weather. Severe weather takes priority over all other news activities, and when necessary, stations will often preempt hours of expensive prime-time programming. News producers know that in times of severe weather, people usually turn to the broadcast media for information. Not only is severe weather a public service, it can save lives. Emergency services such as police and fire departments often depend on the severe weather information they receive from broadcast services. In many cases, severe weather reports on radio and television can mean the difference between life and death.

Televised Tornadoes

Perhaps no time in history have severe weather reports made as much difference as they did on May 3, 1999. That's when a series of tornadoes, some of the strongest ever seen in the Midwest, ripped through the Oklahoma City area, killing 38 and wrecking more than a thousand homes, apartments, and businesses.

The devastation would have been much worse if it had not been for the constant weather updates provided by the local television stations. Sophisticated technology allowed television forecasters to follow the path of the tornado street by street and pass that information directly to their viewers. "We were watching on TV and they said the twister's now passing Penn Avenue," said Oklahoma City resident David Lawrence. "So I could go outside and watch it pass by. We knew when it was time to go inside and get under the mattress."

According to KWTV-TV meteorologist Gary England, "For the first time in my 27 years, I was able to look at that storm, tell people exactly where it was and where it was going. I could see it was at least an F4 tornado, in terms of intensity, and I could say to people that they were going to have to be below ground level to survive."

The American Meteorological Society awarded special citations to KWTV and the other Oklahoma City television stations for their actions during the tornado "which prevented untold deaths and minimized the impact of the devastating storms." England later published a book on surviving deadly storms and tornadoes.

SOURCE of quotations: Lyman (1999).

Weather forecasters can often predict severe weather situations and plan accordingly. This gives the producer time to sit down with the weather department and map out how the coverage will look. Producers have to make important decisions regarding how the news department will help the weather anchors cover the story. Usually, the weather forecasters will stay at the station, giving updates, warnings, and forecasts. News reporters and photographers will often fan out across the area and send back pictures and reports on the impact of the weather situation. In some cases, the weather anchor will talk live with the reporter by phone, so the reporter can update the audience about what's happening in a particular place. In this way, the reporters provide additional depth and material to the story.

The public can also play an important part in this process. Many will call into the station and report on weather situations in their particular area. Sometimes the weather anchor will put these people on the air for a live phone conversation. Even if viewers aren't used on the air, they often give information about rainfall amounts, wind speed, and local damage.

This points out how interactive broadcast weather has become. Television and radio weather people get quite a bit of important information from the general public, especially those people who have an interest in the weather. Many of these people will volunteer to become station "weather watchers," giving daily updates about temperatures, precipitation, or other weather happenings. Digital technology has also made it possible for people to take pictures of severe weather phenomena and send the pictures electronically to the weather station. Many of these pictures are used on the air to illustrate the effects of severe weather.

Some weather watchers have a genuine interest in the weather, but others simply like to have their names mentioned on television. Whatever their motivation, viewers have become much more involved in the weather process, especially during severe weather.

In some cases, severe weather will sneak up on a station with little or no warning. Those are the most difficult situations for news producers, in that they have very little time to make decisions. In most cases, a decision is immediately made to interrupt programming, and other details are figured out on the fly. Even with the most careful planning, most severe weather is done impromptu. The weather anchor always works without a script and basically responds to whatever is happening at the moment. The producer can communicate with the weather anchor through IFB or by simply passing written messages to the set. Other newsroom personnel also work to help coordinate information.

Severe weather can be a time-consuming effort, depending on how slowly a storm moves and the danger it presents to community. In some cases, stations have gone for hours before returning to regular programming, which usually doesn't happen until the threat of severe weather has completely passed through the area. Even after the immediate threat has passed, weather personnel can work long into the night giving periodic updates. It's not unusual for a weather anchor to spend all night at the station during periods of severe weather, and many have small cots or beds at their stations for this reason.

Once severe weather has ended, coverage usually passes from the weather to the news department. This is when the producer has to think about aftermath coverage. Where does the station need to focus its efforts? Are there any particularly hard-hit areas? What are appropriate topics for coverage? Should more emphasis be placed on rescue efforts, devastation, economic impact, or some other aspect? The news director, producer, and other station personnel will sit down and address these questions. In the case of an extremely devastating storm, aftermath coverage could last for several days or even weeks.

It's also important for the producer to give a personal side to aftermath coverage. Damage totals, cost estimates, and other numbers can lose their significance if the audience can't attach them to names and faces. More stations now concentrate their aftermath coverage on the people directly affected by the storm. This could include survivors, rescue workers, and the like. The important thing is to remember that all stories are ultimately about people. A tornado that flattens an empty farmhouse is a much different story if the farmhouse is filled with family members.

CREDIBILITY

Credibility is, obviously, an important issue for the news department at any station, and it is also important for the weather department. People want to know that their station is delivering the most accurate and up-to-date weather information possible, especially during times of severe weather. Most stations promote their weather departments as having the most reliable forecasts, the most sophisticated technology, and the most credible weather anchors.

But the actual presentation of the weather segment depends a great deal on the personality of the anchor. Most anchors fall into one of two categories: the "no-nonsense" type or the "entertainer" type. No-nonsense weather anchors deliver information in a very straightforward, businesslike manner. They take a very serious approach to weather and realize that in some situations, lives are actually at stake. Jim Rasor, who has worked at WSIL-TV in southern Illinois for several years, would be a good example of the no-nonsense weather anchor. He doesn't engage in a lot of "happy talk" with the news anchors or make any jokes during his weather segment.

By contrast, entertainers focus more on the delivery of the weather segment. These weather anchors want to deliver accurate information, but they put more emphasis on doing it in an engaging, interesting style. Jeff Lyons of WFIE-TV in Evansville, Indiana, would be a good example of an entertaining weather anchor. On Halloween, he occasionally delivers the weather in costume, whether it's Elvis or a gorilla. His personality is also particularly suited for doing weather live on location.

Weather Production: Jeff Lyons

Jeff Lyons had a hard act to follow at WFIE, as he replaced legendary weather anchor Marcia Yockey. The two had very similar personalities, as Yockey did various weather segments dressed as a witch, an astronaut, and as Lady Godiva. Lyons has spent most of his 17-year weather career in Evansville, where he was born and raised.

Meteorologist Jeff Lyons,
WFIE-TV, Evansville, Indiana

Q: Do you have a specific philosophy about producing weather? Are there certain things you try to do every day, no matter what the weather is like?

A: My philosophy about weather is that it is a story, just like a news or sports story, and must be told in an interesting and informative way each day. I look at the weather segment in a newscast as a chance to teach the viewer something he or she might not have known. I try to include something extra in every weathercast, like trivia, viewer-submitted photos, etc. I think the successful weathercaster is one who establishes a familiar bond with the viewer by being personable on the air.

Q: For weather people who are more personality oriented, such as yourself, is credibility a concern?

A: Credibility, in my opinion, is a highly subjective quality that viewers perceive in a weathercaster. I think that if the weathercaster is confident, accurate, and straightforward during important weather events, the audience will accept him in a lighter role when the weather is nonthreatening. The worst thing that can happen is to be in the entertainment mode when severe weather strikes (out at a county fair on a live shot when a tornado strikes a distant part of the viewing area). In these cases, it is essential to change modes immediately and get back to the studio environment to establish coverage.

Q: For someone producing a weather segment, what would you say is the most difficult part?

A: The most difficult part is determining what is the most important weather element of the day—the headline in weather—and then creating graphics and animations that explain what is going on. Calm days can be like slow news days in that the weathercaster must come up with something to make the weathercast stand out from the others in the marketplace. This is when it is good to go out on a remote live shot or do something else that may provide entertainment value, as well as weather information.

Q: What is the relationship between the weather person and the newscast producer and the news director?

A: The weathercaster works closely with the newscast producer to determine how much time the weather segment gets, if there will be any video elements within the weathercast, and if the weather will be produced in the studio or on location that day. The news director in our station (market 98) serves as an executive producer, so he also has a say in what I do and how I do it. How much input do they have in the weather presentation? I provide the weather information and they may suggest related sidebar items. On a big weather day, when weather is the lead story, they may build the entire news block around weather.

Q: Can you describe what it's like during severe weather?

A: In a severe weather situation, the most important thing is to be on the air with critical information as soon as possible and as often as is necessary. Research shows that severe weather coverage tops the list of things viewers want from the local TV station. It is important to remain calm on the air but to issue the call to action when viewers should take cover. The weathercaster must use a lot of equipment (radar, character generators, phone-in spotter reports, Internet, tower cameras, etc.) just to get the word out and receive timely information. It can become very hectic as news-people come in and out of the studio with information to be put on the air.

Q: How important is it to include the audience in the weather segment (weather watchers, storm chasers, etc.)?

A: I think it is absolutely essential to have audience involvement. If the viewers feel they have a stake in the show, they will be more likely to watch regularly. In severe weather, they are more likely to participate by giving reports of damage, etc. to the station.

Q: When you look back on some of the best weather segments you've done, what made them successful?

A: In every case, they were segments that were either extremely helpful to viewers (tornado coverage) or ones that entertained (Halloween costumes, county fair remotes, etc.) and involved the audience in such a way that they talked about it for days after the show.

SOURCE: Jeff Lyons (personal communication, April 2003).

There are ways for entertaining weather anchors to increase their credibility. Many stations now require their weather anchors to obtain a seal of approval from the American Meteorological Society. The AMS seal requires additional hours of training and education in meteorology, although it doesn't have anything to do with the anchor's on-air presentation skills. It should be noted that in many small television and radio markets, people who are giving forecasts on the air might not have any weather training at all. They're simply reading material supplied from the National Weather Service or other sources, such as the Weather Channel. When a weather anchor has an AMS seal, stations usually heavily promote that fact on the air. In most larger markets, it's required for the weather anchors.

Because so much of the weather presentation is tied into the anchor's personality, there's not much producers can do on the issue of credibility. If the producer feels like the weather segment is sacrificing too much credibility for entertainment, he or she might sit down with the weather anchor and the news director to discuss the matter. In extreme cases, some weather anchors have been fired for outrageous behavior on the air. But for the most part, audiences seem to enjoy a weather segment delivered in an entertaining way, as long as it's not during severe weather.

GOOD RELATIONSHIPS

You can see how often the news department depends on the weather department and vice versa. That's why it's so important for a producer to develop and maintain a good working relationship with the weather anchor. This relationship is built on mutual respect, in which both sides acknowledge the authority of the other.

The producer must realize that weather personnel have editorial control over the weather segment. Weather people are the ones who figure out the forecast, put together the maps and graphics, and ultimately present the information on the air. Most of this is done without the aid of any script, and weather anchors must be good ad-libbers who can fill minutes of additional time when needed. The only structure they have is the order in which they put their weather elements. Producers need to give them the flexibility to create these elements and allow them to change when needed.

At the same time, weather anchors must realize that they are only one part of the overall newscast. The producer does have authority over weather in certain situations, including timing and placement. Just as weather anchors get extra time for severe weather, they should not be surprised if their time is reduced for situations like breaking news or calm weather. Producers also expect the weather department to take part in live shots or other formats that help the news presentation.

Understanding these roles can lead to a better working relationship between news and weather and may help to prevent potential conflict.

Sports

In many ways, the sports and weather departments at a station are very similar. Sports departments produce their own material, with little or no input from the news producer, yet depend on the producer for time allotment and placement within the show. When a sports event or story becomes big enough, the sports department will also contribute material to the news segment. This type of situation is probably the most common example of the news and sports departments working together.

In such situations, news takes precedence, and the stories are worked into the first block of the newscast. Sports anchors often complain about this, because they say it doesn't leave them with much to say during their own segments. But there are effective ways of coordinating coverage between the departments.

Consider a typical (hypothetical) example: A local all-star athlete is arrested on drug charges. Usually, news and sports departments will work together to cover different angles of the story. Some of the presentation possibilities for the station are shown in Table 6.1.

SPECIAL SPORTS PROGRAMMING

News producers will also work with the sports department to help create special programming oriented around a major sporting event. Such events usually involve a lot of money and fan interest and go beyond simple sports coverage, such as when a local team goes to the Super Bowl or the NCAA basketball tournament. Stations usually spare no expense in these situations, sending dozens of reporters, photographers, and anchors to the scene for extensive live reporting (WTMJ-TV in Milwaukee sent 31 people to cover the Packers in Super Bowl XXXI). A smaller station faced with a similar event would have a much more scaled-down effort, probably including only one or two people at the scene and some live satellite transmission.

Many stations broaden the appeal of these shows by including news and feature reports. News producers can have a variety of roles, including scheduling assignments, show rundowns, satellite coordination, on-scene production, and so on. These kinds of productions involve so many duties that stations usually assign the show several producers. Some work on site and others coordinate coverage back at the station.

From an editorial standpoint, producers should focus on the people and personalities of the event and leave the hard-core sports coverage to the sports department. For example, when a local team goes to play in the Orange Bowl, the sports department will probably cover team practices, player and coach interviews, and then the game itself. News coverage could include reports of Miami nightlife, interesting tourist attractions, or fan activities.

Producers also face the challenge of trying to make these special shows unique. They should realize that other stations and outlets in the market are probably considering or doing much the same thing. If there's a big professional golf tournament in town, chances are that all the other stations will have some sort of special programming. That's why it's important for

Table 6.1   Sports and News Working Together on a Story

Situation	Comments
News anchors throw to sports anchor for story, either on live shot, on set, or in sports office	This is an extremely popular way to handle the story, although it makes it difficult for the sportscaster to come up with fresh material for his own segment. Having the sportscaster in the news segment lends the sports department credibility and lets the audience know that this is not just another story. The downside is that it can lead to overkill on a story.
Sportscaster produces some sort of sidebar or related story that runs in the news block	This method is also very popular, and it allows each department a fresh angle on the story. Usually, the news department would handle the "harder" edge to the story: the details of the arrest and reaction from community members. The sports department would then handle a related angle, such as the prevalence of drugs in the local athletic community or how the arrest will affect the athlete's status on the team or chances for a college scholarship.
Team coverage of the story, involving both news and sports	Team coverage involves allocating almost all the station's resources to the story, including reporters, photographers, engineers, and the sports department. At least two or three reporters would provide different reports on the story, all covering a different angle. Proponents of team coverage say it allows a station to give a story the in-depth attention it deserves; critics call it excessive overkill. Again, the main problem for the sportscaster is that it leaves very little new material to use when the sports segment rolls around.
Story runs exclusively either in news or sports, but not both	This is very seldom done, for a variety of reasons. Skipping the story in the news segment sends the signal that it's not a very important story and also runs the risk of other stations getting the jump on coverage. Running the story exclusively in news might miss the viewers or listeners who don't tune in until the sports segment. It also gives people the impression that the sports department isn't on top of things.

the show to have its own unmistakable identity and something that separates it from the competition. Identity can be accomplished in several different ways, including emphasizing the personality of the anchors, the quality of the photography and graphics, or the types of stories presented.

Obviously, exactly how these shows are produced depends on the money and resources committed by the station. Many stations will send almost their entire news team to the event and produce several hours of special programming. Other stations will send only one or two crew

Figure 6.2   Sports Producers Perform a Variety of Duties to Help Get the Show on the Air, Including Taking Sports Feeds and Editing Stories

members and limit their coverage to some live reports within the newscast. Many times, the sports department will handle all the production needs on site, and there won't be a need to send a news producer. The producer will simply help coordinate coverage from back at the station.

No matter how the station approaches the event, it will require thorough planning and preparation. The news producer should consult with the sports department, news director, engineers, and other station personnel to map out a strategy for the entire production. The ultimate success or failure of the production depends largely on planning done ahead of time.

SPORTS PRODUCERS

In smaller to medium-sized television markets, most sports anchors produce, write, shoot, edit, and present their own material. However, in some larger markets, the person in the position of sports producer handles many of these duties. The very biggest stations and all-sports outlets such as ESPN have several sports producers.

The sports producer is responsible for almost all aspects of the show, except for anchoring. Note the job description for a sports producing job at KSTP-TV in Minneapolis, which gives you some idea about what the position involves.

Duties of a Sports Producer

JOB: Sports Producer
QUALIFICATIONS:
- Experience producing and/or reporting daily commercial TV sports
- Must have exemplary command of language with superior communication skills
- Expertise using technical, verbal, and audio tools of TV essential
- Must have solid journalism background
- Experience making sound, ethical decisions within tight deadline
- Must have ability to motivate, inspire, coach, and lead others

ESSENTIAL JOB DUTIES:
- Write and approve scripts and graphics
- Edit videotape
- Establish and maintain quality control systems
- Coordinate the execution of special projects
- Sustain an on-air look that is clear, consistent, contemporary, and focused on the needs of the viewers

---

SOURCE: KSTP-TV, Minneapolis.

Note from the author: KSTP-TV ran the ad in March 2003, so please don't contact them.

Many of the things a news producer does in creating a newscast (see chapter 3) apply to the sports producer putting together a sports segment.

Always Start With a Rundown

Again, this is simply a list of the stories you plan to cover for the day and how you plan to cover them. A rundown generally includes the list and names of your stories, how you plan to present them (highlights only? sound on tape? a full package?) and other important information for the director.

Your rundown is your blueprint for the show and will often change before the sportscast. Some stories will come in late and have to be delayed; others will not come at all and will have to be dropped entirely. You may also have to drop stories if the news has run long or if your own show has taken longer than expected. Therefore, it's always a good idea to have some sort of backup plan in mind. In the case of our sample rundown, your reporter might tell you that the interview with the coach wasn't possible. You would have to change the story from a VO/SOT to perhaps just a VO and consider adding another short reader or story to make up the time. The key to the rundown is flexibility and being prepared to make changes at any time.

Table 6.2   Typical Sports Segment Rundown

Slug	Story Type	Tape No.	Still Store	Length	Total Time
HS FOOTBALL	V/O	S-147	Football	:40	:40
SCORES	CG	——	——	:30	1:10
COLLEGE PREVIEW	VO/SOT	S-148	Tigers FB	:45	1:55
COACH JONES	PKG	S-149	——	1:50	3:45
BASEBALL TRADE	RDR	——	Cubs	:15	4:00

Note: CG indicates character generator; FB, football; HS, high school; PKG, package; RDR, reader; V/O, voiceover; VO/SOT, voiceover and sound on tape. Numbers indicate time in minutes and seconds.

It's important to work with the newscast producer and let him or her know exactly what's in your show. The sports producer (or anchor) should provide a copy of the rundown to the newscast producer and keep that person updated on any changes. The newscast producer has the final authority to adjust sports time and approve any last-minute changes.

Make a List of the Resources You Expect to Use for the Show

What stories you want to cover obviously depends on what's available. How many photographers are available to shoot? How much time will it take to edit? What's coming down on the network sports feed? What's on the national wires? What are the most important local events going on? Does anything warrant live coverage? These are some of the questions you should be asking yourself as you start planning out your show.

As previously discussed, most if not all stations now subscribe to the Associated Press broadcast wire and some type of video newsfeed service (Table 6.3). Newsfeeds come almost continually during the day, although most of the sports content comes at specific times. Usually, newsfeed organizations will provide sports feeds at least three times during the day: sometime in the morning, for which the feed will include highlights and interviews from the previous night's games; late afternoon, which includes the major sports news of the day and any afternoon games; and late evening, which focuses on highlights of games played that night and updates major stories from earlier in the day.

Be Realistic About What You Can and Can't Do

Obviously, you want to give the best possible coverage to each and every story in your rundown, but just as obviously, there are technical and logistical handicaps that make your job much more difficult. It would be

Table 6.3   Typical Network Sportsfeed Rundown

Time	Slug	Format	Source	Length
4:30:15	TYSON HEARING	VO/SOT		1:30
4:32:05	YANKEES PARADE	V/O	WPIX	1:00
4:33:30	FSU PREVIEW	VO/SOT	NCAA	3:00
4:37:00	ILLINOIS PREVIEW	VO/SOT	NCAA	2:56
4:40:15	PAYNE STEWART	PKG	WCPX	1:50
4:42:30	BLAUSER FILE	V/O	MLB	:35
4:43:15	SANTIAGO FILE	V/O	MLB	:30
4:45:00	CARDS PREVIEW	VO/SOT	KTVK	1:30
4:47:10	JAGS PREVIEW	VO/SOT	WJXT	1:20
4:48:45	BEARS PREVIEW	VO/SOT	WFLD	1:45
4:50:45	CHIEFS PREVIEW	SOT	KMBC	:45

Note: FSU indicates Florida State University; PKG, package; V/O, voiceover; VO/SOT, voiceover and sound on tape. Numbers indicate time in minutes and seconds.

great to have a live report from the state championship basketball game, but is it even technically possible to get a live shot from the arena? And what's the cost involved? If you don't go live, what's the next best way to cover the game? A package seems logical, but will your reporter have time to drive back to the station and edit a piece together? Would a look-live (a taped segment made to appear live) be more appropriate or even a phoner?

Sports producers waste a lot of time spinning their wheels because they try to do too much. Certainly, unexpected breakdowns and problems will occur—more often than you like. But pushing the envelope too far only increases your chances for frustration down the line.

Coordinate Your Coverage as Much as Possible

This means coordination at every level—the newsroom, event management, and especially other station departments. The news department should be fully aware of what you're trying to do. Not only does this avoid unnecessary conflict; the news department may be able to provide some unexpected help. If a news reporter is covering a story in the same town where you need an interview with the baseball coach, you might be able to kill two birds with one stone and save yourself the trip. But don't be surprised if you're asked to return the favor someday.

The engineering department also needs to know what's going on, especially if there's any satellite or live coverage involved. If you're taking a satellite feed, the engineers need to know details such as coordinates and what time the material will come down. Live shots have to be set up well in advance to overcome possible problems such as signal interference.

As much as possible, check with coordinators of the event you're going to cover. Find out about credentials, parking availability, directions to the event, places where you can shoot, and what to do about getting postgame interviews. On the high school and local level, many of these decisions are left up to you. College and pro events, on the other hand, have very strict guidelines regarding the media, and failure to follow the rules can lead not only to embarrassment but possibly to not getting to cover the game at all.

Have as Many Local Stories as Possible

Not too long ago, broadcast television stations were the only game in town and the only way for people to see highlights of national sports events like the Kentucky Derby or Indy 500. Now, there are literally hundreds of cable and satellite channels, some of them completely dedicated to sports. Virtually the same highlights you want to show will run on ESPN, CNN, and the like. Add the Internet and online services, and viewers can get their national sports stories from almost anywhere.

That's why it's essential that you emphasize your *local* sports scene, because it offers your audience something they can't see anywhere else. This means primarily the traditional sports, such as football, basketball, and baseball. Many stations have now expanded their weekend shows to 10 or 15 minutes with one goal in mind—show as many high school and local college games as possible.

Local coverage also means nontraditional sports presented in nontraditional ways. Feature stories about inspiring athletes overcoming adversity or unlikely champions have become quite popular because they interest the nonsports fan. The hard-core sports segment (remember, only about a third of the total audience) is going to watch no matter what you show. It's the other two thirds you need to reach, which can be done with well-crafted feature pieces. Such stories provide much of the real challenge of sportscasting because they force you to get away from scores and highlights and become more of a storyteller.

It's important to keep up with what's going on locally. Make a file (sometimes called a *futures* or *tickler* file) of upcoming events and read the local sports section every day. Develop local contacts who can keep you informed of any breaking situations. Many exclusives have been scored because of innocent conversations or phone calls that came in to the sports department.

One final word about sports producers. Many people become sports producers in the hope that it will eventually lead to an on-air sports position. For the most part, this never happens. There are certainly cases in which someone has made the jump, but these are isolated examples and extremely rare. In general, sports producers are behind-the-scenes positions with no opportunity for anchoring. If you are interested in working as a sports anchor, it would be better to get an on-air position in a very small market and work your way up than to accept a sports producing position in a large market with the idea that it will lead to anchoring.

WORKING WITH THE SPORTS DEPARTMENT

Just as a news producer must cultivate good working relationships with the weather department, the same holds for the sports department. The relationship might be a little more strained in that sports is not considered as important to the overall newscast as is weather. Sports people are very protective about their work and the time they get within the news. If a news producer is constantly reducing the time for sports or using sports material within the news block, this can create problems.

However, most sports anchors have become accustomed to the constraints of the job. Like John Campbell, most are professional, dedicated team players who will work with a news producer in almost every situation.

Sports Production: John Campbell

John Campbell got his start as a sports broadcaster in Wisconsin but has become a fixture at KCRG-TV in Cedar Rapids, Iowa, where he has worked for more than 20 years. Campbell covers a variety of sports but especially likes the outdoors. His weekly segment "Big Ol' Fish," for which viewers send in pictures of their big catches, is so popular that there's almost a year-long backlog of material waiting to be used.

John Campbell, Sports Director, KCRG-TV, Cedar Rapids, Iowa

Q: *Do you have an overall philosophy for producing a sportscast? Has it evolved or changed over the years?*

A: I always try to think ahead and work ahead. If you make every show a "buzzer-beater" [running into the studio to beat the deadline], you will burn out quickly. Remember, there are other people like directors who need your information in a timely manner. The more you get it to them early, the more they will make an effort when you must give them things at the last second. Believe me, there will be enough of those sportscasts.

Q: What are the characteristics of a good sportscast?

A: Sometimes the best casts have been theme casts. We will take a subject and not be afraid to go with it for 3 minutes. In contrast, some of the best shows I have done have had a lot of different stories and video. I think I'm most satisfied when we have a good, up close and personal story in the 'cast. You have to think about what people will remember most about the show.

Q: What are the most difficult parts of putting together a sportscast (and why)?

A: I think the most difficult part is figuring out a lead when there is no lead. Sportscasts can be like baseball games—sometimes you have to "manufacture" a run. Sometimes this involves using bites from something that took place 3 weeks ago, and sometimes it means localizing a national story. Many times, if there's a national baseball story, we'll use our local minor league affiliate as a way to get at the story.

Q: There's been a lot of talk about reducing the time for sports within the news, due to its relative lack of audience interest. Do you see this as a growing problem?

A: The same news director who tells you people don't care much about sports, and if he had it his way would get rid of the sports, is the same one who wants to lead the news-cast with sports when the local university hires a big-name coach. Cutting time for sports is a problem. For example, we get 3 minutes at 10:00, but with a commercial break in it, it's actually more like 2½ minutes. The time problem makes it imperative that you work well with producers. Many times on slow days I offer time to the news producers. It's something that usually pays off in the long run.

Q: For many reasons, many sports segments are becoming much more "funny" or entertainment oriented. Is this a good thing? Does it create a credibility problem for the sportscaster?

A: That's a hard one to answer. I think you need to get the feel for your audience and go from there. You will usually get feedback that tells you if it's working or not. Take some chances, but most of all, be yourself and be open to new ideas.

Q: How important is it to make the sportscast more interactive?

A: We don't do polls or contests, but "Big Ol' Fish" is extremely popular. I'm usually about 8 months behind showing the pictures. Our "High School Athlete of the Week" feature lets the viewers nominate the kids, then vote on the three finalists we select. So it's a very popular segment.

Q: What has been the impact of all-sports networks like ESPN in the way you put your own show together?

A: We cannot compete with the ESPNs of the world, so we stress local sports stories, and I'd say we're now about 99% local. Football, baseball, and basketball just don't cut it anymore. I still think stories about people are the most interesting. Have the guts to cover the state wrestling tournament, but instead of showing 12 matches, find that one interesting story and focus on it.

SOURCE: John Campbell (personal communication, April 2003).

Thinking More About It

Consider taping a series of local newscasts for a content analysis (for more information on content analysis, see "Thinking More About It" at the end of chapter 2). Analyze the newscasts and consider the following:

1. How much time (in minutes) do sports and weather get for each show? Is this fairly consistent on a nightly basis? Do you feel like there was too much or not enough time devoted to these segments? Why?

2. Where are the weather and sports segments placed within the show? Are there any occasions when sports or weather were incorporated into the news segment? If so, why? Do you feel this was justified?

3. Did the weather and sports segments seem to fit in with the overall style, tone, and organization of the newscast? In other words, was there a logical flow between segments? Did the presentation style of the weather and sports anchors seem to match that of the news anchors? Were sports and weather stories presented the same way as news stories?

4. In terms of the overall presentation of the sports and weather segments, how important was the "style" of the anchor? Were the anchors more serious or more entertaining? How did this affect the credibility of the segments? Did it make the segments better or worse?

5. Considering the news, weather, and sports segments of the newscast, on which segment do you think the station placed the most emphasis? Why? Do the weather and sports segments seem to be an integral part of the newscast, or are they presented more as an afterthought?

6. How do the weather and sports segments compare with weather and sports at other stations in the same market? Are they about the same, or have the competing stations tried to make the segments different or unique?

7. If you were producing weather or sports at one of these stations, what would you do, and why? Would it look much as it does now, or would you make changes? What factors should you consider before sitting down to produce these segments?

Producing for Radio and the Internet 7

There's no doubt that television is the most influential electronic medium today when it comes to news. Research confirms that more Americans get their news from television than from any other source, which has been the case for several decades. But this dominance faces a strong challenge from other new media, such as the Internet. And although television dominates the landscape, radio still plays an important role in the broadcast news process.

Radio

News has always been an integral part of radio programming, going back to the first broadcast of presidential election returns in 1920. Between the 1920s and 1950s, national radio networks were vital news links for Americans, especially those living in rural areas. Radio demonstrated the power of broadcasting to provide instant coverage of important news events. Special events, such as the crash of the Hindenburg in 1937 and Edward R. Murrow's descriptions of London during World War II, have become broadcasting landmarks and demonstrate the power of radio news to serve a national audience.

The arrival of television had obvious consequences for radio, particularly radio news. National advertisers flocked to television, forcing radio to reinvent itself as a format medium devoted to local audiences. Many stations reduced the time devoted to news and concentrated instead on music, which became an important part of radio with the development of FM. Something of a news renaissance occurred in the 1980s, as the tremendous growth of talk radio reminded stations of the value of news programming. Almost all of today's radio stations broadcast news in some format, either as an all-news presentation or as periodic updates throughout the day.

HOW PEOPLE USE RADIO NEWS

Before we can begin producing a radio newscast, we must understand how audiences use radio news and why they listen. In 2000, the Radio and Television News Directors Foundation (RTNDF) conducted a national survey of the radio news audience. The American Radio News Audience Survey was designed to find out how Americans use radio today and how this compares to their use of other media (Future of News and Journalism Ethics Projects, 2000).

As for general findings, the survey reported that most people listen to news during the morning hours of 6:00 to 10:00 a.m. This is not surprising, given that most people are driving to work during that time. Not only is news usage the heaviest during the morning hours, it declines steadily throughout the day. The only minor exception is during evening drive time, 3:00 to 7:00 p.m. (see Table 7.1).

Drive time is an extremely important part of the radio news day. People get most of their radio news when they're driving to work or returning home. In fact, in regard to when people listen to radio news, drive time is second only to the time when people first wake up. It's clear that the morning hours are extremely important for radio news listeners; that's the only time radio news listenership exceeds television. As the day continues, radio news listening drops dramatically, as more people switch over to television. Again, the only exception is evening drive time (Table 7.2).

No matter what time people listen to radio news, they want it to be local. More than 90% of respondents in the survey (RTNDF, 2000) thought that it was important for radio news to focus on people, events, and issues in the

Table 7.1   Average Time per Day Spent Listening to Radio News

Time of Day	Time in Minutes
6:00-10:00 a.m.	30
10:00 a.m.–3:00 p.m.	22
3:00-7:00 p.m.	23
7:00 p.m.–midnight	13

SOURCE: RTNDF American Radio News Audience Survey, 2000. Reprinted with permission.

Table 7.2   When People Listen to News

Time of Day	Radio News Listeners (%)	TV News Viewers (%)
First waking up	34	31
Getting ready for day	35	29
Commuting	78	3
Evening time, after dinner	3	50
Getting ready for bed	7	43

SOURCE: RTNDF American Radio News Audience Survey, 2000. Reprinted with permission.

local community. In addition, respondents were 40% more likely to say that local news was important to their selection of a radio station, compared to national news. In this way, radio is much like television—local stations must focus on local news to attract local listeners.

The survey broke down the radio audience into three distinct groups, each of which wanted something different from the news. Respondents who listened on all-news stations wanted more information. Those who listened to talk radio wanted their news to have more opinion and perspective, but music audiences put more importance on brevity. Obviously, how you produce a newscast depends a lot on the type of station involved.

NEWS ON TALK RADIO AND ALL-NEWS STATIONS

As noted, people who want more information turn to all-news or talk radio stations. But there are many different ways of presenting information. One could take the same piece of information and present it in different ways, depending on the medium. You wouldn't necessarily present the information the same way for television, radio, and the Internet.

For example, television is more "appointment" viewing: People make an appointment with themselves to sit in front of the set and watch in specific time increments, usually an hour or half an hour. Although people can do other things while watching television, usually their attention is specifically focused.

It used to be the same for radio in the days before television, when receivers were very large and families would "make appointments" to sit around and listen to specific programs. In today's environment, radio has become a background medium, meaning that people usually listen to the radio while doing something else. Transistors and miniaturization have allowed radios to go in cars, to the beach, or to the ballpark. As a result, people don't listen to radio in specific blocks of time but become occasional users, listening for a few minutes here and there throughout the day. When people listen depends in great part on when they have access to radios, which is why drive time is so important.

Because radio is relatively hit and miss, the main goal of a newscast is consistency. In other words, the news should be presented in the same format and at the same time day after day. This creates habit for the listener, who becomes accustomed to tuning in at a particular time of day to hear certain news information.

One way to create consistency is though a "news wheel" (see Figure 7.1). At first glance, the news wheel looks like a pizza. In actuality, news and program directors will cut a broadcast hour into several "slices" of minutes. Individual news segments can then be put into the slices, depending on the wants and needs of the particular station.

In our example, the hour leads off with national news, which runs from :00 (the top of the hour) to :03 (three minutes past). That's followed by local news, a short commercial break, weather and traffic, business, another commercial break, then entertainment and sports. Stations will usually repeat this format twice during an hour and sometimes even four times. That is, national news would be done at :00, :15, :30, and :45, and local news would air at :03, :18, :33, and :48. Other elements would repeat at their corresponding time slots.

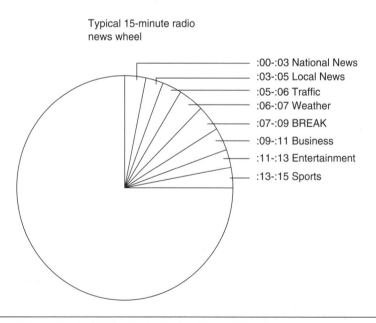

Typical 15-minute radio news wheel

:00-:03 National News
:03-:05 Local News
:05-:06 Traffic
:06-:07 Weather
:07-:09 BREAK
:09-:11 Business
:11-:13 Entertainment
:13-:15 Sports

Figure 7.1   Typical 15-Minute Radio News Wheel

The types of elements in the show and their placement will vary, but what's important is maintaining consistency. That means that the same element hits at the same time for every newscast. This allows the listener to pick and choose certain aspects of the newscast. Those more interested in weather and traffic know to tune into the station at :07, :22, :37, and :52 past the hour. This is especially important in that most listeners will not stay with an all-news station all day long. Instead, they will tune in periodically to catch the news elements that interest them most.

That's why saturation is another key part of producing radio news. Television news has the luxury of running a story once in each show, but if radio news did that, many listeners would miss important stories. Radio producers repeat important stories several times a day to make sure the information is heard no matter when the listener is tuned in. Producers should never assume that a radio audience has heard the story before.

The importance of the news wheel and saturation in radio news increases the workload for a producer. With perhaps the exception of the Internet, no medium is as content-hungry as talk and all-news radio. Producers must constantly write, rewrite, and edit stories, then do it all over again 15 or 30 minutes later. This process will continue throughout the day, or at least for the length of the producer's shift.

As a result, radio producers must have a very keen awareness of their available resources and how to use those resources most effectively. Phoners, live reporting, helicopter coverage, and taped packages must all be evaluated and coordinated many times each hour. In contrast to the television news producer, who probably relies more on human resource management, the radio news producer relies much more on physical resource management. The demands of filling a news wheel don't leave much time for anything else.

The differences between radio and television also dictate what kind of information the producer wants to use. Remember that most people listen to radio news in their car, either on their way to work or coming home. People in their cars listening only for a few minutes at a time have certain news priorities. They want to know if they've missed anything important, how long it will take them to get where they're going, and what problems they might encounter along the way. That's why radio news focuses so much attention on headlines, traffic, and weather.

Despite their differences, radio and television news do share many things in common, especially in terms of producing strategies. Like television producers (see chapter 3), radio producers should strive for local coverage, an especially important point considering that radio has become a medium that serves a niche, local audience. Many stations will start their news wheel with national headlines taken from network radio feeds, and it doesn't make much sense to have local personalities or reporters repeating national stories the network has just provided. In some cases, stations use syndicated material for their national news programming. In any event, local stations should focus on local stories.

"Going local" doesn't always make for compelling news. How long would you listen if someone had simply put an open microphone at the podium of the city council meeting and let it run for an hour? Producers should work to build a newscast that engages listeners and gives them a reason to tune in. Consideration should be given to stories of relevance and interest to the local audience. Why should someone listening care about the story? How does it affect him or her?

As mentioned previously, personalization and interactivity are good ways of making stories interesting and relevant. *All stories are ultimately about people.* Listeners care more when the news focuses more on people than on events, things, or even issues. A proposed ordinance to ban smoking in public places could be treated by simply focusing on the facts—how, when, where, and why. But attaching the story to people (who's affected? who's fighting it?) would make it more interesting.

Interactivity is important in radio and is the lifeblood of many all-news and talk stations. Many people listen just for the opportunity to call in and voice their opinions, and news that has an interactive component can be very successful. Several stations build entire news shows around this concept—giving a bare minimum of news and then opening up the phone lines for listener comments.

Such an approach is an example of how stations can create their own news identity or "brand." Creating a unique news product is extremely important for radio stations because they face much more competition in the market than do television stations. Radio stations must find a way to use their news in a way that distinguishes them from other stations. "Almost all stations are the same in terms of their program libraries and the number of minutes they have in an hour," says Rick Mize, who runs two stations in Oxford, Mississippi. "The difference is how they use what they have to create something unique" (R. Mize, personal communication, February 2003).

There are several ways a radio news program can differentiate itself in the market, including issues of presentation (music, placement in the wheel), content (helicopter reports, phoners, more live coverage), and original programming. The goal of the producer should be to create a branded news program, one that is easily identifiable in the mind of the listener. Many stations try to brand themselves as the "news leader" by flooding the market with constant news programming. This can be a tremendous strain on resources, but producers should try to push the envelope as much as possible. This means maximizing available resources in the best possible way to produce a newscast that is as sophisticated,

Table 7.3 Use of Digital Equipment and New Technology in Radio News

Type of Technology	Stations Using (%)
Digital editing and mixing	74
Digital audio recording	73
Digital or cellular phones	70
Field laptop computers for editing	12

SOURCE: Papper (2000).

up to date, and comprehensive as possible. One of the main ways radio stations can accomplish this is through live reporting.

Unlike television, radio stations can do live reporting at a minimum of cost and effort. The easiest way is doing live reports by phone, which has become even more common with the advent of the cell phone. This allows radio reporters to send back live information from almost any news scene and from places where it would be impossible to get a live television signal.

Phoners remain a staple of radio news, but they do have a drawback in that they can have poor audio quality. This problem can be solved with the Marti, a piece of equipment which does not depend on telephone relay but sends the signal back to the station via microwave. This provides the advantages of broadcasting from venues where telephone lines are unavailable, and because it does not require lines, the costs are almost zero. But the Marti does require a line-of-sight relay connection to the broadcasting station, and the path must be free of obstacles that could impede the signal, such as buildings or trees. It also is considered somewhat big and bulky and has a dependable range of only about 20 to 25 miles. Another development along these lines is known as the Cellcast. Since the Cellcast uses cellular phone technology, it can go anywhere in the country where cell phone service is available. The obvious drawbacks are the uncertainty of cellular service and the expense associated with it.

Research indicates that most radio stations try to incorporate new technology in their news (see Table 7.3). But as with anything else, producers should focus on the basics of good news coverage. Consistency, saturation, and localism should be the bywords for radio producers everywhere, no matter what equipment or resources they have available.

News Production at an All-News Station: Rick Hadley

Rick Hadley is the news director and afternoon news anchor at WBAP-AM, an all-news station in Dallas. He has won numerous awards, including honors from the Press Club of Dallas, the Texas Associated Press Broadcasters, and the Texas Medical Association.

Q: *What are the main duties of a radio news producer?*

A: At WBAP News, the producer plays many roles. He helps plan the day's show by suggesting stories to cover and people to contact. He is responsible for preparing stories to go on the air. He takes feeds from the various networks, reporters in the field, rewrites stories from the wires, and lines up guests for on-air interviews.

Q: *Do you have a specific philosophy about producing radio news? In other words, are there certain ways to try to create a news program or build a show?*

A: Obviously we aim to talk about what people are talking about. We do a lot of hard news (crime, fires, etc.) but also aim to find the hot issue to be part of the package. For instance, when the Fox TV show *American Idol* debuted, winner Kelly Clarkson was from this area. While this certainly was not a hard news story, we gave it lots of play because people in Dallas–Fort Worth were buzzing about it. So, the goal is to build a show with the hot story, the breaking news stories, and of course mix in some analysis of ongoing issues. We also like to have some entertaining or in-depth features or series segments on a regular basis.

Q: *What are the specific demands of producing radio news that might be different from other media, like television?*

A: Since radio is an audio-only medium, the use of sound in telling stories is vital. We urge our reporters to file stories with lots of natural sound, quick sound bites, and music. We want to catch the listener's attention. Going on location to cover stories is superior to interviewing somebody on the phone. The other main difference between radio and television is story length. Television pieces can run 2 or 3 minutes. Most of our stories are under 30 seconds, and our long-form interview segments are 2 minutes, tops.

Q: *What is your main satisfaction in producing radio news?*

A: Back when I did produce, my biggest thrill was getting that impossible guest or newsmaker on the air. Try calling someone whose brother killed three people and ask him to be on the air at 6:30 in the morning. It's a dicey prospect at best. I also found satisfaction in knowing that we put together a well-rounded, informative, and entertaining show.

SOURCE: Rick Hadley (personal communication, May 2003).

NEWS ON MUSIC STATIONS

Almost all radio stations have some news content, even if it's extremely minimal. Music stations, for example, will program a few minutes of news each hour. These few minutes are extremely important—there are more adults listening to news on music stations than the number of adults listening to news on talk, news, and public stations combined.

News Production on Music Radio: Mark "Hawkeye" Louis

Mark "Hawkeye" Louis has become one of the most popular country music radio personalities in the United States. He started in San Antonio and now works for KSCS-FM in Dallas as a member of the station's "Dorsey Gang." When he started in San Antonio, Louis was the news person at two different stations—one rock and one country.

Q: *What's it like to do news at a music station?*

A: It's usually just a rip-and-read operation. Stations will pay for the Associated Press wire, but not much more. They may work in partnership with an all-news station, like we do with our sister station WBAP. But even then, it's still just reading material on the air. The news person usually has other responsibilities at the station and hardly ever goes out on stories. The only time I ever went out to cover a story was when the city council in San Antonio was trying to pass an anti–rock and roll ordinance.

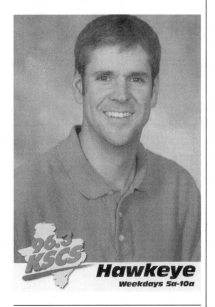

Mark "Hawkeye" Louis, KSCS-FM, Dallas, Texas

Q: *How much time do music stations devote to news?*

A: At our station in Dallas, we do 2 minutes of news every half hour, and I would say that's fairly typical. When we have big breaking news, we'll just turn it over to network.

Q: *Didn't your station recently change its philosophy about news?*

A: We used to have much more news on, about 5 minutes every hour. In fact, we even hired a television news person to come in and do news in the mornings. But our new program director looked at the research and decided we were trying to be all things to all people. If you want to listen to news, you're not coming to our station—that's not what our listeners want to hear. And in some cases, it could actually drive listeners away.

SOURCE: Mark Louis (personal communication, May 2003).

Note: "Rip and read" is a common broadcasting term that refers to using material right from the news wires without any editing. In the old days, when wire copy would print out on a teletype machine, many producers and anchors would "rip" the paper from the machine and read the story on it directly on the air.

At the same time, however, too much news on a music station would be counterproductive. The RTNDF (2000) survey revealed that more people (76%) choose a station based on its music than for any other reason, including news. In addition, the number one thing people like best about news on a music station is its brevity (36%). Only 10% of music station listeners said they value the informative part of the news.

In other words, news on a music station should be like a headline news service. People want the news about the major events of the day, but they want it short and to the point. Some of the comments from the RTNDF (2000) survey indicated that people listen to news on a music station because "it is short, concise, and to the point—then back to the music." Another respondent said, "It gives you the local news and only takes about five minutes of your time."

There are obvious implications here for people who produce news at a music station. The news should be brief, be concise, and touch on the major headlines. This is not difficult to do, considering that the typical music station only programs about 2 minutes of news every hour. And that's not always 2 consecutive minutes; it may be 30 seconds every 15 minutes. That may not sound like a lot of news, but that's the way music listeners like it. People who want more depth or information will generally tune to other sources, such as all-news stations or television.

PUBLIC BROADCASTING

Our discussion of radio news production would not be complete without looking at public broadcasting, which has become an important part of the radio news landscape. National Public Radio produces several award-winning news programs, including its popular *Morning Edition* and *All Things Considered,* which are the main source of national news for millions of Americans.

There are obvious differences between commercial and public broadcasting stations in terms of their mission, revenue sources, and programming schedules. For our purposes, the most important difference is the audience. Audiences for public broadcasting are generally considered to be much older, with higher levels of income and education, and they want different things from a newscast.

Public broadcasting audiences (radio and television) want something more from their news—more depth and more discussion. Thus the stories and news programs are much longer, and the individual stories go into much greater detail. *The NewsHour with Jim Lehrer* on PBS runs a full hour of national news, compared to the half-hour network newscasts. Stories on commercial radio stations typically average less than a minute, but it's not uncommon for stories on NPR to run longer than 5 minutes. After the stories run, reporters and commentators might engage in a discussion of the topic for another 5 minutes. As a result, public broadcasting newscasts have very low story counts but go into much greater depth.

The presentation of the story is also different, usually much more simple and straightforward than stories on commercial stations. Commercial stations must make their presentations more appealing to keep audiences from switching to other stations. By contrast, public broadcasting audiences (although few in number) are not likely to switch. They also have the educational background to understand more complex and in-depth reporting. Public broadcasting also focuses more on nontraditional news topics, in keeping with its mission of providing audiences with an alternative to commercial programming.

News Production on Public Radio: Joe Richman

Joe Richman is producer of the award-winning *Teenage Diaries* series on National Public Radio. Before becoming an independent producer, he worked for many years as a producer on the National Public Radio programs *All Things Considered, Weekend Edition Saturday, Car Talk,* and *Heat.* Here is part of a list of tips he developed for producing engaging stories on public radio.

- *Paint a picture with your voice.* Be the listeners' eyes and ears. Tell them what's going on. Use your voice to take a photograph.

- *Show, don't tell.* Remember that it's more powerful to show something (through details, observations, etc.) than to tell someone about it. It may sound funny, but radio is actually a visual medium. You have to give the listener something to look at, with their imagination instead of their eyes.

- *Use the small details to tell the big stories.* What little things surprise you? What wouldn't you expect? Whether you are doing a story about yourself or someone else, you don't have to give a lot of information, just the *right* information. It's not how you write or talk, but what you write or talk about. Think of it as going deep rather than going wide.

- *Always strive for one memorable moment.* Every story should have at least one little part you just completely love: a great clip of tape, a good scene, a funny anecdote. It's that little thing you run back and tell your friends about. Often the memorable moment turns out to be the unpredictable moment, the part that catches you by surprise. Ira Glass, host of the radio show *This American Life,* says that the point when he knows he has a good story is the moment when he realizes it's not the story he thought it was going to be.

SOURCE: Richman (2002).

In terms of ratings, public broadcasting is no threat to the established news on networks and local affiliates. It has a small but solid place in broadcast news; one that should be respected and understood by all producers.

The Internet

In a little less than a decade, the Internet has completely transformed many aspects of American life, including socialization, commerce, and research. Once just the toy of educators and technocrats, the Internet is now becoming almost as common in the home as television and radio. According to a Harris Poll, more than 137 million American adults are now online, which is 66% of the adult population. In 1995, only 9% of all adults were online. Today's average user spends more than 3 hours per week on the Internet (Taylor, 2002).

The Internet has dramatically influenced news consumption and usage. Not only are more people going online, but they can now instantly access news from all across the world, instead of waiting for scheduled reports on television or radio. As a result, almost all broadcast stations now have a corresponding Internet site, although it is much more common in television (Table 7.4).

INTERNET PRODUCING STRATEGIES

The increase of news on the Internet raises several important questions for station managers and especially for news producers. How stations address these issues depends a great deal on their news philosophy, management style, and available resources.

What Should an Internet News Site Do?

This issue has created serious debate among news executives and station managers, most of whom still don't have a definitive answer.

Table 7.4   Use of Websites by Broadcast Outlets

	TV Stations (%)	*Radio Stations (%)*
Who has websites?	91	68
Which websites have news?	93	32

SOURCE: Papper (2000).

Most stations use their Internet site as a complement to their traditional broadcast news. That is, they want the Internet site to drive people to watch the newscast, and they want the newscast to encourage more use of the Internet site.

This illustrates a concept called convergence, which is one of the hottest topics in the broadcasting industry. The idea is that the technology to deliver news is converging, and the distinctions between broadcasting, print, and the Internet will eventually be eliminated. Media outlets that have converged news coverage will have reporters create stories for broadcast, Internet, and newspaper outlets. For example, a reporter for the Tribune Company, which owns the *Chicago Tribune,* WGN-TV, and WGN radio, might have to produce different versions of the same story for all three outlets.

The problem is that convergence is relatively new, and experts still don't know much about how it works or even if it works. Logically, stations want bigger audiences for both their broadcast news programs and their Internet sites, but no one is quite sure yet how to do that. So far, efforts have been focused on such things as promoting the local news team on the website or having broadcast stories ask viewers to visit the Internet page. But there is no indication yet that such efforts are working. Attendees at the 2002 media conference for the Newspaper Association of America found out that websites have extended the reach of print newspapers only 2% to 5% (Sullivan, 2002).

Another problem is that most stations haven't figured out a way to make money from their Internet sites. It's clear that very few radio and television stations are actually making money, but even more telling is the fact that so many of them simply don't know whether their website is making money. Even though the percentage of stations reporting a profit rose slightly, there is still an overwhelming feeling of uncertainty.

News executives struggle to address these issues; still, they have almost no doubt about the promotional value of the station website. In their study of media websites, researchers Carolyn Lin and Leo Jeffres (2001) found that radio stations primarily use their sites as a promotional vehicle for branding efforts, and television stations try to secure and enhance station brand loyalty. Even if a site doesn't have the latest news, original content, or sophisticated graphics, it can still encourage the site user to go to the broadcast outlet. In some cases, lack of a sophisticated website might be more of a motivation to consume the news on television or radio.

As the Internet continues to evolve, convergence is moving at full speed in newsrooms across America, especially at large organizations that own several different types of media outlets. From that perspective, convergence can be viewed as one solution to the rising cost of news production because reporters and producers must become responsible for more news

Table 7.5   Stations' Economic Evaluation of News Websites (%)

	Profit	*Breaking Even*	*Loss*	*Don't Know*
Television stations	10	19	27	44
Radio stations	8	11	12	69

SOURCE: Papper (2000).

content. But the ideal relationship between a broadcast outlet and its Internet site has yet to be determined.

What Kind of News Should Be on the Internet Site?

It is overly simplistic to say than an Internet news site should provide news. There are several other issues related to this question, including news style, content, and format.

For the most part, stations have simply taken their broadcast material and put it on their Internet site, a process known as *shovelware*. Using shovelware is usually simple, cheap, and an efficient use of resources, especially for smaller stations that don't have the money or expertise to manage a website. In their study of broadcast station websites, researchers Sylvia Chan-Olmstead and Jung Suk Park (2000) noted, "The emphasis on news-oriented content presents a less risky business approach because a station will be able to minimize costs by re-formatting the content it already owns." Typically, stories are simply copied, or "shoveled," from the newscast computer right onto the station's Internet site, a process that can be as simple as moving computer files. The newscast producer might be responsible for this, or perhaps the reporters might have to do it for their own stories.

But as technology improves and Internet users become more sophisticated, they expect more from a news website. Chan-Olmstead and Park (2000) found that "while broadcast stations have diligently transferred their news expertise online and possibly established credibility, they have not capitalized on the essence of the Internet medium." Simply repeating news that has already appeared on a broadcast does not have great appeal, and there has been a tremendous demand for original Web content. "We haven't created the quality of experience yet that makes use of the Web as important to people's daily lives as turning on the television," said Merrill Brown, senior vice president at RealNetworks and former editor-in-chief of MSNBC.com (Jesdanun, 2002).

Some outlets are experimenting with new Internet news content. News sites are already working on various e-mail and wireless news services, and the Associated Press offers packages for media outlets to customize at their sites. Sites like that of *The Washington Post* have been running online chats with key newsmakers. ABC News, among others, runs discussion boards. Reporters for MSNBC.com and the *San Jose Mercury News* remark on news developments through personal online journals.

This type of effort requires an additional commitment of money, equipment, and personnel that most stations cannot afford, especially during poor economic times. Some stations have tried to compromise by requiring a rewrite of news stories so that the Internet version appears new or different, a technique that, obviously, increases the workload for reporters, writers, and producers. In some cases, stories have to be rewritten for three different Internet audiences—morning, afternoon, and night.

Much of what goes on an Internet site depends on the resources available to the station. Smaller stations might have to depend more on shovelware simply because they don't have the resources to create specifically designed Web content. In these situations, the regular news producer or someone else on the staff will be in charge of updating content every so often. The station might even find someone on staff that has the expertise to oversee the technical aspects of the webpage.

One way smaller stations can give their webpages a professional look is to contract the site out to a professional site service, which will handle most of the details of running the site, except for providing local content. These services don't necessarily cost much money (in some cases, networks will allow their affiliates use of a standardized site design), but they aren't very personalized or individualized. If you surf the Internet, you'll notice that the websites of many stations affiliated with the same network look virtually identical.

It has become quite common for stations to combine with other media outlets in the creation of an Internet news site. For example, a newspaper and television station in the same community might host a combined site that offers users the combined resources of both organizations. This is a very effective method that is used in many larger markets. In addition, several companies now specialize in creating websites for broadcast outlets. Such services usually include things like hardware and software, training, and technical support.

For the most part, stations in larger markets prefer to create their own Internet news identity, and they have the resources to do it. Larger stations will hire staff members who are specifically charged with updating and maintaining the Internet news site. Reporters and anchors are also expected to create and contribute material specifically designed for the station's website audience.

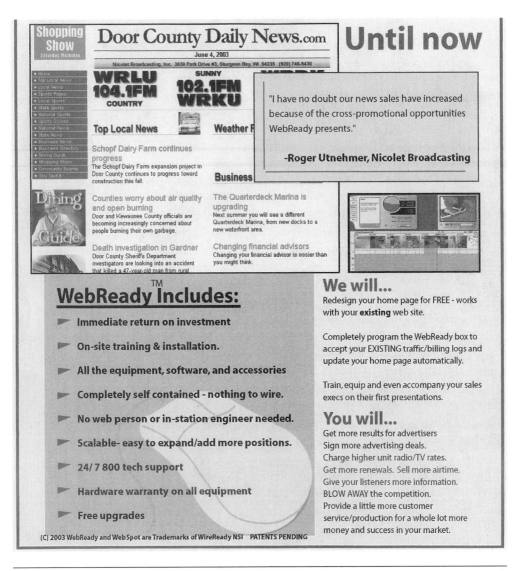

Figure 7.2 WebReady, One of Many Companies Now Helping Broadcast Stations With Webpage Design and Maintenance

SOURCE: WebReady. Used by permission.

News Production on the Internet: Colleen Seitz

The growing importance of the Internet news site has led many stations to hire news producers specifically for that purpose. WEWS-TV in Cleveland is one of the most aggressive stations in terms of Internet news, using five full-time staffers to produce *NewsNet 5*. Executive producer Colleen Seitz has overall responsibility for the content, appearance, and functionality of the site.

In the summer 2003, a major power outage affected the eastern part of the United States, reaching as far as Cleveland. Seitz's comments about how *NewsNet 5* covered the story illustrate not only how producers use the Internet but how important the website has become in television news.

The power first went out in the station, but we never lost our Internet connection. We actually had it on the site before it hit the air, and we were the only website in Cleveland to have the information.

We decided to be aggressive with the way it looked on the website, with several top stories and videos. I worked all night to help with the different aspects of the story. We had miners trapped, gas lines at the only open station, and riders that had gotten stranded on an amusement park ride.

Since people in the area didn't have power, we were guessing that they could power up laptops or palm pilots or were getting relatives in other cities to come to get the latest from *NewsNet5.com*. We wanted to stay on top of it minute-by-minute.

I stayed all night updating information, warning downtown workers not to come to work until after noon. Because I was here, the website ended up providing the newest information to the anchors on the 5 a.m. news.

As power started to come back on, we added updates from the mayor, more video, and the long lists of power and water availability. The assignment desk was getting swamped with closings calls and we shared e-mails to get as much information out as possible. We tried to write stories relevant to viewers' questions, mainly about spoiled food and boiling water.

It was a great team effort, especially between our staff and the newsroom.

SOURCE: Geisler (2003a).

Whether the station is large or small, there are certain things it wants to put on its station homepage (Table 7.6). Again, this goes back to what kind of people are using the site and what they want from their news.

Should Internet News Material Be Any Different From Broadcast Material?

One of the constant themes throughout this book is that producers should know who's in the audience and what they want from a newscast. Research clearly shows that in these areas, there are important differences between Internet and broadcast audiences.

Research indicates that typical Internet users are younger, more educated, and less racially diverse than the general population. More specifically, the

Table 7.6   Common Elements of Station News Websites

Element	Comment
Breaking news	How *NewsNet 5* covered the blackout vividly demonstrates the power of the Internet to cover spot news. The main drawback is that typically people still turn to television or radio for breaking news, and many people still don't have Internet access.
Headlines	In some ways, a station news site functions like a newspaper—users should be able to browse important headlines, then investigate in depth the stories that interest them. Headline writing is particularly important for websites because it not only tells users what's going on but allows them to effectively direct their time and attention.
Weather	Just as with broadcast news, Internet news users are vitally interested in the weather. Steve Outing of the Poynter Institute says weather is one of the most popular categories of online news for several reasons, including unlimited space, the ability to focus on the neighborhood level, and the countless interactive and multimedia possibilities. For example, the weather site for KPNX-TV in Phoenix gets about 500,000 hits per month. "Not an amazing amount, but not bad," says AZCentral.com's Mike Coleman, "especially considering we're predictable with about 330 days of sunshine a year" (Outing, 2002). The key to Web weather is making it as local as possible, right down to the neighborhood. Many stations have enlisted "weather watchers" to contribute to their online content. Sites can also offer expanded content on local weather topics such as dust storms and "snow rollers" (rolls of snow created by high winds). Web weather doesn't necessarily have to go into great detail—many stations simply offer the current radar imagery, current statistics, and a forecast. However, stations should give users access to more weather information if they want it.
Feedback	One of the great features of the station website is its ability to provide audience feedback, especially concerning complaints. Before the Internet, stations wasted countless hours answering phone calls from viewers who were upset, wanted to pass along a news tip, or wanted the answer to a question. Many stations now have specific places on their site for complaints or the answers to frequently asked questions (FAQ). In some cases, individual e-mail addresses for reporters and anchors are delivered on the air, so viewers can contact them directly. Stations and individuals obviously have different levels of commitment regarding their response to viewer feedback.

Element	Comment
Feedback *(Continued)*	The Internet can facilitate many other kinds of feedback, such as the way the *Dallas Morning News* used its website during the invasion of Iraq in 2003. Much of what was on the site came from the audience, including photos sent in from aircraft carriers, military portraits sent in by parents, and comments submitted by soldiers. Oscar Martinez, senior editor of Belo Interactive's Dallas websites, called it "a continuation of the war letters tradition that America has had probably since the Revolutionary War. We talk a lot in journalism about making a connection and establishing a community. Via technology, we have done exactly that here. I'm as proud of it as anything I've ever done in 16 years in journalism" (Geisler, 2003b).
Opinion	We have already discussed the importance of interactivity and how people like to feel their opinion makes a difference. An Internet news site allows users to register an opinion on any number of topics through such things as polls, contests, etc. There is debate in the journalism community over the value of Internet news polls, which are really nothing more than sophisticated man-on-the-street interviews. As long as stations do not try to pass off the results as scientific or of any real news significance, most people consider the polls relatively harmless. They do generate conversation and interest among Internet news users.
Promotion	The Internet website has become as important a marketing tool for the station as billboards, newspapers, or direct mail. Stations try to make sure that their news sites promote the on-air newscasts and, especially, the on-air news talent. In an age in which many newscasts and Internet news sites look the same, anchors and reporters can be used to "brand" the news product and give it an identity. Many stations also provide biographies and contact information for their on-air personalities.

average Internet user is between 18 and 29 years old, college educated, and White. Even though these differences are slowly disappearing, there is still a significant "digital divide" that news producers should take into account.

The younger Internet audience has grown up with computers, but not necessarily with traditional broadcast news. Broadcast news is usually delivered in a straightforward, chronological style, but Internet users like the freedom they have to jump in and out of different stories at will. Internet news producers should structure their content in this nonlinear style and not focus so much on conventional broadcast news style.

Table 7.7   What Stations Put on Their News Websites (%)

	Images	*Audio*	*Video*
Television stations	70	30	36
Radio stations	27	22	N/A

SOURCE: Papper (2000).

Among other things, this means that producers should provide a lot of *hyperlinks*. Hyperlinks are the portions of Internet text that allow users to jump to another part of the story or even to a completely different story. If the story is about a big fire downtown, hyperlinks should allow the user to investigate other information related to the story, such as rescue efforts, damage totals, and pictures.

The emphasis on video and audio should also be a major consideration in producing Internet news. In effect, the Internet combines both print and broadcast news. The text looks very much like a newspaper story, but it can also be supported with pictures and sounds. In our fire example, the user should ideally have the ability to look at video of the fire or hear an interview segment with the fire chief. Most stations incorporate these features into their websites, along with the ability to view the reporter's version of the story as it appeared on radio or television. See Table 7.7.

The written material of an Internet news story should be simple, straightforward, and much like an inverted pyramid newspaper story, where the facts are presented in descending order of importance. Internet users are notoriously impatient—the average user spends only 55 seconds at a particular site before moving on—and they don't want to wait for the important details. There should be an emphasis on headlines and news briefs, with an opportunity for users to explore stories in greater detail if they want.

In many ways, an Internet news story should be produced much like a video game—it should be high intensity, visually engaging, and easy to understand and access. Many of the people who use the Internet regularly are very comfortable with video games and can understand news much better when it is presented in a friendly format.

THE FUTURE OF INTERNET NEWS

Each passing day makes the Internet a more powerful tool for delivering news. Some stations are reluctantly getting on board with online news; others have embraced it enthusiastically. ABC belongs to the latter group and got really ambitious in spring 2003 with the debut of a 24-hour news service available only to Internet users. Called *ABC News Live*, the service was initially more like C-SPAN than CNN, using live feeds of breaking news with some anchored coverage, news summaries, and rebroadcasts of ABC News programs. One ABC News executive described it as "baby steps toward the first Internet news network" (Outing, 2003). Given such events, it's not so much a matter of where Internet news is headed, but who's willing to go along for the ride.

Thinking More About It

1. Listen to all-talk, all-news, and all-music radio stations in your area for part of the day and consider the following:
   a. Do those stations have an identifiable "news wheel" or consistent news programming strategy? If so, sketch out what that station's news wheel might look like. Do you feel like the news wheel is an effective strategy for radio news? Why or why not?
   b. How would you characterize the way news is covered at these different stations? What are the main differences?
   c. How does the radio news coverage compare to television? Was it better, worse, or about the same in terms of amount of information, coverage of stories, and story presentation? If you could rely on only one source for all your news, which one would you choose?
   d. There are probably elements of these newscasts that you feel could be improved. What changes would you make to the news formats at these stations, and why?

2. Pick a local television station that also has an Internet site (you can usually find these stations by typing the call letters into a Web search engine). Watch a newscast on this station and consider the following:
   a. What is the relationship between news content on the Internet site and the television news? Is the news on the Web unique, or does it seem more like shovelware?
   b. What are the ways in which the television news tries to get you to go to the Internet site? In what ways does the Internet site try to get you to watch the television news?
   c. How would you characterize this station's commitment to Internet news? Does it seem like the station has committed plenty of resources to the site, or is it more like an afterthought? Do you think this site provides all the news you need or want?

    d. What are the dominant themes or segments of the Internet site? Does the station put more emphasis on news? On weather? On sports? Do the stories have more of a hard edge, or are they more consumer-friendly?

    e. What opportunities are there for viewer feedback at the Internet site? Does the station seem to emphasize this area?

    f. Would you consider the site easy to use and viewer-friendly? Could you find the news stories you were looking for? If you wanted more information about a specific story, could you find it easily?

Surviving the Newsroom 8

By now, you've probably figured out that producers spend most of their time inside the newsroom. On some occasions, producers will go into the field to help with special on-location programs, but the day-to-day responsibilities of a newscast require the producer to work at the station. This is obviously the best way for producers to perform their assignments, communicate with other personnel, and make adjustments to the rundown.

But staying in the newsroom also has its disadvantages. Even though a producer works in a constantly changing environment, working in the same location day after day can get tedious. Newsrooms are open spaces, usually with desks instead of offices, and this kind of close confinement with coworkers can result in personality conflict. This is especially true considering the producer's unique role in the newsroom. Part management and part labor, the producer can get caught in the crossfire between news directors and other newsroom personnel.

This chapter will focus on some strategies to help producers thrive in the competitive and often contentious world of the newsroom. To better maximize their working relationships, producers must first understand their own management personalities.

Theories X, Y, and Z

We have already discussed the various roles a producer has within the newsroom, including that of manager (see chapter 1). In a typical newsroom structure, the producer has authority over almost every aspect of the newscast, including human resources. Producers must be able to direct, inform, and correct reporters and other newsroom personnel as they relate to the newscast.

Producers have different management styles, depending a great deal on their own personalities and their station's newsroom structure. Generally, these styles fall into categories described by Douglas McGregor (1960) in his groundbreaking work on management behavior. McGregor believed that essentially there were two distinct theories of how to manage people and businesses:

THEORY X

This is the traditional or "old school" view of management, which says that workers are basically lazy and need constant motivation and supervision. It is a very pessimistic view of human nature, in that it espouses the belief that people don't want to work, have little ambition, and are motivated only to pursue their own leisure. Rather than working hard for advancement, most people are content with a steady, secure lifestyle.

As a result, managers need to be very hands-on and provide workers with detailed instructions, motivations, rewards, and punishments. Tasks must be well defined, and workers must constantly be monitored to make sure they are completing their jobs. If given the chance, most workers will start to complain and lose interest in work. The management structure is usually a top-down hierarchy, with a strong authoritarian chain of command. Organizations can be either a "hard X," emphasizing punishment for work not done, or a "soft X," emphasizing rewards for work completed.

In this type of management structure, the producer would spend most of his or her time outlining specific duties and motivating newsroom personnel. Given all the other things a producer has to do, it would be difficult to spend the majority of the day in these areas. It would also be difficult from a human relations standpoint, in that most reporters are college graduates and possess specialized skills. Treating them in an authoritarian fashion would be likely to create suspicion, animosity, and maybe even open rebellion. In almost no case would a reporter refuse to do his or her job, but this management style would still increase dissatisfaction and perhaps put either the reporter's or the producer's job in jeopardy.

You can probably see why Theory X has fallen out of favor in recent years. It creates an extremely severe and stifling work environment in which lower level employees are treated almost like drones. However, this style of management was very common during the U.S. industrial revolution of the 1800s, and there are still plenty of organizations (including almost all military structures) which use it today. Again, whether or not a producer uses it depends a lot on personality and the management style of the news director.

THEORY Y

In contrast to the authoritarian style, Theory Y is based more on employee needs and motivations. Workers are viewed positively, and given the right working conditions, it is believed that they will learn, grow, and produce on the job. They are committed to the overall product and allowed to use their imagination, ingenuity, and creativity. Because workers will exercise self-control and self-direction, they do not need constant rewards and punishments.

In many ways, Theory Y organizations have a "bottom-up" structure, in which lower level employees have a great deal of input into upper level management decisions. This comes from the fact that upper level managers understand that the needs, desires, and problems of lower level workers directly affect productivity. An attempt is made to involve all levels of management in problem solving and communication, and the job is viewed as a part of the whole person, which contributes to the growth of each individual worker. The success of Japanese firms on a global scale, especially the Japanese auto industry, convinced many management professionals that Theory Y could work.

For our purposes, Theory Y would be difficult to implement in news production. For one thing, it would require a total commitment on the part of the entire organization. With such high turnover in the broadcast news industry, there is little consistency in management styles. A producer may work for several news directors, each with a different management style, within a period of just a few years. Reporters and other newsroom personnel also come and go, making it more difficult to invest time and energy in employee relations.

Perhaps more important, the deadline pressure of news producing requires someone in charge to make quick decisions. Much of a producer's day is spent making a series of snap decisions; producers simply don't have time to canvass the feelings and attitudes of other people connected to the newscast. Someone has to take control and make these last-minute decisions, which are usually determined more by experience and the demands of the unfolding situation. Even after the newscast is over, there is little time for feedback or input, as producers must get ready for the next show.

THEORY Z

Although not mentioned by McGregor, a hybrid of his management theories has emerged that attempts to combine their best elements. Theory Z retains a central authority figure but still respects the integrity of each individual worker. The management structure is an integrated meshing of hierarchical levels, with different managers at different levels all contributing input. Feedback is emphasized as a way of making workers feel they have more of a stake in the final product.

On paper, Theory Z seems the most appropriate for a broadcast environment, in that it retains the central command structure necessary for quick decision making yet also takes into account the contributions of each individual worker. However, in practice, it may not be ideally suited for the broadcasting business, because growing consolidation is putting much more of an emphasis on the bottom line in news. In most cases, strategic management decisions are made from a corporate headquarters hundreds of miles away from the station. This distance, both geographical and emotional, makes it much more difficult to integrate employee concerns into the overall management system. Employees are much more likely to be treated as commodities rather than as human beings with unique attitudes and perspectives.

Almost all broadcast managers and producers fall into one of these three management styles. CNN founder Ted Turner, for example, was very hands-on in his approach to management, and would most likely be characterized as a proponent of Theory X. Your management category as a producer will probably depend on several factors (see Table 8.1).

Newsroom Relationships

Even though the station manager or owner has the final authority for everything that goes on at the station, he or she usually delegates responsibility for the news department to the news director—the single most important person to the producer at the station. A good relationship between news director and producer is a key determinant in the quality of the newscast and can make for a satisfying work environment. A bad relationship can mean not only a bad newscast but frustration, anger, burnout, and sometimes job termination.

WORKING WITH NEWS DIRECTORS

News directors expect a great deal from producers. They want the producer to assume responsibility for individual newscasts so they can be free to concentrate on issues like budgeting, scheduling, and administrative work. News directors certainly don't spend all their time on such things, but they are important for setting the tone and direction of the newscast. News directors expect producers to carry out most of the detail work and get a quality newscast on the air.

Ask 100 different news directors what they want in a producer, and you may get 100 different answers. Still, there are common themes mentioned by news directors throughout the industry.

Versatility. News directors want someone who can do it all, both the technical and nontechnical parts of the job. The technical side includes such things as rundowns, blocking, writing, editing—all the skills involved in actually getting the show on the air. The nontechnical part is just as

Table 8.1 Determining Your Management Style

Personality	Probably the single most important determinant because it dictates so many things about work relationships. Some people are more autocratic by nature and others are more accommodating and willing to compromise. More trouble is caused in newsrooms because of personality differences than probably anything else. The important thing is to be yourself and not to try to change your personality to fit the work environment. Try to find a work environment that matches your personality.
Station management structure	Both the station manager and the news director have direct authority over the producer, and the way they manage sets the tone for the entire organization. Producers take their cue directly from the news director and adjust their own management styles accordingly. For example, if the news director is very hands-on, the producer must focus more on chain of command and delegation of duties. A more informal news director allows the producer freedom to concentrate on things such as planning and strategy.
Newsroom personnel	Just as there are all different types of news directors, there are all different types of reporters and newsroom personnel. These personalities and the experience of these people often dictate a producer's management style. Small markets, for example, often have very young, inexperienced reporters who need more supervision and direction from the producer. Larger markets usually have older and more experienced personnel, and the producer does not have to be as hands-on.
News commitment	Each station has a different level of commitment to news, including some that run it 24 hours a day and others that air just a few minutes. Obviously, the news demands at some stations are much greater, and this requires a much more intense effort on the part of the producer. All-news outlets would seem more appropriate for the "Type A" producer personality—intense, hard driven, and completely focused. All producers must have those traits to some degree, but there certainly are news situations that are not as demanding.
Station ownership	As noted, station ownership plays a major role in management. It's probably a generalization to say that all corporately owned stations are more bottom-line oriented, but it is true that important changes have taken place in the industry because of increasing consolidation. It would seem that producers (and other employees) might have more discretion and management freedom at a "mom and pop"–owned station, where the owner is directly involved in the station's day-to-day operation.

important and includes newsroom leadership, human relations, planning, and so on. A producer must bring all of these things to bear every single day. Al Tompkins (1999) of the Poynter Institute says, "Producers are the glue that holds the newsroom together. You set the tone. You regulate style. You shape content. Wars have been fought over the struggle of who would get the authority that you hold daily."

Initiative. News directors want producers to take charge of the newsroom and the newscast. Come to work with definite ideas about what you want to do with your show and take risks to make it happen. News director Angie Kucharski of KCNC-TV in Denver wants her producers to come to her and say, "This is what I want to do with my newscast today!" (Sloan, 2002).

Producers need to take initiative because oftentimes news directors simply don't have the time to do it. This is especially important for critiques and feedback, which often get overlooked because of the requirements of getting another show ready to air. Any good producer wants to know how to get better, and the only way to do that is through feedback. Don't wait until something goes horribly wrong to sit down with the news director to discuss the show.

Communication and Delegation. Perhaps nothing is more valued than good communication between news director and producer, and producer and newsroom. Kucharski says she wants producers to stop by her office—accosting her if necessary—to go over the show and review places for improvement (Sloan, 2002). Tompkins (1999) says to learn the skills of communication. "Remember to use active listening. You manage things, but you lead people." Delegation of responsibility is important because for the most part, news directors don't expect producers to do everything. This depends a lot on the size of the news operation and the resources available: In many small markets, the producer *does* have to do it all.

Newsroom Relations. At least in theory, most directors prefer a producer with a Theory Y or Z management style: one who takes the opinions of other newsroom personnel into account when making decisions. "Value the judgments and contributions of others," says Tompkins (1999). "Listen to reporters, directors, photojournalists, and respect their ideas and expertise." Producers should develop good working relationships with all newsroom personnel, as difficult as that might sometimes be. In an Ohio University study (Fox, 2002), on-air radio personalities felt the most discouraging aspects of their jobs were communication breakdowns with management and the resulting problems associated with working for a large corporation. Good working relationships improve morale and the ultimate product—the newscast.

Creativity. News directors want more than a producer who knows how to stack, block, and fill out a rundown. With broadcast news audiences evolving and shrinking, producers must be able to create newscasts that are interesting, compelling, and engaging. Sometimes this is accomplished with technology, such as graphics and live reporting, and other times the approach or focus to the story is the essential element. Good producers find a way to make the story relevant to their local audience.

What Stations Want in a Producer

WBNS-TV in Columbus, Ohio, ran the following ad for a producer in 2001, so please *don't* call them. The ad illustrates the emphasis stations are now placing on producers who can go beyond the technical demands of the job and think "outside the box."

WBNS-10TV seeks a News Producer who knows how to produce informative, compelling newscasts with true viewer benefit. We give you multiple crews, two SNG trucks, several ENG vans, a chopper and DC Bureau to get the job done . . . the rest is up to you. Strong news judgment, great storytelling and creative writing skills a must. Must be able to show strong conceptual ideas and high production values.

SOURCE: WBNS-TV. Used by permission.

Leadership. Producers do not only take over leadership of the newsroom, they must show management leadership. Depending on the size of the station, news directors encourage producers to take an active role in planning, budgeting, promotion, and long-range news issues. "As a producer, you have a right to a list of expectations and a clear vision," says Kucharski. "Most news directors welcome producers who will be partners in that vision" (Sloan, 2002). It's also important to note that many news directors don't necessarily have a background in management, budgeting, or leadership and may rely heavily on producers as they get on-the-job training.

It's important for the producer to understand things from the other side—what are news directors like? This is an important question not only to create a good working relationship, but also because so many producers wind up as news directors. Like many newsroom positions, it's a very stressful job with a high potential for burnout, and the average news director lasts only 2 years. It's also a position that requires a lot of on-the-job training. There are very few schools or programs that teach specific station management skills or how to become a news director. Most people learn through experience and generally follow a career path of producer, executive producer, assistant news director, and then news director. Although this is as high as you can go in the news department, many news directors eventually become station managers.

Even with all the turnover in a news department, some news directors have survived to carve out long careers at a particular station. Probably the dean of news directors is Lee Giles at WISH-TV in Indianapolis, who has held his post since 1967 and has been with the station since 1963. "You have to get a lot of lucky breaks to stay for that long," said Giles, who has lasted through seven general managers and about that many ownership changes. "I think his longevity is due to a few things," said WISH general manager Scott Blumenthal. "His knowledge of good journalism, gut instinct in terms of talent and people and he is a nice man" (Whitney, 2003).

News directors do have a little more stability, depending on the corporation that owns their station. At Gannett's NBC affiliate KARE-TV in Minneapolis, stability of the operation has played a role in the longevity of news director Tom Lindner, who has held the job since 1996. KARE has the reputation of encouraging stability, and the average length of stay for any employee is 11 years. Lindner believes in regular training and education for both staff and news director, and KARE often sends staffers to workshops and retreats.

Stability in the news director position benefits producers in several ways, including a more consistent work relationship and more security in their own jobs. But it is more likely that producers will work with a variety of news directors over the course of their careers. In those cases, producers will have to go through a transition period in which they learn the expectations, demands, personalities, and habits of their new boss. This can be very difficult, especially if the producer and news director don't share the same news philosophy.

Ideally, a producer will stay at a station until he or she is promoted or offered a better job somewhere else. But it is not uncommon for producers to start looking for work elsewhere when a new news director takes over. For example, Patti Dennis became the news director at KUSA-TV in Denver in 1996, with the goal of rebuilding the news brand. She revamped the newsroom and eliminated some associate producer positions to add more reporters. The number of reporters at KUSA has grown from 23 to 30, but at the expense of several producers, who found themselves either reassigned or out of work.

Producers can make their own lives much easier by understanding their news directors—their personalities, their expectations, and their news philosophies. In some situations, however, no amount of understanding can help improve the relationship, especially when a clash of personalities is involved. Producers must realize that news directors have the ultimate authority to hire and fire, and they will use it when necessary. At the same time, producers should also take charge of their own careers and be willing and able to move on to a different opportunity.

WORKING WITH ANCHORS

The relationship between producers and anchors can cause a lot of friction in a newsroom and can eventually lead to someone having to look elsewhere for work. Many anchors view producers as frustrated, behind-the-scenes desk jockeys—people who really want to be on the air but have to settle for producing because they don't have the talent. Likewise, many producers view anchors as overpaid, lazy prima donnas who can't do much more than read news on the air and who often manage to mess that up.

The ideal situation is one in which anchors and reporters share mutual respect, work together for the good of the show, and complement each other's contribution to the newscast. This is often difficult to achieve because of the anchor's unique status in the newsroom. Technically, producers have final responsibility for everything related to the newscast, including the anchors. If a producer wants to make a last-minute change to the rundown, the anchor should have no problem with that.

However, some anchors become a very powerful "de facto" presence in the newsroom. Whether it's because of seniority, salary (anchor is often the highest paid position in the newsroom, even higher than that of the news director) or celebrity status, anchors can and do often insist on greater control of the newscast. This situation has led to some terrible newsroom conflicts that not even the news director can address adequately.

The problem for producers is that anchors have the star power and celebrity status that are important to stations. A personable anchor who can deliver ratings is as good as gold, and stations will try to hold on to them for dear life. Newsrooms also invest heavily in the recruitment and payment of anchors, and high turnover can not only cost money, it can lose viewers. By contrast, producers are considered easily replaceable and not nearly as important to the station's overall success. This is not a value judgment but simply a description of how most station managers think.

All of this means that in the worst-case scenario of a dispute between anchors and reporters, stations are much more likely to side with anchors. For example, in fall 2002, executives at the *Today* show decided to replace executive producer Jonathan Wald, despite the fact that *Today* still had a solid lead over *Good Morning America* in the ratings. According to *Electronic Media* magazine, "Though Mr. Wald's relationship with the staff and talent of *Today* appeared to settle down, he never seemed to win the confidence of [anchor Katie] Couric, co-host Matt Lauer or key network executives" ("Breaking news," 2002). Couric had recently signed a contract that would pay her $14 million per year. Why would NBC get rid of her and keep Wald?

Again, this is not to comment on the value of producers or to suggest that anchors are more important. But the reality of the business suggests that producers had better learn to get along with anchors or else. Creating a good work relationship, opening lines of communication, and building a newscast that showcases the strengths of the anchor are all things a producer should be doing. There are certainly going to be situations in which producers and anchors simply can't seem to work together or even get along. If these are strictly personality issues, not much can be done. Many producers would expect their news director to back them in such situations, but the unfortunate fact is that such support may be hard to get.

WORKING WITH REPORTERS

Reporters make a very significant contribution to the show, but unlike anchors, most of them usually don't have the clout or power to challenge a producer's authority.

Producers depend on reporters to create quality broadcast stories that fill up much of the show's news hole. At the very least, reporters are expected to do their assigned stories, meet their deadlines, and fill their required time. Reporters that don't do this can make a producer's life miserable and probably won't be around very long.

Reporters also contribute in other ways, by keeping producers informed of what's going on with their stories and advising them as to any necessary changes. They also can sit in on editorial meetings, suggest news coverage, and be flexible enough to do what the producer needs in the event of changes to the rundown. In short, the success of the producer and the entire show is often directly tied to the performance of the reporters.

As with anyone in the newsroom, producers should try to create a good working relationship with reporters. This includes such things as trust, mutual respect, and, above all, communication. No one likes to be surprised with last-minute changes, and producers should keep in constant contact with reporters to let them know what's going on. If reporters feel like the producer is trying to make an effort in this regard, they will be much more likely to accept and accommodate rundown changes. At the same time, if reporters feel like they're treated with respect, they will be more willing to accept the producer's authority.

Producers and reporters have different styles and different ideas of how the news should be put together (Table 8.2). Both parties need to respect the value of the other and put aside differences to help build the newscast. If the relationship between reporter and producer breaks down, the entire news product will suffer.

PERSONAL RELATIONSHIPS

This book isn't about personal relationships, it's about producing. But producers certainly have personal relationships that affect their work, and the work environment also shapes many of the producer's outside relationships. It would, then, seem wise to spend a brief amount of time

Table 8.2   Comparison of Producers and Reporters

Producers	Reporters
• Have more experience in television news • Have worked at more stations • Likely to have pursued television news careers for more pragmatic and less idealistic reasons • Less critical of their stations' newscasts, which previous studies suggest might mean they are less professional than reporters • Much more interested in the editorial control they wield	• More critical of practices within their own newsrooms • More critical of the visual quality of their station's newscast • Expect producers to choose presentation values over journalistic ones
Should a story about a school levy be dumped to make room for live coverage of the mayor returning from an out-of-town trip?	
No Slightly more producers than reporters were inclined to keep the school levy story	No Reporters were more likely to believe most producers would use the live shot at the expense of the school levy story, especially if producers were being pressured by management to use live coverage regularly

SOURCE: Smith and Becker (1989).

discussing the role of personal relationships and what producers can expect when they get into the workplace.

No person has more impact on a single newscast than the producer. News directors give producers a lot of freedom in the shape, content, and presentation of a newscast, but with that freedom comes responsibility. Producers are expected to arrive to work early, stay as long as it takes to get the job done, and go home late. There is no such thing as a 9:00-to-5:00 schedule or a standard work week, and producers will routinely work 60 to 80 hours a week. A producer may finish a long day and then if important breaking news occurs, find himself working straight through another shift. News directors also like producers who keep in touch with the newsroom on their days off and take the initiative to come in when needed.

You can see how this could affect a producer's personal relationships, and indeed, many newsroom personnel find that their work environment

Figure 8.1   News Often Demands That Producers Work Far Beyond the Normal 8-Hour Shift

takes a toll on their personal lives. In a study of reporters, producers, and anchors, Vernon Stone (2000) found that most respondents (75%) found their news career satisfying. But at the same time, half the respondents who were single and worked in television reported job-related problems in their personal lives and said that the medium's long and odd hours made relationships difficult (Table 8.3).

Some of the comments from respondents in the study reflect the difficulty of working in broadcast news. Said one female producer, "[I have] difficulty in getting out to meet people who are not in the business—and being used by men who want to get into the business." A weekend anchorperson and producer commented, "[I] broke up with my live-in girlfriend because she felt my job meant more to me than she did. And it does" (Stone, 2000).

Again, this is not a comment on how producers should act in their personal lives or what they should be doing outside the station. Rather, it is intended as a sobering look at what the professional news environment can do to personal relationships. Producers should enter the industry with their eyes wide open.

Table 8.3 Relationship Issues for News Television Personnel (%)

Issue	Single	Married
Job-related problems	52	30
Relationship problems	17	2
Odd hours	13	6
Would move far away for a better job	51	32

SOURCE: Stone (2000).

Newsroom Relationships

A view of the dynamic relationships between news producers and other newsroom personnel from a variety of industry professionals:

Mike McHugh, former executive producer, WBBM-TV, Chicago: Most general managers have no background in news and think the producers are not important—kind of like middlemen in the news process. They don't see them on television, so they think they have no impact in luring viewers. They couldn't be more wrong. The news director realizes the importance of producers and how difficult it is to attract and retain them. Reporters appreciate good producers. However, they don't always understand why. Most reporters are always begging or demanding more time from producers and don't always understand how their single story fits in the context of the show, so there's a natural tension between the two. Other newsroom personnel appreciate producers who know what they're doing. If producers are running late, the pressure will be on other team members. Producers have to be conscious and willing to accept, even on their worst days, responsibility for the show.

Matt Ellis, News Director, WBZ-TV, Boston: Even in the top markets, producers work closely with their news directors. Producers attend regular editorial meetings, and it is not uncommon for [them] to approve the producer's rundown and read through the copy. Producers and reporters work closely to shape the raw facts and emotion of a story into a neat package. Communication among the two is critical. Reporters know what's happening in the field but not necessarily how their story fits into the whole of a newscast. It's up to the producer to convey that information as the reporter is relaying the facts the producer needs to make the proper decision for placement and introduction of the story. Perhaps no relationship is more important to a newscast producer than the one he or she has with the [technical] director. This is the person who takes your plan and executes it. A director with good instincts and flair can ensure the broadcast retains the right rhythm. And a director who can think quickly on his or her feet can enable a producer to smartly navigate through the unexpected and excel at coverage of breaking news.

The producer is like a captain leading a team of assignment editors, photographers, videotape editors, and others. A successful producer understands how these men and women bring together the elements that make a successful broadcast. They are the ones in the trenches and they need to be recognized.

Rick Hadley, News Director, WBAP-AM, Dallas: My past experience (as I produced the morning news for a couple of years) was that I had to have good relationships with all of these people. The program director and I had to be on the same page. I didn't always agree with his decisions on what to cover, but since he was the boss I did it. I also had to be on good terms with the reporters and anchors since I interacted with them every day. I had to be able to contact them for more in-depth information on stories and to get contact information for newsmakers we wanted to interview.

Jeff Lyons, 10:00 p.m. meteorologist, WFIE-TV, Evansville, Indiana: The weather-caster works closely with the newscast producer to determine how much time the weather segment gets, if there will be any video elements within the weathercast, and if the weather will be produced in the studio or on location that day. The news director in our station [market 98] serves as an executive producer, so he also has a say in what I do and how I do it.

John Campbell, Sports Director, KCRG-TV, Cedar Rapids, Iowa: It's important to just go with flow most days. As much as I kid about the news director, most have given me control over editorial judgment and let me go about my business in a timely manner. Once again, you should let them know in advance if there are big events coming up or trips you should be planning. The more communication is left open, the better for everyone and the final product.

SOURCES: Personal communications: J. Campbell, M. Ellis, and J. Lyons (April 2003); R. Hadley (May 2003); M. McHugh (March 2003).

Thinking More About It

1. What would you consider your own management style to be—X, Y or Z? Why?

2. Which one of these theories do you think is the most effective for a broadcast news producer? Why?

3. In terms of working relationships in the newsroom, consider the news director, producer, and reporter. Which of these people do you think has the most difficult position in the newsroom and why? From a nonfinancial standpoint, which of these positions seems most suited to you?

4. Which of the three positions seems more likely to result in early career burnout? Why?

5. Many journalism students go into the industry with a false sense of what the business is all about. The best way to learn about the business is to get an internship at a station, but you can also learn more by talking to people now working in broadcast news. If possible, visit one of your local broadcast stations. Talk to the news director, producers, and reporters, with the following in mind:
   a. Do you like your job?
   b. Do you see yourself doing this in another 5 years? 10?
   c. Does your job make your personal life difficult?
   d. How many hours a week do you work? How many days off a year do you get? How many of those days do you actually take off?
   e. Do you feel like your job is stressful? Why or why not?
   f. Are you satisfied with your salary?
   g. Have you ever considered getting out of the business?

Even though the answers might not be what you want to hear, it might be for the best to find out this information now. Some people are simply not suited to meet the demands of the profession. If it seems to you that you are, at least you'll know what you're getting yourself into.

Issues in Producing 9

In the process of getting out a newscast (or in some cases, more than one newscast) every day, producers face a variety of issues. Some of these we have already touched on, such as the multiple duties of a producer (chapter 1), the roles of entertainment and technology (chapter 2), and the relationship of the producer to other key figures in the newsroom (chapter 8).

This chapter will focus in more detail on other issues that producers must face from time to time. They may not come up every single day, but they include some of the most important and widely discussed topics in today's broadcast news industry.

Quality Versus Ratings

You have probably heard the phrase "if it bleeds it leads," used to describe stations that take a "no holds barred" approach to local news. This controversial news philosophy emphasizes crime, sex, and sensationalism. The newscast has high-story counts, high production values (lots of fancy music and graphics), and plenty of live reporting. The assumption is that this type of news will attract more viewers, and results seem to back that up. Stations that have committed to this type of news presentation have often seen a dramatic rise in audience ratings, at least in the short term. News executive Joel Cheatwood turned around floundering news operations in Miami and Boston by offering viewers plenty of crime, pretty anchors, and punched-up music (Bernstein, 2001). Research by Behnke and Miller (1992) confirms that news stories of violence, accidents, and drama receive the highest audience interest.

Results also seem to confirm the corresponding assumption: Audiences will not watch no-nonsense, in-depth news shows focused on serious issues. The belief is that today's audiences are more attracted by glitzy packaging than what's inside the package. WBBM-TV in Chicago put this belief to the test in 2000 by completely revamping its 10:00 p.m. newscast. The station went with only one news anchor, produced news stories of considerable depth and length, and downplayed its news music and graphics. The result was a ratings disaster, as the newscast dropped from a 3.8 rating in February to 2.7 in May and 1.8 in July, and WBBM fell to dead last among Chicago's five evening newscasts. "It takes time for viewers to find a broadcast and develop a loyalty," said anchor Carol Marin, "but we as a society don't give time to many things" ("No frills," 2002).

Assuming that these are not isolated incidents, you would imagine that most stations would produce a "slash and burn" newscast to please their audiences. Marty Haag of TV station group owner A. H. Belo noted, "Covering crime is the easiest, fastest, cheapest and most efficient kind of news coverage for local TV stations" (Grossman, 1997). But many in the industry have strongly resisted what they perceive as a challenge to the fundamental principles of good journalism. Lawrence Grossman of the *Columbia Journalism Review* says that local television news has become "awful" and may eventually give way to newspapers and the Internet as the main source of local news (Grossman, 1997). Warren Cereghino, a television news executive in Los Angeles for more than 30 years, said, "So much of TV news [in Los Angeles] becomes theatrical. It's not journalism, and it's a downward spiral that's getting worse" (Johnson, 1999).

There are some who insist that good journalism and good ratings can go together. "It turns out that viewer preference for murder and mayhem in local news is just another urban legend," says Tom Rosensteil of the Project for Excellence in Journalism (Schulberg, 1999). In a study by the project, stations that scored high in quality also did well in the ratings. However, the study also noted that local television news is still heavy with "the superficial and the reactive," and stories that "require little planning or knowledge from the reporter" (Schulberg, 1999).

It may well be that quality broadcast journalism will eventually win over the audience. "*60 Minutes* is often used as an example of something that took a few years to catch on," says Marin. "But once it did, it became and remains one of the most successful news magazine shows ever. We still believe, and I believe, we could have built it [WBBM's 10:00 p.m. newscast]. But it was going to take some time" ("No frills," 2002). The problem is that in today's media environment, not many stations want to take the time, or the risk. Deborah Potter, executive director of NewsLab, a nonprofit group that encourages quality in local news, said, "I worry about a chilling effect. Local television is imitative, and I hope this isn't a situation where people say, 'See, I told you so'" ("The future of," 2001).

News Production Philosophy

Each producer has a unique style or philosophy behind putting a show together. Much of this philosophy is developed through years of experience working with news directors and other station executives. Below are some sample thoughts from men and women who have produced news at the highest levels of the broadcast industry.

Al Tompkins (1999), The Poynter Institute: Step back from the show and ask if the broadcast you are about to present truly reflects what happened in your community that day. Discover all you can about your audience and seek to serve them. What do you think about all day? You are what you think. Think about serving the viewer and serving your community.

Angie Kucharski, News Director, KCNC-TV, Denver: Your responsibility is good journalism, but you need to see the big picture too. Focus your energy and take the initiative. Be a risk-taker and a "doer" (Sloan, 2002).

Dow Smith (2002), faculty member, Syracuse University; former news director: Producing is not a list of things to get done every day. Producing is about the different roles a producer plays in creating and executing a newscast. Every task you do fits within the basic producing roles of journalist, news writer, production expert, promotion writer, team leader, researcher and lawyer/ethicist.

Mike McHugh, former assistant news director, WBBM-TV: Two words are the key—energy and warmth. If you have that, you've got it. Sure you want it to be visually stimulating, intellectually rewarding, yadda yadda, but if your result gives you these two magic words, the rest falls into place. Oh yeah, it better be clear and easy to understand. My personal philosophy is, don't make it too complicated.

Matt Ellis, News Director, WBZ-TV, Boston: TV news viewers can be a finicky bunch. They want information but they are busy and can't always devote their full attention. Knowing that, I believe the most important thing is to give them stories that are important to their lives and the lives of their families. The late Thomas "Tip" O'Neil, U.S. Speaker of the House from Massachusetts, once said, "All politics is local." All news is local as well. Stories that people will watch are stories they can relate to. Of course, as broadcasters, you have to reach the broadest audience possible. And that's the challenge. As a news manager, I believe in empowering producers to make decisions and take chances. One of the great things about producing television news is that every day you get the chance to prove yourself. No one newscast will make or break a career. So take chances. Look for different ways to tell stories and package them. It is only by taking some risks that a producer can truly challenge him- or herself.

SOURCES: M. Ellis (personal communication, April 2003), M. McHugh (personal communication, March 2003), Sloan (2002), Smith (2002), Tompkins (1999).

The issue of what is perceived as quick ratings versus quality journalism has polarized many in the broadcast news industry. On one side stand the traditionalists like Lawrence Grossman and Carol Marin, who believe that the quick-fix approach is eroding the quality of local news. You can also count Jim Lehrer, host of *The NewsHour with Jim Lehrer* on PBS, in that group. Lehrer and former co-host Robert MacNeil launched the newscast in 1983, devoting the entire hour to quality coverage of serious issues. The show has won more than 30 awards for quality journalism, and Lehrer has won two Emmys, a Peabody, and the Fred Friendly First Amendment Award.

Not surprisingly, Lehrer (2002) has serious issues with today's broadcast news. "Journalism at times continues to embarrass me, to annoy me and to anger me occasionally," he said. "There's a tendency for [it] to be something more akin to professional wrestling—something to watch rather than to believe." Lehrer blames the growing influence of news cable channels like CNN, MSNBC, and the Fox News Channel and their constant demand for news content. "The cable news operations have airtime to fill, excitement to generate, and that may not always be tied directly to the true value and weight of a particular story."

But many of today's young news executives and producers would answer, "So what?" They point to declining news viewership and fragmenting audiences and reason that broadcast news has to provide a reason for viewers to tune in. All the quality journalism in the world won't get you anywhere if no one is there to see it or hear it. Let Jim Lehrer pontificate, they seem to say. The ratings for his nightly news show are microscopic. (In recent years, *The NewsHour with Jim Lehrer* has averaged a 1.5 rating, while the evening network newscasts average between 7 and 8. A single ratings point represents about a million homes.)

If millions of people are going to watch *Survivor* and other reality shows, it would be foolish not to capitalize on that in news. On CBS, *The Early Show's* senior executive producer, Steve Friedman, boasted, "We'll have four of five days when we're dealing with either *Survivor or Big Brother.* When you get a show that everyone's talking about, that's nirvana. We're in television nirvana right now" (Grossman, 2000).

Lehrer, Grossman, and many others would have a different word for it.

Live Reporting

I have already briefly touched on the role of live reporting in a newscast (see chapter 3). Now I want to take a more in-depth look at this issue, which has caused serious debate in newsrooms across the country. Live

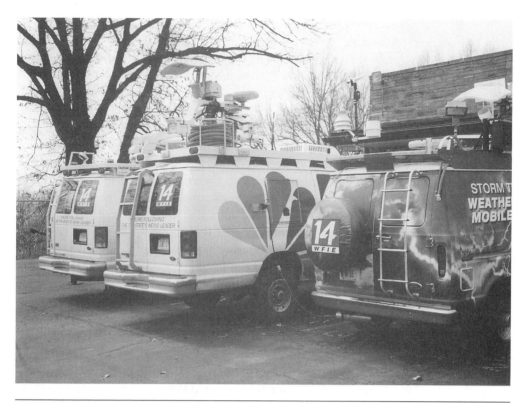

Figure 9.1   Most News Directors Do Not Like to See Expensive Live Trucks Sitting Unused in the Station Parking Lot

SOURCE: Photograph by Brad Schultz.

reporting has become the standard at most stations, but many believe that it is now so overdone that it has reduced the quality and effectiveness of broadcast journalism.

There is no doubt that more and more stations are using live coverage in some form, whether through a local microwave relay, a satellite transmission truck, or with just a simple phoner. New technology has made going live easier but not necessarily cheaper. Live vans and satellite trucks cost hundreds of thousands of dollars, and to justify that expense, many station managers and news directors will demand some sort of live shot in every newscast.

Even if expense is not an issue, stations want to do as much live reporting as possible. Sometimes it's an absolute necessity, such as in cases of tight deadline reporting. Reporting live from a story also sends a message to the audience that the news team "is on top of the story" and committing its major resources to news coverage. Stories covered live somehow seem more important in the mind of the audience, and that helps give the station more credibility. Live reporting is a good public relations tool, in that it gets reporters and other news personnel exposure in the community.

"Does every station in this market attempt to do one or two lives in every broadcast?" asks Tom Bell, news director at WKBD-TV in Detroit. "Absolutely. It's a visual medium. It has to have elements to keep your eyes going, to keep you involved" (Hinds, 2000).

The unfortunate side effect is that much news is now "live for live's sake." That is, many stories are covered live simply because the station has the capability of going live, regardless of whether or not the story has any real news value. Bob Ayra, a reporter for a Chicago cable station and author of a book on live reporting, says he can't count the number of times people have come up to him on a live shot and asked why he was there. "I hear that more and more," he says. "People aren't stupid. They understand when it's a relevant live shot or when it's ridiculous" (Hinds, 2000).

Deciding between the relevant and the ridiculous is one of the main jobs a producer has when considering live coverage (Table 9.1).

In addition to questions of validity and appropriateness, producers must also consider live reporting within a technical context. In the case of live reporting through a microwave truck, topography and weather are important determinants. Microwave relay has an effective range of only about 60 or so miles, and it requires a clear line of sight between the truck and the station. The signal will not work well if it has to go through hills, trees, or other obstacles.

Live shots should not even be attempted during severe weather, such as thunderstorms or high winds. Microwave trucks have a mast that goes close to 100 feet up in the air. It makes an inviting target for lightning. Although not life threatening, high winds can buffet the mast to the point where a reliable signal becomes impossible. Extreme cold or heat can also cause the mast's hydraulic systems to function improperly. Again, these situations are for microwave relay trucks, not satellite trucks.

In many situations, the final decision on going live does not rest with the producer. Some news directors have a standing order that every newscast must have some type of live shot. According to a producer in a small television market, "Every day, my news director says 'so where are we going live tonight?' But as far as I'm concerned, we should NOT go live just because we have the ability to put our truck out there. I argue with my news director about it on a daily basis, unless there is some worthwhile event going on" (Main & Stewart, 1997).

Even when a story appears to warrant live coverage, it can end up problematic. In some cases, the reporter will get to the scene and discover that the story is much different than was envisioned back at the station. For example, a call about a major blaze would obviously send news crews scrambling, but once they get on the scene, they may discover that the "blaze" was very small and was quickly put out by fire crews. And even though the story might not now warrant live coverage, the station has already committed valuable resources for that purpose. Many stations will go ahead with the live shot simply because they've already committed to do one.

Table 9.1   Relevant Versus Ridiculous

Legitimate	Comments
Breaking news	Most breaking news situations (fires, explosions, etc.) warrant live news coverage, but even this isn't an all-inclusive category. Does the breaking news affect a majority of the audience? There are some cases that are not as relevant and could be handled just as easily in another way. However, live reporting from the scene of a breaking story has several advantages, including the ability to provide the audience with instant updates.
Immediacy	Sometimes a live report is important to put the audience at the scene of the story and make them feel a part of what's going on. The most obvious example is breaking news; another example is out-of-town coverage. Stations that cover news outside their home area rely on live reporting not only out of necessity but also for credibility and prestige.
Deadline	Stories that take place close to a newscast deadline are much easier to handle with live coverage. If city council is debating an important new law, that's obviously big news. But many city council meetings don't start until 8:00 p.m. or so, and they may drag on long into the night. In such cases, a simple live report from the scene can provide the latest information. A live report doesn't always have to include a reporter: Many stations will use their live equipment to feed back video or sound bites from the scene of a late-breaking story. In our city council example, a sound bite could be transmitted live (or taped) from the scene while the newscast is in progress.
Other time or space restrictions	Aside from deadlines, there are other restrictions in getting a story. Maybe the political candidate you want to feature doesn't arrive at the scene until newstime, or perhaps the only time to get an interview is for 5 minutes during the newscast. The nature of the story and the schedules of the people related to its coverage will often necessitate live reporting.
Compelling sound or video	Even if a story doesn't have tremendous news value, it can have live appeal. A giant sinkhole that appears in a city park might qualify as visually interesting. But again, many of these stories could be handled just as easily in other ways, without the effort and risk of a live shot.

(Continued)

Table 9.1 (Continued)

Legitimate	Comments
Lack of sound or video	Some stories just aren't very exciting (such as budgets and council meetings) and may not provide much in the way of video or sound. A simple live report with a minimum of video or sound can be an effective way to communicate these types of stories. This is especially appropriate for coverage of trials, where cameras are barred from the courtroom.
Demonstration	Some stories might require the reporter to demonstrate something, such as what happened at a crime scene. This works well for a live shot but can also be accomplished with a stand-up in a reporter package.

Illegitimate	Comments
"Live for live's sake"	It goes without saying that just because you *can* go live doesn't mean you *should*. If there are no legitimate news reasons for doing a live report, producers should try and resist the temptation of doing so.
"Face time"	Many stations use their live reporting as a way to promote their reporters or anchors. The audience gets to see the reporter in action, but the live shot does not otherwise add anything to the newscast. Using a live shot for the sole purpose of getting more "face time" for reporters is not an appropriate use of resources.
Detracts from the story	Live reporting can sometimes shift the focus of the story toward the reporter and away from the story itself. This is particularly true if the reporter has an overly engaging presentation. Many reporters will use their live reports to make themselves part of the story (for example, putting on a hard hat and swinging a hammer at a construction site). This type of reporting not only looks silly but diverts the audience's attention away from the real story.

In such situations, or in cases of legitimate live coverage, there are things producers can try to make the station's live reporting look better (Table 9.2).

News Cutbacks

The growing dependence on technology in broadcast news is ironic because in other areas news departments are cutting back. Perhaps

Table 9.2 Making a Better Live Shot

Technique	Comments
Perspective	Any live shot looks better when there is some context involved. In other words, there should be something interesting or compelling behind the reporter that helps communicate the story. If the report is from a protest rally, put the protesters in the background. Just as obviously, avoid brick walls and plain settings. Late-night live reports are often less effective because many times the audience can only see darkness behind the reporter. The background should provide context for what's going on in the story. However, some of these decisions are outside the producer's control. For example, at a crime scene, police may dictate exactly where reporters and live trucks can set up. There are other situations where it's not possible to choose your background. Logistical realities and other considerations may force a reporter to use an undesirable location. This is especially true in group live shots, where several stations are trying to send back material from the same event.
Motion	One current trend in live reporting is the "walk and talk," where reporters will move as they deliver a live report. It could be a demonstration of something going on or just an interview conducted during a walk. Many news directors believe that reporters should "do something" in their live shots to make them more appealing, even if it's something very simple. What reporters actually do depends a great deal on the type and location of the story.
Simplicity	Effective live reports don't always have to be elaborate. One way to visually demonstrate what the weather is doing is a simple weather live shot. Many stations now do this by going live from a "weather patio" directly outside the station. Such live reports are extremely simple, and viewers don't know if the shot is 10 miles or 10 feet away. Simplicity also works well because live reporting is demanding in terms of technology and resources. Any number of things can happen to keep a live shot from getting on the air or to knock it off while it's airing. Lights can get kicked over, plugs can accidentally be pulled, microphone batteries can die—you name it. Producers should always remember that live shots come with a built-in level of risk, and the more complicated they get, the greater the chance is that something will go wrong.

Table 9.3   Digital Television Conversion Costs per Station

Digital Service	Estimated Cost (per station)
Tower	$500,000-$3 million
Transmitter	$400,000-$1.25 million
Antenna	$300,000-$500,000
Encoder	$200,000-$500,000
Switcher	$200,000-$400,000
Studio	$150,000-$250,000
Downlink	$90,000-$120,000
Decks and monitors	$90,000-$120,000
Upconverter	$80,000-$120,000
Router	$60,000
Total costs	**$2.2-$6.5 million**

SOURCE: Dickson (1998).

because new technology is so expensive, stations and owners must reduce expenses in other areas. A good example is the conversion to digital television, which almost all stations must eventually make. The National Association of Broadcasters estimates that by the time digital is established, stations will have spent more than $16 billion in the conversion process, including the purchase of all-new transmitters, towers, cameras, editing equipment, and so on (Table 9.3).

There are other reasons why news has become more cost conscious, including the increasing consolidation going on within the broadcast industry. We have already noted how more stations are now owned by large media corporations, and those corporations are putting much more of an emphasis on the bottom line (see chapter 2). Stations must also deal with eroding audiences and a weak economy. The additional media options consumers now enjoy, such as cable, satellite, and the Internet, have fragmented and splintered viewing audiences, making it more difficult for stations to turn a profit. Recent years have also been a tough time for the broadcast advertising market and the economy in general. Broadcast stations began to feel the advertising pinch in 2001, when NBC led the major networks in selling advertising inventory at

Table 9.4   Broadcast News Staff and Budget Changes, 2001-2002 (%)

	Increased	Decreased	Stayed the Same
TV news staff	19	54	27
Radio news staff	20	10	70
TV news budgets	30	31	36
Radio news budgets	16	9	49

SOURCE: Papper and Gerhard (2002b).

Note: Where percentages do not add up to 100, the remaining responses were "don't know."

cost-per-thousand decreases of 5% compared to the previous year ("Network upfront," 2001).

All of these factors have resulted in deep cutbacks in news coverage, personnel, and equipment, even for the major networks. Staffing seems to be more affected than budgets, and television news seems especially vulnerable in that news staffing and budgets both declined (Table 9.4).

It should also be noted that 40% of all television stations either added more news content or planned to add more news in the future—all of which means that today's producers are expected to do more with less. News directors expect the same high-energy newscast with good production values, but they want it done on a tighter budget. In smaller markets, this certainly means that producers will have to take on more responsibilities than ever. Most people will not only produce but also write, report, shoot, edit, and even anchor.

While serious, time-consuming, and costly news coverage has declined, cheap content has rushed to fill the void. We have already discussed how many stations are now emphasizing entertainment or feature-type reporting in their newscasts, primarily because such content is relatively cheap and easy. Instead of exposing corruption at city hall, many stations find it more profitable to report on what Michael Jackson is doing (as witnessed by his three network "news" specials in February 2003). When the Dixie Chicks complained about President Bush's war policy during one of their concerts, hundreds of stations across the country turned the event and its fallout into headline news stories.

This is not to suggest that radio and television stations are not doing high-quality, important stories. If not for the work of John Ferrugia at KMGH-TV in Denver, the entire sexual assault scandal at the U.S. Air Force Academy in 2003 might have gone unreported. Nevertheless, everyone should be aware of the realities and pressures of producing broadcast news in today's media environment.

Market Size

If you've ever had the chance to watch or listen to news from various places around the country, you know that the news in New York, Chicago, and Los Angeles looks and sounds much different than the news in Utica, Pensacola, and Topeka. The news at stations in bigger markets usually looks more professional and more sophisticated (although not necessarily "better") than it does at smaller stations. The obvious reason is that big-market stations have more money and resources available to their news programs (Table 9.5).

Large-market stations have more news staff, bigger news budgets, and more sophisticated news technology, compared to small-market stations. The question is, does this really make a difference in the way news is produced? "Honestly, in a lot of ways, producing in the nation's biggest TV market is very similar to producing TV newscasts anywhere else in the country," says Jason Gewirtz (2002), formerly a producer with WABC-TV in New York and now with CNBC. "But it's truly on a much bigger level. Simply put, more stuff happens here, and it happens fast. When I first arrived in 1999, it was mind-boggling."

Table 9.5   Differences in Market Size for Television News

Market Size	Full-Time News Staff	Stations Increasing Their News Budgets (%)
1-25	58	49
26-50	46	17
51-100	35	26
101-150	22	29
151+	16	36

SOURCE: Papper and Gerhard (2002b).

Note: The average major market radio station had a full-time news staff of 3.28, compared to 1.10 for small-market stations.

Figure 9.2   Bigger Stations Have More Resources, But Does That Make the News Better?
SOURCE: Photograph by Brad Schultz.

But Gewirtz (2002) does admit that the demands of producing at a big-market station can influence news coverage.

> There are days when I'm amazed at how little attention certain awful, shocking and disturbing stories get. The reason they get so little time is because there is so much going on all the time. The area is huge, covering the five boroughs of New York City and is enough to deal with, then there are the massive suburbs, Long Island, Connecticut, and of course New Jersey where a huge portion of our viewership is. Just about any portion of our viewing area is significantly bigger than most entire TV markets.

Gewirtz (2002) says that the competition in many large markets has forced stations to become "news factories," with more emphasis on getting news on the air and less emphasis on creativity and presentation.

> This market is cutthroat. If you get beaten on a story as a producer or reporter, you almost always have to answer for it. Nobody likes losing, and just about everyone here is very competitive. Sometimes that means we

don't personalize stories like other markets, but we do a great job of covering the news. I would argue nobody does "breaking news" like we do here.

There seems to be an admission that perhaps the news in smaller markets might be a little "better," if that's the right term. Perhaps it's more correct to say that small-market producers can invest in more creative and engaging presentations simply because they don't have to face the same competition and demand for news. "You'll often see better journalism done in smaller markets because people who are there are often working harder to prove themselves," says Mike McHugh (personal communication, March 2003), who has produced news in some of the biggest (Chicago, market 3) and smallest (Bluefield, West Virginia, market 149) markets in the country. "They're more creative, more willing to take chances. More people, staff and experience doesn't always make better programs. From a producing standpoint, I think the best newscasts in the country are in markets 10 through 30."

At least in terms of a producing philosophy, most producers are not willing to say there's a difference between big and small markets. Matt Ellis (personal communication, April 2003), once the head writer for *Good Morning America* in New York and now at WBZ in Boston, got his start in a small market. He admits there are obvious differences in terms of resources and staff, but he believes there are very few differences in the way newscasts are approached. "Philosophically, there shouldn't be much difference," says Ellis. "News producers are like the chefs cooking the raw food and adding the spices so it comes out just right. That's the job whether you are in market 151 or market 1."

Rick Hadley (personal communication, May 2003), the news director at WBAP-AM in Dallas, would agree. He also worked in small markets for several years before coming to one of the biggest radio markets in the country.

I believe the slogan "all news is local" applies in either case. Whether it's a large or small market, you must program based on the hot issues of the day. One major difference I've noticed is your accountability in the small market versus large. In a small-market station, you're more likely to run into that newsmaker at a restaurant or the mall than a newsmaker in a large market. So if you've done negative reports about that small-market newsmaker, of course make sure the information is accurate before airing it. And be prepared to defend or explain yourself upon a chance encounter with that newsmaker. In the large market, the people you report on, especially public officials, expect to be interviewed and are used to the media game. It's not always the case in small market. You might not be able to get the mayor or police chief on the air at a moment's notice like a producer in a major market can usually do.

Ethics

Just like anyone else in the news business, producers must deal with a variety of ethical issues. Some of these are issues that producers face alone; others are shared with other members of the news station. In no particular order, here are some of the key ethical issues producers will have to address.

HONESTY

It sounds silly even to mention this, because every journalist is taught the values of accuracy, impartiality, fairness, and objectivity. This issue really isn't about out-and-out lying but more about the various gray areas between truth and falsehood. Consider the now infamous mug shot of O.J. Simpson that appeared on the cover of most of the major news-magazines after his arrest in 1994. *Time* darkened the photo to give Simpson a sinister, almost guilty appearance. Even in the face of almost unanimous condemnation, *Time's* managing editor defended the photo, writing, "The harshness of the mug shot—the merciless bright light, the stubble on Simpson's face, the cold specificity of the picture—had been subtly smoothed and shaped into an icon of tragedy" ("Ethics in," 2000).

Producers may never deal with anything like that, but it does illustrate how easy—and tempting—it now is to shade the truth in certain directions. It might be that a station heavily promotes its coverage of a local protest rally only to find that few people bothered to show up. Would a producer then write or edit the story to make it look like a major protest, complete with angry citizens? And what about "pseudoevents"—news events staged only for the benefit of the camera or microphone? Does the producer have the responsibility to let the audience know that all the protesters left once the cameras stopped rolling? Roy Peter Clark (2002), Senior Scholar at the Poynter Institute, has a simple answer: "[There are] two cornerstone principles: Do not add. Do not deceive."

Technology has certainly made it easier to manipulate the truth. On New Year's Eve 1999, most major television networks gathered in New York's Times Square to report on the momentous change to the year 2000. NBC has a very prominent logo in the area, which CBS decided to replace, using digital technology, with the CBS eye. Ethical small potatoes, or did a news organization dedicated to presenting the truth misrepresent itself and the facts? Argued CBS, "Covering the Jumbotron was an aggressive move that is going to put some noses out of joint. People can disagree as to whether this is an appropriate use of technology" (Vercammen, 2000).

Similar digital alterations have become quite common at sporting events, where station promotional announcements and, most especially, advertising are made to appear part of the action. Using advertising in this way has become very popular, as companies move away from traditional commercial breaks toward "product placement." "We are heading in a lot of dangerous ways," says broadcast journalist Linda Ellerbee. "It's not necessarily bad. It's just that as journalists, I believe we have to pay particular attention here" (Vercammen, 2000).

VISUAL BIAS

Producers can also fall into the trap of visual bias—using or emphasizing certain stories that have a high visual appeal, whether or not the stories have any news value. A man engaged in a life-and-death struggle with an alligator makes for interesting pictures, even if the story takes place thousands of miles away and has no relevance for anyone in the local audience. Even when stories do have news value, the visuals can confuse or dilute the message. During the 2003 war in Iraq, viewers were so fascinated with exploding bombs and night-vision warfare that they often paid no attention to the news behind the pictures. At the same time, some reporters were content to let the video become the story and report nothing more than what people could clearly see.

There is no doubt that television is a visual medium, and producers must constantly be aware of the temptation to run a story simply because it has interesting pictures or high production values. A consideration of what makes a story newsworthy is certainly appropriate (see chapter 3), but newsworthiness is not always the first consideration. The type of station (especially in regard to size and amount of resources), its overall news philosophy, and the needs of an individual newscast will often determine what role visual bias plays in a producer's decision-making process. For example, visually interesting stories are much more attractive on slow news days or when the producer has trouble filling the news hole.

There is always a tendency in broadcast news to overdo a good thing—in this case, run compelling video until people actually get tired, annoyed, or even angry. In September 2001, images of planes crashing into the World Trade Center became so ubiquitous on network television that thousands of viewers finally called to complain. Bob Steele (2001), who directs the ethics program at the Poynter Institute, says,

> I'm not opposed to the use of graphic photos and video. Journalism is inherently intrusive and invasive. There are many times—in our obligation to be fair, accurate and authentic—when we must tell the painful truth with words and images. But we should strive in our reporting techniques and publishing decisions to avoid causing unnecessary harm.

Producers should also realize there's an opposite side to visual bias—avoiding stories that don't have good visuals. Complex stories regarding local government, budget issues, and court rulings are often downplayed or ignored because they don't translate well to television. There are ways to get around these types of stories, such as the innovative use of graphics. Although the audience does expect television stories to have a certain level of sophistication, that should not become the primary consideration. Perhaps the best solution is for producers to ask themselves this question: Would I run this story on its merits, regardless of the video involved?

PERSONAL BIASES

There is another type of bias that all producers (and everyone else in the business) must recognize. Every journalist has a distinct set of personal beliefs and biases based on such things as personality, upbringing, and education. No matter how much the industry preaches about fairness, objectivity, and impartiality, these biases can sometimes get in the way of producing the news.

One of the important jobs of the producer is that of agenda setter: someone who directs the news agenda for a particular newscast. Producers often decide what goes in the newscast and what gets left out, and often-times these decisions can be influenced by personal motives. According to media researcher Wolfram Peiser (2000), "There is at least some reason to believe that the journalist's agenda may contribute to our understanding of the media agenda."

For years, there has been a claim that the national news media has a liberal bias and is more sympathetic to Democratic Party candidates and causes. Former CBS television reporter Bernard Goldberg (who is generally not considered a conservative) wrote a book alleging extreme liberal bias in the national media. Among Goldberg's (2003) claims:

- The media cite sources who are in agreement with the liberal world-view of journalists but fail to give sufficient attention to sources who disagree.

- The media suppress information that doesn't fit in with their liberal beliefs.

- The networks follow the lead of the liberal *Washington Post* and *New York Times* in deciding what is newsworthy and in deciding what spin to put on the news.

- For these reasons, the public is deserting the mainstream news media.

The last point is interesting because it laid the foundation for the rise of the conservative media, through Rush Limbaugh and the Fox News Channel. An ironic result is a rise in complaints about a conservative bias, from such powerful political figures as Senate Minority Leader Tom

Daschle (D-South Dakota). It was Daschle who compared Limbaugh's conservative radio show to "violent Middle East rhetoric, which led to the September 11 hijackings and mass American deaths" (Thomas, 2002).

The point here is not to come down on one side of the debate or the other but simply to recognize that journalists do bring to bear their own distinct beliefs, prejudices, and biases. Most producers are relatively young, and many are fresh from college. Young, idealistic people in their 20s are often more likely to have a liberal bent. According to media researcher Vernon Stone (2001), the median age of a television news person is 30 years and has changed little over the years. The median age for a radio news person is 31 years.

But even if liberal bias is a myth, in a very practical sense, there is no such thing as absolute journalistic impartiality, fairness, and objectivity. Newscasts aren't produced in a theoretical vacuum—they're produced by real people in real newsrooms. Every day, producers make dozens of decisions related to the newscast based on experience, personality, and judgment. Although some of these decisions must be made in a matter of seconds, others give time for more reflection. A producer should recognize the influence of his or her own personal biases in decision making and, when possible, seek out other newsroom personnel for different perspectives.

CREATING THE NEWS

Producer Duties

KVBC, Channel 3, is seeking a creative, hard working, news junky to produce daily stories and long term projects in the fastest growing city in the country. Las Vegas is a place where there is always a connection to the big stories and there is never a slow news day. We have the toys and a commitment to dig a little deeper to find the investigative angle. This is not a job for beginners.

Note from the author: KVBC-TV in Las Vegas ran this ad in March 2003. Please do not contact them about it.

In the KVBC-TV ad shown here, the truth was stretched a bit, because from time to time there are slow news days even in an exciting place like Las Vegas. The long, hot summer months can get especially slow for the news business, no matter what the size of the market or how many "toys" a station has to produce the news.

It is especially tempting during such times for producers to "create" news to fill a news hole. There are various definitions for creating news, but typically it involves giving extensive coverage to a relatively insignificant story or issue or making the station part of the story. If there's no important news in the area on a slow summer day, the station might devote a lot of news time to its charitable program of delivering electric fans to the needy. Although admirable, such a program probably shouldn't merit more than 30 seconds of air time. But on a slow news day, it can be stretched to fill several minutes, which not only solves the news hole problem but serves as good promotion for the station.

In scenarios like this, stations can come under criticism for creating news. All journalists are taught to remain passive observers of the news and simply report what's going on. More and more, however, journalists are becoming more actively involved in news creation, and not just on slow news days. It could be something relatively harmless, such as having a reporter take part in a local news event. For example, it has become quite common for reporters to run in marathons, serve as emcees for an organizational meeting, or accompany a group in foreign travels.

The danger is when the media no longer report the story but actually become the story. CNN's Walter Rogers covered the 2003 Iraq war embedded with an Army unit, and constantly faced live fire "like a John Wayne movie" (Johnson, 2003). At one point, he and his cameraman were saved by a solider who shot an Iraqi creeping up on them. "Being captured is a real possibility, and it is not something I look forward to," he admitted. If Rogers, or any other reporter, had been killed or captured, that would have been a story in itself, and the reporting focus would have shifted away from the war.

Sometimes, reporters inadvertently make news. Many reporters, notably men such as World War II correspondent Ernie Pyle, have been killed or taken prisoner as a result of their war coverage. In 2002, the capture and execution of *Wall Street Journal* reporter Daniel Pearl became a legitimate news event and part of the ongoing media coverage of terrorism. But reporters and producers should avoid situations in which they can become more important than the issues they're covering.

This can be a problem if the producer has a different news philosophy than the news director or other station executives. What the producer might recognize as "creating the news," or as a pseudoevent, the news director might view as legitimate. It's often difficult to maintain one's personal ethics and values, given the pressures of producing broadcast news—and this is especially true when the boss is breathing down your neck.

This points up the lack of ethical guidelines and training now in place at stations across the country. Most stations say they want to act ethically, and they usually subscribe to some form of ethical principles. Yet ethical standards vary from place to place, as do the sanctions when ethical norms are broken. What might be considered a serious ethical breach at one station might be rewarded at another as "good, hard-hitting journalism."

Hardly any stations have the time, inclination, or resources to make a big investment in ethical training, with the result that producers have to make their own ethical decisions.

No one would seriously disagree with this comment from Bob Steele (2002), head of the ethics program at Poynter:

> Indeed, ethical principles and values provide the moral compass and the moral gyroscope that give us direction and balance. And that direction and balance is essential in this era of intense economic pressure. A moral gyroscope is needed as we sail the choppy seas of new media products, partnerships and inter-media competition. A moral compass is essential as we travel roads littered with dangerous land mines reflecting the range of complex and controversial issues we must cover, from race relations to gun control to school violence. Simply put, we need clarity on our principles and values more than ever.

In reality, ethical clarity is very hard to come by.

Consultants

The mere mention of the word *consultant* is enough to send many producers into a state of panic. Consultants wield a tremendous amount of power in hundreds of newsrooms across the country, and their decisions often have a direct influence not only on the newscast but on the producer's career. No wonder that the role of the consultant has become one of the most discussed and most controversial in broadcast news.

A consultant is a representative of a media research firm that can provide several different services to broadcast stations, all for a hefty fee. The original consulting firms developed in the early 1960s and concentrated on delivering qualitative data to broadcast clients. This was during a time when stations had access to the ratings numbers—how many people watched or listened—but didn't know why people watched or how they felt about the news. Early consulting firms such as McHugh and Hoffman did thousands of surveys with what they called the "middle majority" who watched television news (Allen, 2001).

The research of these firms showed a big difference between what people wanted to see in news and what stations were actually doing. As the influence of these consultants grew, the look of television news began to change. It began in the 1960s with the popularization of "eyewitness news" and its emphasis on excitement, graphics, and "happy talk" between anchors. In the 1970s, consultants used their research to help many weak stations climb to the top of the news ratings.

Their success fueled the growth of the consulting business. Firms branched out beyond simply providing data, and many now consult in all areas of news presentation, including talent recruitment, training, and placement. Many consulting firms even critique the anchor's appearance, including hair and makeup. Consulting is now a $50 million a year business, and consultants operate in more than 80% of local television newsrooms across the country. The largest firms, such as Frank Magid Associates and Audience Research and Development (AR&D), have offices all over the world.

Typically, a consulting firm will contract with individual stations to provide its services on an exclusive basis. Once a station is signed up as a client, the consulting firm usually sends a representative to visit the station once or twice a year. Usually the representative is a former news director, producer, or reporter with several years experience in the business. This representative will meet with and interview key newsroom personnel, such as the news director, producers, and reporters. Everyone will meet together as a group and critique newscasts. These meetings, along with the interviews and research data, will help the consultant come up with ideas to make the newscasts better. Most times, it's simply a matter of fine tuning the news, such as having the reporters do more live reports or having the producer increase the show's story count. For some weak or under-performing stations, there might be drastic changes in store, such as different anchors or a new news set. For the sake of consistency and creating a good working relationship, consulting firms try to have the same representative visit the same group of stations.

This process is seemingly straightforward and simple, yet over the years it has generated a tremendous amount of controversy at local news stations. Many producers and reporters don't like outside consultants trying to tell them how to do their jobs, especially producers, who are usually very protective of "their shows." Local news people reason that they know better than anyone the demands of the local market, especially as consultants usually live somewhere else and may visit the market only once a year. "[News] decisions should be made inside the station, not in Marion, Iowa [Magid headquarters] or Dallas [AR&D headquarters]," says Mark Berryhill, News Director at WHDH in Boston (Aucoin & Jurkowitz, 1999).

In addition, a lot of local news personnel resent the growing power wielded by consultants. Stations spend thousands of dollars every year for consulting services, and because news directors don't like that money to go to waste, they are often willing to implement any and all suggested changes. "[Consultants'] role has expanded over the past 10 years or so," says reporter John Henning of WBZ-TV in Boston, a 35-year news veteran. "They used to just advise on how anchors ought to dress or what sets should look like, but now they are almost telling news organizations what kind of news people want to hear" (Aucoin & Jurkowitz, 1999).

This last statement typifies a strong feeling on the part of many local news people that consultants have ruined broadcast journalism. They argue that consultants want all stations to look and sound the same, with an emphasis on crime, sensationalism, and high-energy graphics. "They alter the impact of journalism," said Donald McGaffin, a former West Coast anchor and reporter (Aucoin & Jurkowitz, 1999). "Consultants have made television non-journalistic." One Boston television reporter refers to consultants as "one step above used car salesmen" (Aucoin & Jurkowitz, 1999).

Naturally, consultants defend their business. "If there was ever a time when formulas worked, formulas long since ceased to provide results for clients," says Doug Clemensen of Clemensen and Rovitto. "The needs of a particular station or client vary enormously from place to place" (Aucoin & Jurkowitz, 1999). According to Jim Willi, a partner at AR&D, "At AR&D we are not news doctors—that's old school thinking. We are station strategists. To win in today's cluttered marketplace, you must have the entire station, all departments, working together on a single mission" (Audience Research & Development, 2002).

Love them or hate them, consultants are an established part of the broadcast news business, and producers must learn how to deal with them. Almost every newsroom has a horror story about a knock-down, drag-out fight between producer and consultant, but, obviously, open hostility doesn't benefit anyone. It certainly doesn't win points with the news director, who's often caught in the middle between consultants and the newsroom. A key point here is to respect the consultant as someone who does know about the business and genuinely wants to make the newscast better.

It's important to keep an open mind about the value of the consultation. A producer who has already prejudged the consultant as a used-car salesman is highly unlikely to give any of the recommendations a serious chance to work. This could be a serious mistake because consultants often do have valuable advice. "We're a very well-informed set of eyes and ears," said John Quarderer, vice president at Magid. "[But] it's up to the stations to look at what we do and what we suggest and say 'Is this what we want to be?'" (Aucoin & Jurkowitz, 1999).

That's probably the bottom line. The news director and producers at the individual station will eventually decide what (if any) changes will be made to the newscast. It might work out better for producers to keep an open mind with consultants and save any serious reservations for the news director. Remember, it's the news director who has the final say, and he or she has the ultimate authority over any consultant recommendations.

Consultants: John Quarderer

As both an industry professional and an academician at the University of Missouri's School of Journalism, John Quarderer has a unique perspective on consultants. He must like something about the business because he's now a vice president at Frank Magid Associates in Marion, Iowa.

Q: Is there a way to define what consultants do?

A: We're in the service business, the relationship business, and the teaching business. It's more like "let me help you do it better," and stations recognize the need for depth of knowledge and access to a data set that is developed over time.

Q: How do consultants help stations create their own identity or "brand"?

A: We try to help stations define the brand they already have. You don't dictate a brand in the minds of the audience. You may think you're "Channel X" and better than the competition, but the audience may think differently. Then it's a matter of working with stations to alter their brand perception to gain audience share. It's much different than branding a product like toothpaste, which has a set price. In TV news, there are three or four products all about the same, all on at the same time and all free. We have to create value; there's no magic formula.

Q: What about the criticisms of consultants, especially by those in local news?

A: I don't think most clients feel that way. They recognize the need for information and for critical eyes to evaluate not only what they're doing but the broad landscape of their news. A lot of it has to do with the fact that the environment has changed, so that a strong station sees the local Fox affiliate, with fewer staff and a radical news philosophy, eating into their ratings. The older generation that was so resistant is starting to get out of the business. Today's generation understands the value of market research and the need to change. I don't believe we're trying to make everyone the same. In fact, I don't think you can define a "Magid client." For example, two of our traditional clients have been WCVB in Boston and WPVI in Philadelphia. They were as different as two stations could possibly be: WCVB was the serious journalism station that won DuPont Awards, while WPVI was an "action news" station. Yet both were strong ratings leaders in their markets, and both were very good clients.

SOURCE: John Quarderer (personal communication, October 2003).

Thinking More About It

Consider taping a series of local newscasts for a content analysis (for more information on content analysis, see "Thinking More About It" at the end of chapter 2). Analyze the newscasts and consider the following:

1. Where do you think the station falls on the "quality versus ratings" line? What specifically was in the newscast that suggests which direction the station was leaning? Or do you think the station tried to "play it down the middle," with a combination of both?

2. Based on your observation of how the station presented the news, do you think it was effective? Was it a "good" newscast? Did it hold your interest? Why or why not?

3. How many live reports did the newscast have? Would you characterize these as "relevant" or "ridiculous?" Why? Were there any stories in the newscast that were not presented as live that you would have done live? Why?

4. Do you think these same news stories would have been presented differently if this station was in a different-sized market? How do you think they would have been presented?

5. Were there any stories that raised ethical questions in your mind? Which ones and why? Was there a story that you saw that made you think, "I can't believe they did that."?

6. Did the news stories seem to have a particular bias to them? Do you feel like the reporters presented the stories impartially and objectively, or did they interject their own biases into them?

7. Did the newscast seem to have a familiar "sameness" to it that might suggest the work of consultants? In other words, did it look or feel the same as other stations in other places? Did the graphics look similar to those of other stations? Had you heard similar opening or closing music at another station?

The Job Market 10

Producers generally have an easier time finding jobs than do on-air talent. For one thing, more people are trying to get into the business in front of the camera than behind it. There are probably many more people wanting to become anchors and reporters than there are people wanting to be producers, technical directors, or photographers. In addition, stations like to keep on-air positions fairly stable to maintain some consistency with the audience. That's not to say that reporters and anchors never move on or lose their jobs, but for the most part, there's a little higher turnover in the behind-the-scenes positions. The growth of news content on the Internet, cable, and satellite has also created more news openings, and producers are in especially high demand at broadcast news outlets across the country (Table 10.1).

That doesn't mean it's easy for producers to find work. This chapter will focus on the realities of the job market for producers and specific things you can do to make yourself more attractive as a job candidate.

The Numbers

If you've taken an economics class, you know about the basic law of supply and demand. When the supply of any product rises above the demand for that product, there is a surplus, and the price charged for the product drops accordingly. The same situation applies in broadcast journalism. Every year there is a tremendous supply of eager college graduates looking to make their mark in the business. Think of how many people just at your school want to get into the business and then multiply that by hundreds of thousands of colleges, universities, and trade schools all across the country.

Table 10.1   Amount of News Planned in 2002 Compared to 2001 (%)

	Increase	Decrease	Stay the Same	Not Sure
All television	26	2	62	10
Major networks	27	2	61	10
Other commercial	13	0	63	25

SOURCE: Papper and Gerhard (2002b).

Note: Does not include changes in news at cable television or radio stations.

In general, the supply of people wanting to get into broadcast journalism far exceeds the demand for their services, making it extremely difficult for recent graduates and others already in the field looking for a new job. The situation has been made even worse in recent times because of a poor over-all economy. Research shows that in 2002, the number of journalism graduates who got full-time jobs dropped 12%, and salaries declined by nearly $1000 a year. "The job market is harsh with a capital 'H,'" remarked a recent broadcast journalism graduate (Becker, Vlad, Huh, & Daniels, 2002).

Even in good economic times, new broadcast journalism graduates don't make much money in their first jobs (Table 10.2). This is true for producers as well, although in recent years the income levels have risen more than 12%. Don't get overly encouraged by the "maximum" figure of $115,000, which is for the most experienced executive producers at the network level and for those in the largest markets. It's more likely that producers coming straight out of college will work at or near the minimum salary level. Also note that radio lags far behind television in terms of salaries.

Unlike much of the broadcast journalism profession, news producers are predominantly female (Table 10.3). There is a higher percentage of women working as broadcast news producers than there is in any other newsroom position. This reflects an overall trend of more females getting into the business, especially in the positions of news anchor and reporter. There's also a relatively high percentage of minority news producers. In 2002, 20% of the total television workforce was minority, compared to just 8% for radio, and the radio minority figure has continued to shrink since 1994.

These figures suggest that the "typical" news producer is White, female, and makes less than $30,000 per year. That's an obvious generalization, but it does reflect the current state of the job market. There are more women than men at journalism schools across the country, and many are taking the career path into producing. Although the national economy has kept broadcast salaries flat, producing salaries have risen a bit, perhaps as a reflection of the increase in broadcast and cable news opportunities.

Table 10.2   Broadcast News Salaries

	Average	Maximum	Minimum
Television executive producer	$48,900	$115,000	$18,000
Television news producer	$29,000	$100,000	$15,000
Television news director	$73,800	$250,000	$18,000
Radio news producer	$29,400	$42,000	$21,000
Radio news director	$31,400	$72,000	$10,000

SOURCE: Papper and Gerhard (2002a).

Table 10.3   Television Positions by Gender and Race (%)

	Male	Female	White	Minority
News producer	36	64	85	15
Executive news producer	50	50	89	11
News director	74	26	91	9
News anchor	43	57	79	21
News reporter	42	58	74	26

SOURCE: Papper (2002).

Some of the decline in minority employment can be attributed to the elimination of the equal opportunity guidelines that pertained to the broadcast industry.

Finding a Producing Job

There are some considerations you need to make before you start looking for a producing job. These include such things as what qualifications you should have, where to look for jobs, and techniques for the actual job search process.

WHAT STATIONS WANT

It's good to start with an understanding of what stations and news directors are looking for in a producer. Consider KNXV's advertisement for a news producer, which gives an indication of type of skills and resources you'll need as a producer.

News Producer Advertisement

Qualifications

EDUCATION: College diploma or equivalent experience required.

EXPERIENCE: 2-3 years television broadcast experience required. 2-3 years news experience with promotion writing/editing preferred. Production experience a plus.

EQUIPMENT: Must be able to master newsroom equipment within a 90-day period.

LICENSE: Must have a valid driver's license and provide proof of insurability.

SKILLS: Must be creative, yet factually accurate writer, possess excellent communication skills and be able to work under deadline pressures. Flexible hours and some travel are required.

Job Description

1. Supervise the organizing, writing and editing of assigned newscasts. Directly participate in the management of the newscasts as they air from the control room.

2. Write all news copy not supplied by anchors, writers or reporters [as needed].

3. Initiate and participate in the formulation of processes and the innovation of newscast formats or systems in the newsroom which support the assigned newscasts.

4. Perform other duties as needed and directed by the News Director.

SOURCE: KNXV (website).

Note from the author: This ad was run by KNXV Phoenix in 2002. Please do not call them about it.

This ad gives you a general idea of what stations want in a producer. Most producers will need a college degree, although it need not necessarily be in journalism. Many people now in the industry, including several highly paid network anchors, got their degrees in history, English, philosophy, or political science. In very rare cases, some people can get in the business without a degree. Some of these people skipped college and went right into the industry, working their way up from studio camera operator or some other lower level job. However, the competition in the business today almost demands that job applicants have some sort of college degree.

Another reason college is important is that almost all stations now require some producing experience, and many schools have stations or news labs for that purpose. Even stations in the smallest markets would prefer that new producers have experience, even if it's just at the college station. The more training producers can get in school, the less on-the-job training they'll need at work. This is especially important for smaller stations, which have a lot of turnover and don't want to spend too much time training employees who are eventually going to leave.

Bigger stations, such as KNXV in Phoenix, want producers to have experience beyond the university level. Generally, they expect producers to spend at least a year or two at a smaller station before trying to get into a bigger market. This is not to say that recent graduates can't get producing jobs in medium and large markets, but it is extremely rare, and graduates might be better off cutting their teeth at smaller stations for awhile.

The requirement about "mastering the newsroom equipment" is just another way of saying that producers will have to learn the station's computer software system. There are only a half-dozen or so competing programs in use by stations, and it really doesn't take that long to figure them out. In some cases, the producer may already have been using the system at the college broadcast station. Once hired, a producer may want to go in during off hours to learn more about the intricacies of the program.

Notice how the ad also emphasizes the skills of writing, communication, and working under deadline pressure. These are the main skills a producer uses on a daily basis—writing to fill most of the news hole, communicating with other newsroom staff, and making sure the show is on time and ready to go. "Flexible hours" is a nice way of saying you'll probably be working a lot of odd hours and overtime. Travel will be necessary if you produce shows on location or out of town (see chapter 5).

The main element of the job description is everything that goes into producing a newscast. Typically, each newscast will have its own producer, but there are situations in which a producer might be responsible for two newscasts per day, such as the 6:00 p.m. and 10:00 p.m. shows. Again, the emphasis is on the organization, writing, and editing involved in putting a show together and after that, overseeing it from the control room.

There are also planning and management components to producing, such as "initiate and participate in the formulation of processes and the innovation of newscast formats or systems in the newsroom which support the assigned newscasts." Producers should be leaders and innovators in the newsroom, coming up with both short- and long-term visions for their newscasts. Most stations and news directors want producers to take an active role in how their newscasts will look, now and in the future.

Figure 10.1   New Producers Must Learn How to Use Specific Station News Software
SOURCE: Photograph by Brad Schultz.

WHERE TO LOOK FOR JOBS

Technology has made the job search process much easier, but it has also increased the pool of competitors for each position. Because of tools such as the Internet, there are often hundreds of applicants trying to get the same broadcasting job. Media researcher Vernon Stone (2001) says that for every entry-level position in a television newsroom, the typical news director gets 60 to 70 resume tapes. News director Jeff Kiernan of WTMJ-TV in Milwaukee says whenever he has an on-air opening, he usually gets around 200 resumes (J. Kiernan, personal communication, April 2000).

The most obvious place to look for producing jobs is within industry sources, such as in trade magazines and on websites devoted to broadcast journalism (Table 10.4). Online industry magazines such as *Broadcasting & Cable* and *Electronic Media* have job listings sections that feature broadcast openings all across the country. But again, everyone else looking for a job has access to these sites, and many sources charge a fee to access listings.

Most universities and some journalism schools also have placement offices. These offices offer job-seeking strategies and have information

Table 10.4   Places to Look for Producer Openings

Source	Examples
Industry sources	*Broadcasting & Cable,* http://www.tvinsite.com *Television Week,* http://www.tvweek.com National Association of Broadcasters, http://www.nab.org/bcc
Journalism job sites	http://www.journalismjobs.com http://www.tv.jobs.com
State broadcasting groups	Texas Association of Broadcasters, http://www.tab.org Mississippi Broadcast Association, http://www.msbroadcasters.org
Individual station sites	http://www.100000watts.com provides a listing of every television and radio station in the country, along with links to their home pages

Note: Web addresses were current as of fall 2003.

about current job openings. Visit your office and talk with the placement counselor about getting your career started.

There are some websites specifically dedicated to people looking for jobs in journalism or broadcasting, such as http://www.journalismjobs.com and http://www.tvjobs.com. More and more of these sites seem to pop up each day, and the best way to find them might be through an Internet search engine.

Many states have organizations dedicated to the broadcasting business, and their websites often have a placement section. These are often invaluable sites to visit because they often feature openings that are not widely advertised. Finding them may be a bit difficult, but again, a search engine can be an invaluable help.

Finally, almost every station will advertise job openings on its own website. Federal regulations require stations to advertise and announce positions, and many find this an easy way to do it. A complete listing of all radio and television stations in the country, including websites, is offered at http://www.100000watts.com and other sites. If you're interested in working at a particular station or in a certain part of the country, you can easily find if there are producing jobs available there. A general search is much more difficult, as it must be done one station at a time. Typically, a station will advertise in several places, including its own website. But going through the station website might help you find an opening that not too many others know about.

The Job Search Process

The actual job search process is pretty much the same no matter what size station is involved or where it's located. Almost all stations will require a cover letter, a resume, and a resume tape before they will consider inviting qualified applicants for a personal interview.

THE COVER LETTER

Sample Cover Letter

Date
[Mr. or Ms.] [News director's name]   *(use real name)*
Station address

Dear [Mr. or Ms.] [News director's name]:

In response to your advertisement for a television   *(get to the point;*
reporter at [station call letters], I am enclosing a tape and   *don't waste time)*
resume for your consideration.

My name is [your full name], and I believe I have the   *(tell them how*
combination of credentials you're looking for. I have worked   *you can help*
during the past year at the campus television station at the   *them)*
University of Mississippi, where I gained experience as a
reporter, writer, anchor, editor, producer, and photographer.
I also worked at the campus radio station and wrote stories   *(show your*
for the *Daily Mississippian* newspaper.   *versatility)*

I will graduate with a journalism degree this spring and am
anxious to put my experience to work at [station call letters].
I am extremely interested in meeting with you face to face at   *(show interest)*
your convenience to discuss this opportunity. If you need more
information or simply need to reach me, feel free to contact
me at any time.

Thanks for your time and consideration,   *(they are doing*
                                                               you a favor)

[your complete name]   *(complete contact*
1934 Rewind St.   *information)*
Oxford, MS 38655
(662) 333-1234
biff@yahoo.com

The cover letter is important not because it can land you a job but because it can keep you from getting one. Many applicants have been immediately rejected because they tried to get "cute" with their cover letters, such as the person who stapled a packet of instant coffee to his resume and invited the news director to "have a cup of coffee on me while you consider my qualifications." Others have tried to grab attention by putting their cover letters on fancy paper or including small gifts.

A cover letter should play it fairly straight—tell the station who you are, why you want the job, and why you should get it. There are many different ways of creating a cover letter, but all should try to include certain things. It's very important to address the news director by name and to make sure you spell the name right. Including the name is not only courteous, it makes the news director feel like the application is personal and not just some form mailing (avoid "Dear News Director" at all costs). Find out how to spell the name correctly, because a wrong spelling sends a signal that you're either sloppy or didn't do your homework.

News directors are very busy, and they probably have innumerable resumes to read through. Get right to the point with your cover letter and don't waste a lot of time on introductions or warm-up material. They don't care about your life history—just tell them who you are and why you're applying. If you've been recommended by someone who knows the news director, that gives your application more credibility, and the cover letter is the place to include that information.

The next section should deal with the two things news directors want to know most: (a) How can this person help us? and (b) What skills and experience does he or she have? Employers already know what they have to offer (salary, benefits, vacation, etc.), and it goes without saying that you shouldn't even ask about those things at this point. Instead, tell them what you have to offer and what you can do to make the station better. An emphasis on your versatility is especially appropriate because stations are looking for producers who have a variety of skills and experience. You might want to mention your combination of job-related skills or what experience you have that would help you in the job.

It's important to show interest and let them know that you really want *this* job. Producers coming out of college certainly have different skill levels, but for the most part, everyone's at about the same place. When news directors have two or more candidates that are roughly equal, they often make their decisions based on who has the best attitude. Many times, they would rather spend a little extra time training a willing producer with a good attitude than hire a more skilled producer who shows no initiative or interest. One way of showing interest is to volunteer to meet the news director or travel at your own expense to the station, and many jobs have been filled simply because people showed this type of persistence. But don't go overboard. There's a fine line between persistence and annoyance, and news directors don't like to be pestered—especially close to news time.

Always remember that the station is doing you a favor by considering you and that the news director probably has dozens of other applicants to consider. It never hurts to say thank you.

THE RESUME

Your resume should allow the news director to see at a glance the important things about you—your education, work experience, skills, and contact information. Therefore, it should be concise, easy to read, and ordered in a way that makes it easy to find information.

Sample Resume

Personal:	Biff Producer, 1934 Rewind St., Oxford, MS, 38655 (662) 333-1234 biff@yahoo.com	*(Complete contact information)*
Education:	BA, Journalism, University of Mississippi, 2003	*(Don't worry about GPA)*
Experience:	Channel 12 News, University of Mississippi News anchor, reporter and producer Summer internship, CFCF, Toronto, 2002 Helped in newscast production and editing	*(Be specific and detailed. List anything you did that demonstrates your ability to do the job. DO NOT put non–journalism-related experience, such as Burger King, Pizza Hut, etc. News directors don't care. Tell them only how you can do the job.)*
	Proficiency in using IMAC Movie and digital editing	*(any skills you might need in a newsroom, such as digital editing, newsroom software, etc.)*
Awards and Honors:	Outstanding Journalism Student, UM, 2001	*(Add only if the award or honor relates to the job. DO NOT put fraternities, social clubs, Magnolia Queen, etc. News directors don't care. Tell them only how you can do the job.)*
References:	*Your references should* • reflect positively on you • *be able to describe you as more than a student* • *be able to testify not only about your abilities, but about your character and dedication*	

Focus your resume on those things that news directors care about and forget the things that don't matter. The only personal information you really need is your name and contact information. You do want to indicate if you have a college degree, but grade point average (GPA) is not really necessary because your GPA is not the best indication of how you would do on the job. It might be that you sacrificed grades to get valuable experience at the college radio or television station. If you have a good GPA, feel free to put it down, but it certainly isn't a requirement.

Work experience is absolutely essential, provided it somehow relates to journalism or broadcasting. News directors do not care if you worked at Pizza Hut or J. C. Penney's; they want to know about your journalism skills and experience. This is where you can describe not only what you did in college but what specific skills you learned. The more things you did, the better, and don't be afraid to go into detail. If you have zero journalism-related experience, you might want to include information about some of your other jobs. But if you don't have any journalism experience, chances are you aren't getting this job.

Internships are also valuable work experience and should be included. In fact, anyone considering a career in broadcast journalism should make every effort to work a summer internship at a cable, television, or radio station. Not only does it provide great experience, it can help you sharpen your career path. It's not uncommon for students to be very excited about broadcast journalism until they get their first internship and find out what the business is like in the "real world." Internships are also good for students who don't have access to stations, equipment, or labs in their college environment.

Be sure to consider carefully what you'll be doing during your internship. It looks pretty impressive to have an internship with WJLA-TV in Washington, DC, on your resume, but at really big news organizations, that internship might consist of nothing more than answering phones and getting coffee. You're probably better off going to a smaller station that will allow you to get more directly involved in the news process. You'll learn skills that directly transfer to your resume.

As with work experience, you can list awards and honors you won in college as long as they might pertain to the job you're seeking. Journalism honor societies and honors you've received for student journalism contests are fine, but news directors don't care if you were fraternity pledge chairman or voted "most popular" on campus.

The use of references often depends on the station, and some will specifically request at least three. It might be a good idea to include references whether the station asks for them or not as a sign that others think highly of you and your work. Remember that references should always reflect positively on you, and you should check with the person giving the recommendation before listing them on your resume. Many times, someone will ask for a recommendation and then be surprised to hear later that the recommendation was very poor. Don't assume that the reference you choose is always going to say good things about you.

Recommendations from those working in the industry carry a little more weight than recommendations from teachers because they indicate how well you can do on the job. You should always try to include recommendations from professional people and not rely solely on professors and college people. In addition to a professional recommendation, you should get someone to write something about your character. As mentioned, attitude is a very important part of the job search process, and news directors want to make sure they're getting committed workers. No station wants to spend the time and money on a job search only to find out that it has hired a "troublemaker" with a bad attitude.

THE RESUME TAPE

The resume tape is the single most important tool most broadcasters have in their job search process. It can also be important for producers because it reflects their news philosophy and how they put a newscast together. However, some stations do not require a tape when asking for applications, probably because it would take too much time for a news director to go through them all. It's more common for stations simply to ask for a resume and cover letter.

When a station does ask for a tape, there are all kinds of theories about what should be on it. An entire show would take at least 30 minutes to view, so it's perhaps more advisable to include just one or two news blocks. This can still give the news director an idea of how the producer approaches the news and what tools he or she uses to put it on the air. Obviously, producers don't want to include shows that have a lot of problems or errors, but news directors aren't really looking for perfection. Certainly, the producer can't help it if the anchors have a bad night on the set.

The tape should include things that show the producer's strengths. This would include not just such producer essentials as blocking and stacking but any special techniques or strategies. News directors are always interested in how a producer approaches breaking news or special programming, and those shows might be especially appropriate to include.

Although anchors and reporters live or die by the resume tape, it's not quite as important to news producers. News directors assume that producers have the basic skills required to get a show on the air, and they often put more emphasis on leadership, vision, planning, and other important qualities. It's also true that even the best producer is limited by available technology, which may influence the quality of the newscast. Stations want to look more at the producer as a person, as opposed to the sophisticated toys he or she used in creating a newscast.

THE INTERVIEW

After news directors have sifted through the cover letters, resumes, and resume tapes, they will narrow down their list of applicants to the top two or three. The station will then notify those people and bring them in for a personal interview. Once you agree to a personal interview, you can assume the station has a very high level of interest. Bringing in job candidates requires a lot of time and money, and stations don't like to waste their resources on unqualified prospects. But don't confuse station interest with commitment. There are no guarantees, and in some cases stations have called off the process after interviewing all the candidates.

If a station calls you for an interview, there are some things you can do to help your chances. One thing is to research your prospective employer. Find out about the station, who owns it, and what the news programs are like. It is also useful to learn about the community, such as important businesses or local events. Thanks to the Internet, this type of research is now extremely quick and easy.

As mentioned, attitude plays a key part in the interview process. How you get along with the news director, the answers you give, and even the questions you ask reflect what kind of attitude you would bring to the work environment. At the very least, you should show a high level of interest in the station and the position and a willingness to "do whatever it takes" to get the job. Interviewees who immediately start asking about vacation time, sick leave, and benefits usually raise red flags for the news director.

Salary is another area you should probably avoid until you're surer of the station's commitment. Asking too early could be a sign of jumping the gun and assuming that you've already got the job. Based on our discussions of the broadcast pay scale earlier in this chapter, you should have something of an idea of the station's salary structure. It's fine to ask about a general salary range before you agree to visit the station. But most stations have a very definite idea of what the job will pay, and often this is nonnegotiable. The large supply of qualified applicants allows the station to play a successful game of hardball. News directors will simply give you a take it or leave it offer, and further negotiation is at your own risk. If you can't accept the salary that's offered, it's acceptable to say so—if you're prepared for the news director to pull the offer and look for someone else.

The prospective producer should also use the interview as a time to get a closer look at the station and the community. It could be that the situation is not just right for whatever reason—too far away, a news director who seems hard to work with, or other workers at the station who warn you not to come there. Just because you've got an interview doesn't mean you have to take the job. At the same time, jobs in broadcast journalism are extremely precious and hard to come by. Pass on a job now, and it might be months before you get another good offer.

SUMMARY

Obtaining a job as a broadcast producer can be a frustrating, exhaustive, and maddening process. Perseverance pays off, because 100 news directors might say "no" before one finally says "yes." Those already in the business know to stick with it and not give up. Your first job will probably be the hardest one to get.

News Production: The Job Market

Those already in the industry say the first job is often the toughest to get. Here are some of their thoughts about getting your foot in the producing door.

Mike McHugh, former producer, 10:00 p.m. news, WBBM-TV, Chicago: There are tremendous opportunities available for those who want to produce newscasts. The reality is few people want to do any more. I'll give you an example. My cousin graduated from college. He had been a sports intern in Philadelphia for a semester, and of course, couldn't find a sports job. I recommended he be a producer. He gets hired to work the assignment desk in New Bern, NC. Two weeks later, he's producing the morning news. Eight months later he's producing the weekend in Harrisburg, PA. Two months later, he's producing the 6:00 p.m. show. Less than year after that, he's hired at KYW-TV in Philadelphia as a writer-producer. Two months later, he's named the weekend morning news producer, and last week the producer of the 6:00 p.m. He's a good guy, really, but within 2 years he produced a main show at a top 5 station.

That's what's it like out there for producers. [News director] Jim Labranche tells me when he advertised for a reporter in Bluefield, West Virginia, he got more than 100 resumes. The producer opening got only six resumes, including mine. The only problem is that long term it's so demanding, nobody can do it forever.

Matt Ellis, News Director, WBZ-TV, Boston: For me, the switch from on-air reporting to producing led to a successful career path. I found I was able to move quickly into bigger markets as a producer than I was as a reporter. It's worth noting that some people are better suited to producing. I had the organizational skills and the desire to have a larger voice in what was included in the newscast.

One interesting difference between producers and reporters: A producer is judged in quantifiable terms. Any news manager can check to see that all the news that should be included is included, that all the facts are correct, and that the right video is used to illustrate what's being said. It gets trickier to judge a reporter. One news manager may not like a reporter's voice or haircut. It takes someone with a thick skin to succeed on the air.

SOURCE: M. Ellis (personal communication, April 2003), M. McHugh (personal communication, March 2003).

Thinking More About It

1. Investigate the journalism job sites at some of the websites suggested in the chapter. Of all the job sites on the listing, how many interest you as places at which you might want to pursue a possible career? For how many of the jobs do you feel reasonably qualified? For those jobs you really want, what do you still need to do to make yourself more attractive to prospective employers? Do you feel like you will leave your school program with the skills and education necessary to get the job you want? Why or why not?

2. What are some ways to find jobs that most people might not know about? Where are places you can look?

3. Create a sample resume, resume tape, and cover letter and have your instructor critique these materials. What needs to be changed, and why?

4. Develop a plan for getting your first job. What specific strategies are you going to use? What time frame have you set for getting an internship? Creating a resume tape? Sending out resumes? Where are you going to look for work? What people could you use as references? What contacts have you made in the industry that might help you?

References

Allen, C. M. (2001). *News is people.* Ames: Iowa State University Press.

Audience Research & Development. (2002). *Strategic specialists.* Retrieved March 22, 2004, from http://www.ar-d.com/strategist.html

Aucoin, D., & Jurkowitz, M. (1999). Outside consultants play a key role in shaping broadcasts. *Boston Globe.* Retrieved March 19, 2004, from http://www.personal.kent.edu/~glhanson/readings/tv%20news/bglobe.htm

Bagdikian, B. H. (2000). *The media monopoly* (6th ed.). Boston: Beacon Press.

Bartlett, M. (2003, October 24). Fox anchor unveils project. *Daily Mississippian,* p. 1.

Bauder, D. (2003, July 2). "CBS Evening News" hits ratings low. *AP Wire.* Retrieved March 23, 2004, from http://www.miami.com/mld/broward/entertainment/6214030.htm

Becker, L., Vlad, T., Huh, J., & Daniels, G. (2002, November). 2002 annual survey of journalism and mass communication graduates. *AEJMC News, 36*(1), 1-6.

Behnke, R., & Miller, P. (1992). Viewer reactions to content and presentation format of television news. *Journalism Quarterly, 69,* 659-666.

Bergman, L. (2000, May/June). Network television news: with fear and favor. *Columbia Journalism Review.* Retrieved March 19, 2004, from http://archives.cjr.org/year/00/2/bergman.asp

Bernstein, D. S. (2001, November). Breaking news. *Boston Magazine Online.* Retrieved March 19, 2004, from http://www.bostonmagazine.com/ArticleDisplay.php?id=20

Breaking news. (2002, October 10). *Electronic Media.* Retrieved November 11, 2002, from http://www.emonline.com

Byron, G. (1997). *TV news: What local stations don't want you to know!* Retrieved March 19, 2004, from http://www.tfs.net/~gbyron/tvnews1.html

Carter, B. (2003, April 14). Nightly news feels pinch of 24-hour news. *New York Times,* p. C1. Retrieved March 19, 2004, from http://www.nytimes.com/2003/04/14/business/media/14TUBE.html

CBS 2 Chicago. (2004). *CBS 2 team.* Retrieved March 4, 2004, from http://cbs2chicago.com/team/

Chang, H. (1998). The effect of news teasers in processing TV news. *Journal of Broadcasting and Electronic Media, 42,* 327-339.

Chan-Olmstead, S. M., & Park, J. S. (2000). From on-air to online world: Examining the content and structures of broadcast TV stations' web sites. *Journalism and Mass Communication Quarterly, 77*(2), 321-339.

Clark, R. P. (2002, January 24). The line between fact and fiction. *Poynteronline.* Retrieved March 19, 2004, from http://www.poynter.org/content/content_view.asp?id=3491

Curb call on car chase coverage. (2003, February 27). *Herald Sun.* Retrieved March 12, 2004, from http://heraldsun.news.com.au/printpage/0%2C5481%2C6049140%2C00.htm

de Moraes, L. (2003, July 22). CBS news chief defends approach to Lynch. *Washington Post,* p. C07.

Dickson, G. (1998, November 16). The high cost of pioneering in DTV. *Broadcasting & Cable,* p. S37.

Ethics in the age of digital photography. (2000). *National Press Photographer's Association.* Retrieved April 13, 2003, from http://www.nppa.org/services/bizpract/eadp/eadp2.html

Fox, K. (2002). An investigation of factors affecting job satisfaction and career motivation of on-air radio personalities. *National Association of Broadcasters.* Retrieved March 19, 2004, from http://www.nab.org/Research/topic.asp#MANAGEMENT

The future of local news. (2001, February). *PBS Online NewsHour Forum.* Retrieved March 20, 2004, from http://www.pbs.org/newshour/forum/february01/local_news.html

Future of News and Journalism Ethics Projects. (2000). *American Radio News Audience Survey.* Retrieved March 19, 2004, from http://www.rtnda.org/radio

Gavel, D. (2002, October 17). CBS news president Andrew Heyward: An embarrassment of niches. *Kennedy School Brown Bag News Stories.* Retrieved March 20, 2004, from http://www.ksg.harvard.edu/news/news/2002/heyward_101702.htm

Geisler, J. (2001, October 8). Terrorism. Covering the U.S. attack on the Taliban: Minute-by-minute with broadcast news. *Poynteronline.* Retrieved March 20, 2004, from http://www.poynter.org/content/content_view.asp?id=6095

Geisler, J. (2003a, August 14). TV/radio: How newsrooms handled blackout coverage. *Poynteronline.* Retrieved March 20, 2004, from http://www.poynter.org/dg.lts/id.44615/content.content_view.htm

Geisler, J. (2003b, March 20). TV/radio. In newsrooms now: Tips from leaders. *Poynteronline.* Retrieved March 20, 2004, from http://www.poynter.org/content/content_view.asp?id=25790

Gewirtz, J. (2002). *Producer's perspective.* Retrieved March 30, 2003, from http://www.tvnews.com

Goldberg, B. (2003). *Bias: A CBS insider exposes how the media distorts the news.* New York: Harperperennial.

Greppi, M. (2002, August 19). Newspro. Timeout for sports: Local stations debate how much coverage viewers really want. *Electronic Media.* Retrieved March 20, 2004, from http://www.tvweek.com/newspro/081902sports.html

Grossman, A. (2002, December 18). Younger viewers keep NBC atop news net derby. *Hollywood Reporter.* Retrieved March 22, 2004, from http://0-web.lexisnexis.com.umiss.lib.olemiss.edu/universe/document?_m=992f499c798635b92b7ef57a6f6f8118&_docnum=1&wchp=dGLbVtz-zSkVA&_md5=b10d75c0d754a24cd2c1b41276ccc696

Grossman, L. K. (1997, November/December). In the public interest: Why local TV news is so awful. *Columbia Journalism Review.* Retrieved March 23, 2004, from http://www.cjr.org/archives.asp?url=/97/6/grossman.asp

Grossman, L. K. (2000, September-October). Shilling for prime time: Can CBS news survive "Survivor?" *Columbia Journalism Review.* Retrieved March 23, 2004, from http://archives.cjr.org/year/00/3/grossman.asp

Hinds, J. (2000, February 25). A stand up job live! *Detroit Free Press,* p. D1.

Jesdanun, A. (2002, September 30). *News web sites slowly moving away from "shovelware."* Retrieved April 6, 2003, from http://digitalmass.boston .com/news/ 2002/09/30/news_sites.html

Johnson, P. (2003, March 26). Confronting Iraq. Reporters go along with military: Upbeat stories play well at home, but critics see skewed view of war. *USA Today.* Retrieved March 21, 2004, from http://www.usatoday.com/educate/ war15-article.htm

Johnson, S. (1999, July-August). How low can TV news go? *Columbia Journalism Review.* Retrieved March 23, 2004, from http://archives.cjr.org/year/97/4/ tvnews.asp

Lee, M. (2002). One-man band: Digital video and lightweight communications can transform newsgathering. *ABC News.com.* Retrieved March 21, 2004, from http://abcnews.go.com/sections/wnt/WorldNewsTonight/LeeCam_ notebook_feature.html

Lehrer, J. (2002, September). *Returning to our roots* [Red Smith Lecture in Journalism]. Kansas City, MO: Universal Press Syndicate.

Lin, C. A., & Jeffres, L. W. (2001). Comparing distinctions and similarities across websites of newspapers, radio stations and television stations. *Journalism and Mass Communication Quarterly, 78*(3), 555-573.

Lyman, R. (1999, May 6). Fury on the plains: The warnings; residents watched on TV as the tornadoes neared. *New York Times,* p. A31.

Main, A., & Stewart, R. (Eds.). (1997). *The producer book.* Retrieved March 21, 2004, from http://www.scripps.ohiou.edu/producer/thebook/

McGregor, D. (1960). *The human side of enterprise.* New York: McGraw Hill.

Network upfront picking up steam. (2001, June 20). *Electronic Media.* Retrieved June 27, 2001, from http://www.emonline.com/news/web062001.html

"No frills" newscast ends. (2002, October 31). *PBS Online NewsHour.* Retrieved March 21, 2004, from http://www.pbs.org/newshour/media/media_watch/ marin_10–31.html

Outing, S. (2002, September 23). How's the weather on the Web? *Poynteronline.* Retrieved March 21, 2004, from http://www.poynter.org/content/content_ view.asp?id=9464

Outing, S. (2003, March 12). E-media tidbits: Wednesday, March 12, 2003. The first 24-hour Internet news network. *Poynteronline.* Retrieved March 21, 2004, from http://www.poynter.org/column.asp?id=31&aid=24524

Papper, B. (2000, June). News staff pitch in, do double duty on Web site. *RTNDA Communicator.* Retrieved March 21, 2004, from http://www.rtnda.org/ research/web02.shtml

Papper, B. (2002). RTNDA/F research: 2002 women & minorities survey. *Radio and Television News Director's Association.* Retrieved March 21, 2004, from http://www.rtnda.org/research/womin.shtml

Papper, B., & Gerhard, M. (2001, September). RTNDA/F research: 2001 newsroom profitability survey. *Radio and Television News Director's Association.* Retrieved March 21, 2004, from http://www.rtnda.org/research/money .shtml

Papper, B., & Gerhard, M. (2002a). RTNDA/F research: 2002 Radio and television salary survey. *Radio and Television News Director's Association.*

Retrieved March 21, 2004, from http://www.rtnda.org/research/salaries02
.shtml

Papper, B., & Gerhard, M. (2002b). RTNDA/F research: Staffing/amount of news
research. *Radio and Television News Director's Association.* Retrieved March
21, 2004, from http://www.rtnda.org/research/staff.shtml

Peacock, M. (2001, March 26). Train and retain your best for the new television
economy. *MEDIAdvise.* Retrieved March 21, 2004, from http://www.mediadvise
.com/textpages/Survey.htm

Peiser, W. (2000). Setting the journalist agenda: influences from the journalist's
individual characteristics and from media factors. *Journalism and Mass
Communication Quarterly, 77*(2), 243-257.

Postman, N. (1985). *Amusing ourselves to death.* New York: Penguin Books.

Project for Excellence in Journalism. (2002). *Local TV news project.* Retrieved
March 21, 2004, from: http://www.journalism.org/resources/research/reports/
localTV/2002/disappearing.asp

Radio and Television News Directors Association. (1996). Changing channels: Young
adults, Internet surfers and the future of the news audience. Retrieved March 19,
2004, from http://www.rtnda.org/resources/channels/channels. html#toc

Radio and Television News Directors Foundation. (1998). *RTNDF Journalism and
Ethics Integrity Project.* Retrieved March 23, 2004, from http://www.
rtndf.org/research/survey.pdf

Richman, J. (2002). Tips for producing engaging radio diaries. *Straight Scoop
News Bureau.* Retrieved March 17, 2004, from http://www.straightscoop.
org/advice/stu_radiodiaries1.html

Rutenberg, J. (2002, December 9). Wanted: a new personality for MSNBC;
troubled cable news network seeks ways to match its rivals. *New York Times,*
p. C1.

Safran, S. (2003, April 20). Things viewers never, ever say. *Lost Remote.* Retrieved
March 22, 2004, from http://www.lostremote.com/story/viewers_never_say.
htm

Schleuder, J. D., White, A. V., & Cameron, G. T. (1993). Priming effects of television
news bumpers and teasers on attention and memory. *Journal of Broadcasting
and Electronic Media, 37,* 437-452.

Schulberg, P. (1999, January 15). This just in: Good journalism, good ratings go
together. *Portland Oregonian,* p. C3.

Sloan, R. (2002, September 6). Being the brightest and best: A news director's
expectations for producers. *Poynteronline.* Retrieved March 22, 2004, from
http://www.poynter.org/content/content_view.asp?id=9500

Smith, Conrad, & Becker, L. (1989). Comparison of journalistic values of television
reporters and producers. *Journalism Quarterly, 66,* 793-800.

Smith, Curt. (1987). *Voices of the game.* South Bend, IN: Diamond.

Smith, D. (2002). *Power producer* (3rd ed.). Washington: RTNDA.

Steele, B. (2001, June 7). Talk about ethics. Pearl photo: Too harmful.
Poynteronline. Retrieved March 22, 2004, from http://www.poynter.org/
column.asp?id=36&aid=839

Steele, B. (2002, January 1). Ethics. Good decisions and great journalism: The
marriage of ethics and craft. *Poynteronline.* Retrieved March 22, 2004, from
http://www.poynter.org/content/content_view.asp?id=3863

Stone, V. (2000). *Single in television news.* Retrieved March 22, 2004, from http://www.missouri.edu/~jourvs/tvsingle.html

Sullivan, C. (2002, July 15). Publishers should focus on non-readers. *Editor & Publisher.* Retrieved March 22, 2004, from http://www.editorandpublisher.com/eandp/news/article_display.jsp?vnu_content_id=1542100

Taylor, H. (2002, April 17). Internet penetration at 66% of adults (137 million) nationwide. *HarrisInteractive.* Retrieved March 22, 2004, from http://www.harrisinteractive.com/harris_poll/index.asp?PID=295

Thomas, Cal. (2002, November 27). Demos, liberal news media have own examples of "shrill rhetoric." *Salt Lake Tribune.* Retrieved March 19, 2003, from http://www.sltrib.com/2002/nov/11272002/commenta/5865.htm

"Today" co-host Katie Couric renews NBC deal. (2001, December 20). *theEnews.com.* Retrieved March 22, 2004, from http://www.theenews.com/stories/tv/couric-122001.htm

Tompkins, A. (1999, July 1). TV/radio: What news directors want from producers. *Poynteronline.* Retrieved March 22, 2004, from http://www.poynter.org/content/content_view.asp?id=4580

Utley, G. (1997, March-April). The shrinking of foreign news: From broadcast to narrowcast. *Foreign Affairs, 76*(2). Retrieved March 22, 2004, from http://www.foreignaffairs.org/19970301facomment3750/garrick-utley/the-shrinking-of-foreign-news-from-broadcast-to-narrowcast.html

Vercammen, P. (2000, January 25). Digital developments: Networks changing images on your TV. *CNN.com.* Retrieved March 22, 2004, from http://www.cnn.com/2000/SHOWBIZ/TV/01/25/digital.inserts/

Wendland, M. (2000, February 7). TV/radio. Peter Jennings and his cool new tool: The e-mail preview. *Poynteronline.* Retrieved March 22, 2004, from http://www.poynter.org/content/content_view.asp?id=3527

Whitney, D. (2003, March 3). Surviving as a news director: Ratings success, luck among secrets of longevity. *TelevisionWeek.* Retrieved March 22, 2004, from http://www.tvweek.com/newspro/030303newsdirector.html

Zillmann, D., Gibson, R., Ordman, V. L., & Aust, C. F. (1984). Effects of upbeat stories in broadcast news. *Journal of Broadcasting and Electronic Media, 38,* 65-78.

Index

ABC News Live, 143
Accuracy issues, 100-101
Action news format, 31
Active voice, 74-75
Actuality, 41, 84
Advertising:
    commercial breaks, 12
    conflicts of interest, 13
    digital technology, 175
    dropping commercials, 12-13
    ratings and self-censorship, 26
    rundown break times, 47
    sales department, 13
    special news formats and, 97
Alliteration, 80
All-news radio format, 125-129
Alternative news formats, 90-91
    advertisers and, 97
    breaking news, 99-101
    call-in show, 96-97
    debate, 94-95
    election coverage, 95-96
    live on-location, 91-93
    long-range planning for, 3
    producing strategies and issues, 98
    roundtable discussion, 93
    town hall meeting, 94
Anchors, 27-28
    anchor-driven morning programs, 56
    rundown and, 41
    scripting, 64
    sports, job opportunities, 119
    weather, 108-111
    working with, 152-154

Arlin, Harold, 23
Assignment editor, 5-7
Associated Press (AP), 38, 116, 131
Attribution, 78-79
Audience generation gap, 28
Audience interaction.
    See Interactivity
Audience ratings, 26, 161-163
Audience Research and Development
    (AR&D), 181, 182
Audience retention, 52-54
    interactivity, 58
    localism and, 57
    maximizing resources, 58-59
    teases, 53-54
    "things viewers never say," 59-60
    thinking "big picture," 59
    understanding audience preferences,
        54-56
    See also Interactivity
Audio:
    natural sounds, 82-83
    personnel, 8
Authoritarian management style
    (Theory X), 146
Ayra, Bob, 166

Backtiming, 44-45
Backup plans, 7
Bagdikian, Ben, 25
Beat system, 38
Bell, Alan, 54
Bell, Tom, 166
Bergman, Lowell, 26, 29

Berryhill, Mark, 181
Blocks, 47-48
  finishing, 60-62
  lead, 48-50
  "11 at 11," 48
  stacking guidelines, 48-52
  stories following lead, 50-52
Blumenthal, Scott, 152
Bottom line, 25-26, 170
Breaking news, 99-101, 167
Brinkley, David, 27
Broadcast news producer.
    See News producers
Broadcast news trends:
  action news, 31
  anchors, 27-28
  bottom line, 25-26
  cutbacks, 168, 170-171
  entertainment, 28-29
  historical perspective, 23-25
  implications for local producers,
    31-34
  interactivity, 30
  technology, 29-31, 89
  See also Quality
Brokaw, Tom, 27
Brown, Merrill, 136
Budget cutbacks, 168, 170-171

Cable news, 26, 27, 162
Campbell, John, 119-120, 158
CBS, 24, 26
Celebrities and entertainers, 28
Cellcast, 129
Cereghino, Warren, 162
Chan-Olmstead, Sylvia, 136
Character generator (CG), 64
Cheatwood, Joel, 161
Chyrons, 8, 64
Clark, Roy Peter, 175
Clemensen, Doug, 182
Close segment, 45
Closing stories, kickers, 46-47
CNN, 27

Commercial breaks,
    12-13, 47, 52-53
Communication skills, 150, 189
Competition, 52,173
  cable and, 27
Conflicts of interest, 13
Conservative media bias, 177-178
Consultants, 24, 180-183
Content analysis, 34, 69
Control room, 8, 66-68
  staff communication technology,
    67-68
Convergence, 135
Coordinated news coverage, 58-60
Couric, Katie, 27, 56, 153
Cover letter, 192-194
Creativity, 150-151
Credibility, 108
Credits, 62
Crime, sex, and sensationalism,
    161, 182
Cronkite, Walter, 24, 27

Daschle, Tom, 177-178
Debate, 94-95
Delegation, 150
Dennis, Patti, 152
Digital technology, 8, 30
  conversion costs, 170
  manipulating the truth, 175
  radio news, 129
Disney, 25
Drive time, 124, 126

Editorial meetings, 4, 5
  story suggestions, 37
Educational requirements, producer
    jobs, 188-189, 195
Election coverage, 95-96
Electronic Media, 153
Ellerbee, Linda, 176
Ellis, Matt, 32, 68-69, 157, 164,
    174, 198
E-mail feedback, 30, 58

Emergency services, 106
Employment opportunities, 185-187.
    See also Job search
Engineering department, 9-10
Entertainment, 28-29
Equipment, 9
Estimated running time (ERT), 43
Ethical issues, 175
    creating news, 178-180
    guidelines and training, 180
    honesty and deception, 175-176
    personal/political biases, 177-178
    sales department and, 13
    visual bias, 176-177
Experience requirements, for
        producer jobs, 188-189, 195

Federal Communications
        Commission (FCC), 25
Feedback, 30. *See also* Interactivity
Ferrugia, John, 171
Fox News, 27, 177
Frank Magid Associates, 181, 182, 183
Futures file, 118

Geisler, Jill, 30
Gender:
    audience preferences, 56
    news producer trends, 186-187
General manager (GM), 3, 157
Gewirtz, Jason, 172-174
Giles, Lee, 152
Glass, Ira, 133
Goldberg, Bernard, 177
Grammar, 78
Graphic artists, 8
Graphics, character generators (CG)
        or chyrons, 8, 64
Grossman, Lawrence, 162, 163

Haag, Marty, 162
Hadley, Rick, 32, 129-130, 158, 174
Hard lead, 76
Henning, John, 181

Heyward, Andrew, 29, 31
Honesty and deception, 175-176
Hook of story, 77
Humor, 53
Humorous lead, 76
Huntley, Chet, 27
Hyperlinks, 142

Information overload, 72
Initiative, 150
Interactivity, 30, 58
    radio news, 128
    severe weather news, 107
    station website, 140-141
    town hall meeting, 94
Internet news sites, 30, 58, 134-143
    accuracy issues, 100
    audience characteristics, 139, 141
    common elements, 140-141
    convergence, 135
    full-time staffers, 138-139
    future of, 142-143
    hyperlinks, 142
    interactivity, 140-141
    power outage coverage, 139
    profitability issues, 135
    promotional value, 135, 141
    shovelware, 136
    use by broadcast outlets, 134, 137
    video and audio, 142
    weather service, 140
Internship, 195
Interruptible frequency broadcast
        (IFB), 67-68
Interview, employment, 197
Interviews, story format, 41

Jennings, Peter, 27, 30
Job market, 185-187, 198. *See also*
        Job search
Job search, 187-198
    cover letter, 192-194
    industry professionals'
        observations, 198

interview, 197
resume, 194-196
resume tape, 196
skills and qualifications, 188-189
where to look, 190-191
Journalistic ethics. *See* Ethical issues

Kickers, 46-47
Kiernan, Jeff, 190
Kucharski, Angie, 150, 151, 164
Kuralt, Charles, 24
KVBC-TV, 178

Large-market news staff, 19-21
Late newscast audiences, 56-57
Lauer, Matt, 56, 153
Lead stories:
    live reporting, 48
    stacking guidelines, 48-50
Leadership, 151
Leads, story, 76-78
Lee, Mike, 30
Liberal media bias, 177-178
Limbaugh, Rush, 177
Live reporting, 41, 48-49, 164-172
    accuracy issues, 100-101
    appropriate and inappropriate
        situations, 167-168
    breaking news, 99, 167
    engineer concerns, 9-10
    lead stories, 48
    "live for live's sake," 166, 168
    making live shots, 169
    on-location programs, 91-93
    radio, 128-129
    reporter "face time," 168
    sports, 112
    technical concerns, 166
    weather, 105, 166
Local news:
    audience preferences, 57
    importance for radio news,
        124-125, 127-128
    sports programming, 118

Log, 12
Long-range planning, 3, 16
Louis, Mark "Hawkeye," 131-132
Lynch, Jessica, 29
Lyons, Jeff, 34, 109, 158

Management styles, 18, 146-148, 149.
    See also Newsroom working
    relationships
Managerial roles and authority, 15-16
Marin, Carol, 162, 163
Market size, 172-174
Marti, 129
Master control room. *See* Control
    room
McGregor, Douglas, 146
McHugh, Mike, 16, 17,
    157, 164, 174, 198
McHugh and Hoffman, 180
Media corporations, 25, 170
Media news convergence, 135
Media political biases, 177-178
Microwave transmission,
    9, 105, 129, 166
Minority employment, 186-187
Moonves, Les, 29
Morning news show audiences, 55-56
Murrow, Edward R., 24
Music radio station news, 130-132

National Association of
    Broadcasters, 170
National Public Radio (NPR), 132
Natural sound, 82-83
News anchors. *See* Anchors
News blocks. *See* Blocks
News commitment, 149
News cutbacks, 168, 170-171
News cycle, 89
News director, 4-5
    longevity, 151-152
    managerial style, 18
    newscast critique, 68
    working with, 148-152

News hole, 12

News media convergence, 135

News producer job market,
     185-187, 198

News producer job search. *See* Job
     search

News producers:
     comparison of producers and
          reporters, 155
     gender and minority trends,
          186-187
     personal relationships, 154-158
     roles of, 1-3, 15-16, 68-69
     satisfactions, 69
     working hours, 155

News producers, skills, 68, 150-151
     communication and
          delegation, 150
     creativity, 150-151
     employment requirements,
          188-189
     initiative, 150
     leadership, 151
     newsroom relations, 150
     sports producer duties and
          qualifications, 115
     technology, 32-34
     versatility, 148

News producers, working
     relationships. *See* Newsroom
     structure; Newsroom working
     relationships

News production, historical
     development, 23-25

News production philosophy,
     163-164

News production software, 45, 189

News releases, 38

News tips, 38

News updates, 57

News value, 39, 40
     personal biases, 177-178
     visual bias, 176-177

News wheel, 126

News wire services, 38, 116, 131

Newscast end, 68

NewsNet 5, 138-140

Newsroom structure:
     assignment editor, 5-7
     engineering department, 9-10
     large-market staff, 19-21
     management style and, 149
     news director, 4-5
     production department, 8
     promotion department, 14
     reporters and photographers, 7-8
     sales department, 13
     small-market staff, 21
     sports and weather, 10-12
     station manager, 3
     station size and resources and, 16, 18
     support personnel, 14
     traffic department, 12

Newsroom working relationships, 145
     anchors, 152-154
     industry professionals'
          observations, 157-158
     management styles, 146-148, 149
     news directors, 148-152
     personality conflict, 145, 149
     producer skills, 149-152
     reporters, 7-8, 154
     staff communication technology,
          67-68
     station ownership and, 149

Nightline, 93

Ober, Eric, 26

One-man bands, 30

Open segment, 45

O'Reilly, Bill, 27

Outcuing, 63-64

Outing, Steve, 140

Packages, 41
     lead stories, 49
     time, 43
     writing for, 85

Paley, William S., 24, 25
Park, Jung Suk, 136
Peacock, Mike, 30-31
Pearl, Daniel, 179
Peiser, Wolfram, 177
Personal biases, 177-178
Personal relationships, 154-158
Personality conflict, 145, 149
Personalization:
    radio news, 128
    story writing, 72-73, 80-81
    See also Interactivity
Pew Research Center for People and
    the Press, 28
Philosophy, news production, 163-164
Phoner story format, 41, 49
    call-in-show, 96-97
Pitches, 46
Political biases, 177-178
Potter, Deborah, 162
Powers, Ron, 28
Producers. See News producers
Production department, 8
Production software, 45, 189
Profit issues, 170
Profitability, 25-26
    Internet news venues, 135
Project for Excellence in Journalism, 28
Promotion department, 14
Public broadcasting, 132-134
Public service announcements
    (PSAs), 12
Pyle, Ernie, 179

Quality:
    budget cutbacks and, 171
    consultants and, 182
    ratings versus, 26, 161-163
Quarderer, John, 182, 183
Question lead, 76-77

Radio, 123-134
    audience listening patterns, 124-125
    creating station identity, 128

digital technology, 129
drive time, 124, 126
early technological limitations, 23
evolving news production trends, 24
live reporting, 128-129
local news importance, 124-125,
    127-128
news on music stations, 130-132
news wheel, 126
personalization and
    interactivity, 128
public broadcasting, 132-134
resources, 127
saturation, 127
talk and all-news formats, 125-129
using natural sounds, 82-83
Radio and Television News Directors
    Foundation (RTNDF),
    32, 54, 124
Rasor, Jim, 108
Rather, Dan, 26, 27
Ratings, news quality versus,
    26, 161-163
Reader-graphic (R/G), 52
Reader story format, 41
Recycling old stories, 38
References and recommendations,
    195-196
Regional audience preferences, 55
Reporters, 7-8
    comparison with producers, 155
    "face time," 168
    package introductions, 85
    story ideas and, 37
    working with, 154
Resume, 194-196
Richman, Joe, 133
Rogers, Walter, 179
Rosensteil, Tom, 162
Roundtable, 93
Rule of threes, 80
Rundowns, 41-45
    break times, 47
    complete, 61-62

first block, 50, 51
running time, 43
skeleton, 45-47
software, 45
sports, 115-116, 117
30-minute newscast, 90
Runtime, 44

Safran, Steve, 59
Salaries, 186, 187, 197
    anchors, 27
Sales department, 13
Satellite feeds, 9
Scripting, 62-66. *See also* Writing
Seitz, Colleen, 138-139
Sensationalism, 161, 182
Sevareid, Eric, 24
Severe weather, 105, 106-108, 110, 166
Shaw, Bernard, 27
Shovelware, 136
Simpson, O. J., 175
60 Minutes, 162
Skeleton rundowns, 45-47
Small-market news staff, 21
Smith, Dow, 164
Smith, Howard K., 24
Smith, Shepard, 27
Soft lead, 76
Software, 45, 189
Sound bite, 41, 84-85
Sound on tape (SOT), 41, 43.
    See also Voiceover/sound
    on tape
Special news programs. *See*
    Alternative news formats
Sports, 10-12, 111-120
    anchors, job opportunities, 119
    audience tastes, 54-55
    coordinating coverage, 113,
        117-118
    live reporting, 112
    local stories, 118
    news-sports interaction, 113, 117
    pitches, 46

resources, 116
rundown, 45-46, 115-116, 117
special event programming,
    112-114
sports producers, 114-119
Stacking, 48-52
    lead stories, 48-50
    See also Blocks
Staff, newsroom structure.
    See Newsroom structure
Staff, working relationships.
    See Newsroom working
    relationships
Staff communication
    technology, 67-68
Station log, 12
Station manager (SM), 3
Steele, Bob, 176, 180
Stone, Vernon, 156, 190
Story count, 56
Story formats, 41
    kickers, 46-47
    rundown, 41
Story ideas, 37-39
Story leads, 76-78
Story scripts, 62-66
Story slug, 41
Story writing. *See* Writing
Supers, 64
Support personnel, 14
Swayze, John Cameron, 24

Talk radio formats, 125-129
TalkBack Live, 94
Tape editors, 14
Tape number, 43
Team coverage, 49, 113
Technical director, 8
    scripting and, 64
Technology:
    broadcast news trends, 29-31, 89
    digital manipulations, 175
    early limitations, 23
    interactivity, 30

live reporting, 166
local producers and, 32-34
producer's role and, 2
producer competencies, 189
production and engineering
    departments, 8-10
weather department, 33-34
Teleprompter, 64
Television market size, 172-174
Television 30-minute news format,
    89-90
Theory X, 146
Theory Y, 146-147
Theory Z, 147-148
Thirty-minute news format,
    89-90
Throwaway lead, 76
Tickler file, 118
Time, 175
Time and timing:
    backtiming, 44-45
    constraints, 1, 8
    end of newscast, 45
    estimated running time
        (ERT), 43
    management style and, 147
    news hole, 12
    newscast end, 68
    producer control, 62, 68
    runtime, 44
Time of newscast, audience
    preferences and, 55-57
Today, 27, 153
Tompkins, Al, 150, 163
Town hall meeting, 94
Traffic department, 12

Umbrella lead, 76
Unions, 14
Updates, 57
Utley, Garrick, 31

Visual bias, 176-177
Voiceovers, writing for, 83-84

Voiceover/sound on tape
    (VO/SOT), 52
    writing for, 84-85
Voter News Service (VNS), 96

Wald, Jonathan, 153
WBBM-TV, 18, 19-21, 162
WBNS-TV, 151
Weather, 10-12, 103-111
    anchors, 108-111
    credibility, 108
    interactivity, 107
    Internet service, 140
    live reporting, 105, 166
    pitches, 46
    producer's role, 104-106
    producer working relationship, 111
    rundown, 45-46
    severe weather, 105, 106-108,
        110, 166
    time constraints, 11
    use of technology, 33-34
Websites, broadcast news outlets. *See*
    Internet news sites
Websites, producer employment
    resources, 191
Willi, Jim, 182
Work experience, 188-189, 195
Working hours, 155
World News Tonight, 30
Writers, 14
Writing, 14, 71-88
    active voice and verb "to be,"
        74-75
    attribution, 78-79
    audience understanding, 73-74
    communicating an idea, 71-73
    creativity and originality, 80
    details, 71-72
    five "W's," 76
    for packages, 85
    for voiceovers, 83-84
    for VO/SOT, 84-85
    grammar, 78

hook, 77
humanizing, 80-81
news clichés, 81
personalizing stories, 72-73
producer skills, 189
simple words and sentences, 79
story lead, 76-78

story organization, 72
teases, 53
using available elements, 73
using natural sound, 82-83
WTVA-TV, 18, 21

Yockey, Marcia, 109

About the Author

Brad Schultz, PhD, is Assistant Professor and Head, Broadcast Sequence, Department of Journalism, University of Mississippi. He has taught a variety of classes, including Broadcast News Writing, News Producing, Broadcast Management, and Sports Broadcasting. Before entering academe, he spent 15 years in local television news at different stations around the country. His experience includes anchoring, reporting, producing, writing, editing, photography, and management. He has won awards from the Oklahoma Associated Press and the Cleveland Press Club for reporting and producing. His first book, *Sports Broadcasting*, came out in 2001. Other academic work has been published in the *Web Journal of Mass Communication Research, Journal of Media and Religion, Journal of Communication and Religion, International Journal of the History of Sport,* and *RTNDA Communicator*. He has made several presentations at the national convention of the Association for Education in Journalism and Mass Communication. He has a Bachelor of Journalism degree from the University of Missouri, a master's degree in telecommunications from Southern Illinois University, and a PhD from Texas Tech University.